THE UNRAVELING

THE UNRAVELING

Reflections on Politics without Ethics and Democracy in Crisis

BOB BAUER

FOREWORD BY JON MEACHAM

ROWMAN & LITTLEFIELD
Lanham • Boulder • New York • London

Published by Rowman & Littlefield
An imprint of The Rowman & Littlefield Publishing Group, Inc.
4501 Forbes Boulevard, Suite 200, Lanham, Maryland 20706
www.rowman.com

86-90 Paul Street, London EC2A 4NE

Distributed by NATIONAL BOOK NETWORK

British Library Cataloguing in Publication Information Available

Library of Congress Cataloging-in-Publication Data

Names: Bauer, Bob, 1952- author. | Meacham, Jon, author of foreword.
Title: The unraveling : reflections on politics without ethics and democracy in crisis / Bob Bauer;
    foreword by Jon Meacham.
Description: Lanham, Maryland : Rowman & Littlefield, [2024] | Includes bibliographical
    references and index. | Summary: "Part memoir, part rumination on the declining moral
    compass of America's political class, this is the first book to place restoring political ethics at
    the center of the renewal of American democracy. The Unraveling will be essential reading
    for anyone interested in American politics of the last 50 years--and the next"-- Provided by
    publisher.
Identifiers: LCCN 2023059135 | ISBN 9781538191842 (cloth ; acid-free paper) | ISBN
    9781538191859 (ebook)
Subjects: LCSH: Bauer, Bob, 1952- | Political ethics--United States. | Democracy--United
    States. | Government attorneys--United States--Biography. | United States--Politics and
    government--2017-2021. | United States--Politics and government--2021-
Classification: LCC JK468.E7 B38 2024 | DDC 320.973--dc23/eng/20240319
LC record available at https://lccn.loc.gov/2023059135

∞™ The paper used in this publication meets the minimum requirements of American National
Standard for Information Sciences—Permanence of Paper for Printed Library Materials, ANSI/
NISO Z39.48-1992

To Nick, Luke, Sophie, and Stephen.

CONTENTS

FOREWORD

Jon Meacham

THE HOUR WAS LATE. OR AT LEAST RELATIVELY LATE; IN THE CLOSING weeks of January 1801, the president of the United States, John Adams, was meeting with his secretary of state, John Marshall. It was an unsettled, and unsettling, season in the nascent American republic. Adams's victory over Thomas Jefferson in the election of 1796 had, in Jefferson's view, led to a "reign of witches" in which Adams's Federalists sought to limit dissent, to target immigrants, and to supplant "that noble love of liberty and republican government which carried us triumphantly thro' the war" of 1776 with "an Anglican, monarchial and aristocratical party." To Adams, meanwhile, the Jefferson interest was radical, Frenchified, and atheistic. The fate of the American experiment seemed to hang in the balance. "Now the crisis is advancing," one newspaper observed.

Everything was at stake, or appeared to be. The election of 1800 had produced a tie in the Electoral College, which in turn sent the decision to the House of Representatives to choose between Jefferson and Aaron Burr. In the chaos of the winter, there was talk of insurrection, of civil war, and possibly of a *pro tempore* president—and the name of John Marshall was in circulation as a caretaker, a suggestion that at once infuriated and frightened Jefferson.

Adams, however, had another idea. The incumbent Chief Justice of the United States, Oliver Ellsworth, had resigned in December 1800, and now Adams, in his last weeks as president, wanted to take advantage of the little time he had left to name a successor. John Jay had refused to return to the post, and so now, sitting with Marshall, Adams went straight to the point. "I believe," he told Marshall, "I shall nominate you." Things then moved quickly, and the secretary of state was confirmed as chief justice before the presidential election could be settled. For Jefferson, who would ultimately prevail in the House on the thirty-sixth ballot on February 17, 1801, it was a frank assertion of power by his defeated rivals. And that was not all: The Federalists also added a number of circuit court judgeships and filled them in the waning hours of the Adams administration. The last-minute campaign, Jefferson said, amounted to "a parasitical plant engrafted" on the "judicial body." It had, however, all been done within the bounds of the Constitution, and Jefferson, as deeply opposed as he was to the worldview embodied by Adams and by Marshall, accepted the new order of things. "It is difficult," the new president told James Madison, "to undo what has been done."

Politics and law, power and justice, ambition and order: There it all was, even in the beginning. The book you are holding now is the latest contribution to an unfolding conversation about the exercise of influence, the importance of elections, and the integrity of the Constitutional ethos. The issues that Bob Bauer addresses here are, in a phrase of St. Augustine's, "ever ancient, ever new"—and ever urgent.

A man of the arena, Bauer is remarkably candid about his own role in defining and in deploying the law of politics—or, sometimes, the politics of the law—in recent decades. In these pages he takes honest account of the conflicts and compromises of an inherently complex sphere of life. Is a political lawyer representing a client—or the Constitution? A campaign—or a set of laws and norms? A particular policy agenda—or the capacity of the American system to make given policy choices for a time, and then revisit those choices in the next election even if you lose this round or that round? These are difficult questions, and they raise the most profound issues about democracy, about ethics, about the rule of law, and about sustaining a free government amid what the Victorian novelist George Eliot once called "the dim lights and tangled circumstance" of a fallen, frail, and fallible world.

In the end, Bauer recognizes a truth that even old rivals such as Adams, Marshall, and Jefferson agreed on: That popular government finally depends less on the letter of the law than it does on the spirit of the people, on the moral willingness of citizens to cultivate and to live according to habits of heart and of mind that put the interests of the whole ahead of the appetites and ambitions of the few. Nothing is more difficult; humankind has been struggling with this conflict since at least the third chapter of the Book of Genesis, when the first creatures made their first selfish choice. No statute can cover all contingencies; no code can resolve every tension. If such statutes and such codes could do so, they would have been drafted and enacted long ago. But politics, like the law, is a human undertaking—imperfect and provisional. The best we can hope for is a common assent to principles that find expression in practice that is commonly accepted as legitimate and fair-minded.

Easily said, of course, but not so easily done. And as a lawyer and a professor of law, Bauer is a doer, a man committed to both thought and to action, to both reflection and to execution. History and our own lived experience in the first decades of the twenty-first century tell us that democracy is not guaranteed; the rule of law is not automatic; the Constitution itself is not a given but a gift. That gift is the beginning of our common life, not the end; it's a the context for a conversation about power and rights and responsibilities, not the last word. And that conversation must be one informed by a moral sense that the social contract that has created a more perfect Union is worth preserving against the designs of those who seek—and who love—power more than they do justice.

If you are a reader like me, you will find, I believe, that you may disagree with Bob Bauer's politics but still be grateful for his devotion to the principles for which he is fighting—principles that would make American politics not an occasion for total war but a realm in which we debate differences, live with ambiguity, and resolve what we can. A politics divorced from conscience is a politics of raw power that plunges us back into Thomas Hobbes's state of nature, with its war of all against all. A proper politics of democracy, as Bauer argues, is a politics of moral choice and of ethical consideration—an arena in which reason and generosity can at least take a stand against passion and selfishness.

Sixteen days after the House removed doubt and elected him president, Thomas Jefferson stood with John Marshall, whom he had asked to administer the oath of office in a gesture of unity amid division. "During the contest of opinion through which we have passed, the animation of discussions and of exertions has sometimes worn an aspect" which might worry "strangers unused to think freely and to speak and write what they think," Jefferson said in his Inaugural Address; "but this being now decided by the voice of the nation, announced according to the rules of the Constitution, all will, of course, arrange themselves under the will of the law, and united in common efforts for the common good." In a voice from the past, a hope for our time, and for all time.

December 2023

PREFACE

On the desk in my study is an empty bottle of white wine. Though not much of a drinker, I bought it to celebrate the conclusion of the 2020 election. This would occur, I was reasonably confident, when Congress met as the Constitution required to complete the final tally of electoral votes and proceeded to declare Joe Biden the winner of 270 electoral votes and the president-elect of the United States. For weeks, I and others on the Biden campaign had been working through Donald Trump's challenges to the 2020 election. We did so in the courts, and then, for some weeks later, we had regular calls with Capitol Hill senior staff about preparations for the electoral vote count on January 6. We considered a whole range of possibilities, including the one that fortunately did not materialize: Mike Pence buckling under pressure from Donald Trump, and either declaring him the winner, or disrupting the proceedings by insisting that the count should be suspended and the battleground states invited to reconsider the results in favor of Joe Biden they had already certified.

Then came the attack on the Capitol, and I was back and forth on calls with my primary source of contact with the Senate leadership, Mark Patterson, who was general counsel to the Democratic leader Chuck Schumer. I've known Patterson for years, having worked with him when he was a senior aide to one of Schumer's predecessors, former Democratic leader Tom Daschle. Patterson is calm, sensible, possessed of excellent judgment. On January 6, I reached him at a secure space to which he had been escorted to protect him from violence as the mob coursed through the corridors, police officers were beaten, guns were drawn, and one was fired. I checked regularly on his safety, and we shared our disbelief at this turn of events. We also remained in touch about the congressional leadership's plans to resume the proceedings and complete the vote after the invaders had been ousted and order restored. This was the key: not allowing the attack to serve the purposes of Trump and his allies to stop the final count and buy time for more groundless challenges to the certified outcome. We convened regular calls to brief Joe Biden.

By 4 a.m. on January 7, and without worrying about having a drink in the vicinity of an early breakfast, I finally had the chance to drink the wine. I thought: *we are on the way back.* Not immediately, of course, as it was clear that those involved in the attack on the Capitol would face investigation and prosecution. In a week the House voted to impeach Trump. But, I thought, the restoration of the normal rhythms of democratic life might now begin. It did not, of course, and by the time of this writing, it is not clear how far along we have come.

It is now 2024, another presidential campaign is underway, and the democracy is being tested once more. Trump and his confederates face prosecution for the events of January 6, and yet his party has embraced "election denialism," proclaiming that the political system is fraudulent to the core, rigged to disfavor Republicans and steal votes for Democrats. Trump is running for president on a platform with this claim front and center, and a solid majority of his party stands behind him.

But it seems wrong to see the crisis as beginning and ending with Trump and assume that his departure from the national stage will allow the corner to be decisively turned. Election denialism feeds a form of antipolitics that rejects the tenets of the free exercise of democratic politics. A democratic politics is defined by the give-and-take of debate and disagreement, acceptance of the diversity of opinion and interests, a shared understanding that elections go one way and then the other, and respect for the institutions that make a free politics possible. In antipolitics, political activity as a means of reconciling diverse opinions and interests is seen as an abject surrender of principle. It is replaced instead by a bullying disregard for the views of the opposition, which is not just to be defeated at the polls but utterly vanquished. Partisans should control elections, all the better to ensure the desired results, and the rule of law, disdained as a political tool, is ready at hand for use against adversaries, to punish and weaken them.

This is not the standard, time-honored cynicism about our politics. I recall reading in 2007 a book titled *The American Lie: Government by the People and Other Political Fables*, which—years before Trump—had nothing good to say about the politics in our democracy. "Millions of Americans see over and over again that politicians and government officials, routinely, deceive, mislead, and misinform them, offering pretexts while masking their true plans and purposes."[1] Benjamin Ginsberg, a political scientist, saw nothing trustworthy in the routine operation of American politics. Even elections serve to control and channel public participation: they are fundamentally "a means of regulating popular political activity."[2] Voters have a choice, but it's a choice between two political parties who vie for victory with slick marketing techniques and limitless mendacity. The established order does not really want voters engaged in the business of politics. Send them to the ballot box every few years: That should do it. That should shut them up.

Many voters—and no doubt, many nonvoters—agree with this grim assessment. Writing many years ago, another close observer of American political culture noted the "common opinion" among the electorate that "American politics are 'dirty' and that the candidates and parties do a major share of their 'dirty work' in campaigns for public office." This, he wrote, "has long seemed to be one of the major and persistent components of the American political system."[3] This picture of grubby, self-interested politics may be overdrawn. It is often enough an expression of disgruntlement about conditions over which politicians may have little but not total control, and it is easier for the public to blame their leadership than to face the complex reasons things are not as many voters wish them to be. Still, it is real enough: There is a dirty side to politics.

For all this distrust and wariness, however overstated, the place in which we find ourselves now is starkly different. Behind the standard cynicism about politics is a wish to reclaim and reinvigorate it, to have it work better. Now we experience a cynicism defined at its core by rejection, the repudiation of politics as a democratic value. When Donald Trump declared that the election results he refused to accept justified "the termination of all rules, regulations, and articles, even those found in the Constitution,"[4] congressional leaders on both sides of the aisle denounced him. But not all. Not, for example, a different generation of senators, such as Rick Scott of Florida and Josh Hawley of Missouri, who said it was really up to the voters to decide whether Donald Trump's arguments for setting aside the Constitution had any merit. I suspect they were in large measure looking to get themselves out of the argument and avoid inflaming the Trump base. But that wasn't all. They were also making a bet: that for a significant portion of the American electorate—the portion on which they depended for their own political advancement—the call for the suspension of the Constitution would have definite appeal.

After all, if the assumption is that our politics is irredeemably corrupt, then the framework the Constitution establishes for the conduct of this politics, including the protections for free speech and free association, may be a contributing factor. If the practice of politics has fallen into disrepute, then the institutions on which politics depends are suspect; and if necessary, the constitutional order that is the foundation for this activity must also be brought into question.

The reasons for how things have come to this point are complex. I feel I have some sense of the explanation, some reasonable notion, but far from a full grasp on the truth. I am convinced that the course we are on is untenable. If there are some who do not adhere to even basic assumptions about democratic politics, what progress toward the restoration of our deteriorating civic life might we expect?

Some of that work of restoration may involve, as it always does, the enactment of legal reform. It can be urgent and bipartisan, and we have a recent example. The two parties came together in 2022 to reform the law governing the congressional vote count at the end of the presidential selection process. The Electoral Count Reform Act was a major achievement, resolving basic questions about the conduct of the congressional proceedings under attack on January 6—and the new law rejected in clear terms the preposterous and dangerous claims that the vice president of the United States could unilaterally either decide the outcome of the election or prevent Congress from completing the electoral vote count. I worked with Democratic and Republican committee staff on that bill, consulted with a bipartisan coalition in favor of reform led by Senators Susan Collins, Amy Klobuchar, Joe Manchin, and others, and testified

before the Senate Rules Committee hearing on the proposed legislation. This experience, one of the most rewarding of my career, showed
that it is not impossible to include legal reform in the work across the
partisan divide that must be done to reconstruct American democratic
institutions.

Nor should too much be read into this experience. Legal reform can
carry only some of the burden of democratic renewal. In times of stress,
each party looks upon the reform proposals of the other as little more
than ploys serving partisan self-interest. The history of reform debates is,
in fact, part of the history of the struggle for political power. It is rare that
a party has actively supported a reform of the political process it did not
believe to be consistent with its own interests or has not been suspected
of having this motive. Suspicions of self-interest boil over in periods of
polarization such as ours and make reform hard to develop and pass on
anything like a true bipartisan basis.

For that reason, many of one party's cherished reforms don't last
long in the face of objections from the losers in the reform debate. There
is always a conflict between legal restrictions on the conduct of politics
and the freedom each party craves to do what is necessary to win. From
1976 to 2004, the country embarked on a major effort to reform the way
we finance our elections. By the end of the period, most of those controls,
for all practical purposes, had crashed to the ground. One party's relentless opposition to campaign finance controls is one chapter in this story,
but it's clear that when the stakes are high, both sides strive to do what
it takes to win. Reforms that are oversold in the first place, and cannot
produce what is claimed, only compound the cynicism, hastening the
descent into antipolitics.

The crisis of democratic politics is a crisis of public faith *in* politics.
To restore faith in government, the role of politics has to be defended.
For this defense to stand any chance of being persuasive, political actors
bear responsibility to demonstrate, in the choices they make, that it can
and should be an honorable and ethical calling. Good politics can be
played hard and passionately but also with respect for the limits beyond
which it cannot go—cannot ethically go. Not all the limits are clear; not
everyone agrees on the limits. However, there has to be agreement that

there are limits of some kind, and that political actors are accountable for honestly confronting choices and accepting responsibility for those they make.

This is the point at which the normal cynicism about politics can be particularly destructive. The cynic scoffs at the very idea that the ethical standards of political activity can be raised, that any such standards exist at all. I cannot agree that politics and ethics are worlds apart, one having nothing to do with the other. Many years ago, an insightful "defense of politics" showed how it was, in fact, a moral enterprise, that "to act morally in politics is to consider the results of one's actions," and that "however convinced [men and women are] of the rightness of their party, they must compromise its claims to the needs of some electoral and legal framework."[5] In a profound sense, democratic politics is ethical in nature, if it can be said to be democratic at all.

In my experience, political actors know the difference between good and bad politics, but many can get caught up in the game, driven by their own ambitions or demons, and they suppress whatever flickers of conscience they may experience. Bad politics is rationalized easily enough: blood sport, or the other side started it first, or the goal is winning and *so very sorry about that, but we did what we had to do.* But politicians, and their aides and advisers, know the critical difference between the good and the bad, and the hard calls in between, and they can and should be held responsible for refusing to pay close attention to them as they go about their business.

In one remarkable instance of an open recognition of unethical politics, Lee Atwater, a leading Republican strategist who directed George H. W. Bush's 1988 election campaign, offered a deathbed apology to Bush's opponent, Massachusetts Governor Michael Dukakis. Atwater was the mastermind behind the infamous Willie Horton strategy, which combined a loud racist dog whistle with a distortion of the facts to paint Dukakis as a capital L, Massachusetts "liberal" whose policies and beliefs were located at an ideological extreme of American politics. Among other claims, the Bush campaign depicted the Democrat as recklessly furloughing convicted murderers who could and would then return to the streets to commit violent crimes. This attack echoed paid advertising by an independent group delivering the same attack with an unmistakable racist message: Dukakis thought nothing of releasing Black criminals to commit violence and rape against white people. At the time, Atwater was proud to "do what it takes to win." Years later, he acknowledged that he employed "naked cruelty" against Dukakis and had relished his reputation as an "ugly" practitioner of "negative politics."[6]

Atwater did not mean for this "negative" politics to be confused with the sharp delineation of differences between candidates, their ideologies, and their positions. He meant a politics so negative in its contempt for facts, fairness, legitimate differences, and moral limits such as abjuring racist appeals, that it borders on or becomes an antipolitics. The opposition becomes the enemy and must be destroyed, not debated, and in this war, anything goes. Atwater's regrets were duly noted, and the political world moved on.

In reflecting on this fundamental difference between good and bad, between the ethical and the unethical in politics, I recall a conversation I had in 2015 with then-vice president Joe Biden about a man we both knew and admired, Nordhoff "Nordy" Hoffman. The vice president, now president, knew him well as the former head of the Senate arm of the national Democratic Party—the Democratic Senatorial Campaign Committee (DSCC)—charged with advising and funding Democratic Senate campaigns. Nordy had exhibited an extraordinary confidence, not widely shared at the time, that a twenty-nine-year-old Delaware Democrat, Joe Biden, could defeat a longtime Republican, Caleb Boggs. I remember this well, as Nordy had given me my first job in politics as a summer intern at the DSCC, and he would declare to anyone who would listen in the summer of 1972 that Biden could do it—he could win the damn thing, no matter what others might think.

Nordy was a former All-American tackle on the fabled Notre Dame championship football teams coached by Knute Rockne. He was massive: when he picked up the phone, the receiver virtually disappeared from view into his meaty grip. He was full of cheer, loud most of the time and more audible, at considerable distances, when excited or angry. He started out as an organizer for the United Steelworkers, then became the head of their lobbying team in Washington, and in his next step, executive director of the DSCC. He was a Democrat from head to toe. In the crowning moment of his career, the Senate Democratic majority elected him the Senate's sergeant at arms, a position as the body's chief administrative officer with a wide portfolio from communications technology to security.

Senate Democrats chose Nordy in recognition of his campaign work on their behalf, and he knew he would hold the position only as long as Democrats held their majority. In 1981, they no longer did, and the Republicans replaced him. But he never failed to grasp that, regardless of his service to the party that had landed him the job, his role as a Senate official called for him to be nonpartisan and work with both Democrats and Republicans and their staffs. He was the Senate's—the whole Senate's—sergeant at arms. As he recounted in an oral history years later, he considered this bipartisan institutional work a "privilege." When he retired, one Republican senator would say of this Democratic warrior: "During my entire acquaintance with Nordy Hoffman, I never saw a flicker of partisan bias."[7]

Nordy did not stop there. He saw this new job as a chance to make a point about democratic values. He believed that "we in America . . . don't spend enough time listening." He believed that good politics requires listening. He arranged for Democratic and Republican administrative assistants (essentially chiefs of staff to the senators) to attend a first-ever, bipartisan, three-hour session on "how to listen." And Nordy noted with satisfaction that of those who attended the listening session, "only two got up and left. Those two who left, their senators lost the next election. I don't know that that had anything to do with it, but at least I got a kick out of it!" It almost seemed that the Democrat Hoffman could have accepted victories by these two Republican senators if they had won because they had learned to listen.

This was pure Nordy: he loved politics, but he wanted to do it the right way and believed that there was such a thing as a right way. Nordy valued—he did not just accept—the limits on political combat and the need to accept disappointing results. In his oral history, recalling two Democrats he admired, Ed Muskie of Maine and former senator and vice president Hubert Humphrey, he regretted that neither made it to the presidency in the year Nixon was elected. "They might have made a change in the country if they had won, but it was not to be; therefore, we had to go along with what we were given by the voters, which is the right way to go. I can't argue with that." This was many years ago, when an old political hand like Nordy Hoffman could say, of the election of Richard Nixon so many Democrats had reviled for so long, that it was a result "given by the voters" and he could not "argue with that."[8]

On that day in 2015, before the start of a meeting about whether he would run the following year, I shared memories of Nordy with Vice President Biden. Biden was visibly moved by these recollections. He had never forgotten Nordy's well-placed faith in his first and improbable Senate candidacy, but our reminiscence turned quickly to Nordy as an individual and political professional and what he represented: that in politics, there is a "right way to go" and that all those active in our public life have an obligation to care about it, and to find it.

ACKNOWLEDGMENTS

It's impossible to adequately credit all who have done so much to shape my thinking about this book, several of whom also commented on chapters, or all, of the drafts.

I'll begin with family members: my wife Anita and my children, all of whom read and commented on the drafts and were constructive—and unsparing, as close family tend to be—in their criticisms. Anita put up with endless questions and requests for advice: The book is so much the better for her help and support. I just have to mention our cats Oscar and Scoop who may have napped and snacked through much of the research and writing but also found time to walk across my keyboard and revise, in their way, a number of passages.

I'm immensely grateful to those who graciously and very helpfully commented on the draft: Matt Bai, Judy Corley, Jack Goldsmith, Tom Griffith, Rick Hasen, Sally Katzen, Fred Kronz, Trevor Morrison, Rick Pildes, Jen Psaki, Jeffrey Weil, and Martin Willard. As always, my close friend over so many years, Fred Martin, encouraged this project from beginning to end and his suggestions were invaluable. Jack Goldsmith, an exceptional writer and scholar, and the co-author of our book *After Trump*, has always given me consistently excellent and badly needed advice on how to address the challenges of book writing.

I presented parts of an early draft to my NYU law colleagues at a faculty workshop, and their questions and comments were simulating and enormously helpful. NYU has provided me with a marvelous home for teaching and writing, and I cannot thank enough the Deans: Ricky Revesz who recruited me, and his successors, Trevor Morrison, and Troy McKenzie. My good friends and colleagues Rick Pildes and Sam

Issacharoff, pioneers in the field of law and democracy, have been models of exemplary scholarship in this area of the law I care so much about.

Boundless thanks as well to research assistants who have helped me over the years with my work on the subject of this book: ethics in politics and government. I fear overlooking someone: but they know who they are. Darby Hopper and Rachel Greene played a special and invaluable role in the final and intense stages of manuscript review. My gratitude as well to the support provided by my assistant at NYU, Quetin O'Berry.

Of course, I owe numerous rounds of heartful thanks to my editor, Jon Sisk, and his team at Rowman & Littlefield. My agents at Javelin, Matt Latimer and Robin Sproul, guided me through this process, and I am grateful for their skill and patience with me.

And last but far from least: I can't and won't name all of those I have been privileged to advise over the years in government and politics. Some appear with express reference and at some considerable length in chapters of the book. Over the course of my career, I have been fortunate to work with real leaders who care profoundly about the health of our democratic institutions and who have worked hard to arrest their unraveling and to repair the damage.

Bob Bauer
January 2024
Washington, D.C.

And since failure lies at the core of who we are, the most important stories we tell about ourselves, as well as those we read about others, are primarily tales of failing. . . . Failure and storytelling are intimate friends, always in cahoots.

—Costica Bratadan
In Praise of Failure

We are blinded in examining our own labors by innumerable prejudices.

—Samuel Johnson
The Rambler, No. 21

CHAPTER I

First Words About a Life in Politics

I choose a life in politics as the son of an immigrant with a passionate love of a healthy American politics and of the institutions that make it possible. As a lawyer for political parties, politicians, and campaigns, I handle a lot of the routine business of helping clients comply with laws and rules, but I also have the good fortune to represent presidents in their campaigns and in office. I gain and enjoy the reputation of a hard-charging lawyer zealously committed to helping his clients win and reflect on the importance of defining and caring about ethical politics. I note how other notable figures in our politics have come to a similar conclusion but doubt that they have gotten it quite right, and I decide to give my view, based on a self-critical appraisal of my own experience.

This is a book about my career as a lawyer in politics—a political lawyer helping clients to win elections or fights about public policy. Not all of that career was spent in the vise of major ethical dilemmas, not by any means. Much of it has been distinctly routine, such as counseling a California biking club on how its members might legally drop leaflets along the trail in opposition to a particular congressional candidate. Or advising a crestfallen minister who quite unintentionally broke the law in funding the early stage of a campaign and had to return quietly to the pulpit while sorting out his legal affairs. Or explaining to a bewildered congressional candidate why her proud father broke the law by giving his own daughter a very large, very loving contribution, but way too much, for her political campaign.

Some opportunities that have come my way have been far from
routine. I have had the good fortune to represent two presidents, Barack
Obama and Joe Biden: the first as presidential campaign counsel and
later White House counsel and the second as personal and political
counsel. I have counseled the Democratic Senate leadership in a presidential impeachment, represented my party and its candidates in House
and Senate recounts of disputed elections, and defended its officials in
congressional investigations. I've made the case for my clients in court,
congressional testimony, and the media. This has all been part of the
political machinery running in the background, which in election years
moves to the foreground of American democratic life.

Through these years, often with deep and misplaced self-satisfaction,
I energetically gave counsel or helped to execute controversial political
strategies—the kind some described as cutting edge, a bull in a china
shop, or take no prisoners. These are the ones on which I have rightly
reflected in sorting out what the tough-minded lawyer owed his clients
in intense political competition and what might, in retrospect, raise issues
I did not see or engage with clearly at the time. As a Democratic party
lawyer, I used a novel legal theory to sue a member of the Republican
congressional leadership over a campaign spending ploy. This move was
condemned at the time, even in some Democratic quarters, as an escalation in the political wars. In another legal strategy of this kind, I pressed
the threat of criminal prosecution not only against a legally sketchy political operation itself, but also the private donors who put up the money.
For this I was criticized for "intimidation" tactics. I was a member of a
Democratic legal team that aided House Democrats in 1985 in challenging the state certification of the election of a Republican candidate for
the House. The House then conducted its own recount and seated the
Democrat, declaring him the winner . . . by four votes.

Certainly, as White House counsel, I understood the difference
between the roles of party lawyer and government lawyer. Still, I was
involved in controversial decisions that some took as an indication that I
was less a reliable government counselor than an enabler of my boss's—
the president's—political and policy preferences. This is a familiar charge
against White House lawyers, and in the past those who made poor

decisions suffered a lasting loss of reputation and even, in the Watergate era, imprisonment. I never engaged in activities that would have brought about the direst of consequences, but if I stumbled in the job, it was because once again—as in a campaign, so too in government—the imperative was to help my side prevail, which clouded other considerations and the better judgment those other considerations would have helped inform.

It is from this vantage point that I have observed at close quarters the toll that an unethical politics has taken on American democracy. To say this is not to engage in any false moral equivalence or what-about-ism in which everyone and every party at all times share equally in the blame for the current state of the democracy. It is not to somehow "contextualize" the ascendency of Donald Trump and his unique dismissal of ethics, taken all the way to utter contempt for the rule of law. I'm second to none in my opposition to all that Donald Trump represents as a politician: the lies, the cruelty, the refusal to accept responsibility, the contempt for institutions, the installation of family in White House jobs, the disdain for expertise, the relentless self-interestedness. These traits hold a special place of dishonor in the history of the American presidency (as does the enabling and protective behavior of elected officials of his own party). Trump has been in politics what he has been in business: a shamelessly unethical actor. I will note his unique and malign contributions throughout this book.

Yet democracy depends on those moments, far from headlines but ones I and others in politics have confronted often enough, when those in positions of political responsibility must recognize an ethical choice and make the right one. Politics, it is said, is a contact sport, and it is naïve to deny that it can be exciting to watch and, for those on the field, to play. Winning is exhilarating. There is also a line to be drawn between hard contact and foul play, and this line separates hardball politics from a slide into attacks on the foundations of the democracy. That line has to be considered—and then, as an ethical politics demands, it has to be drawn—in making choices that arise in the competition for political power.

To speak usefully at all of political ethics requires clearing away every temptation to play favorites and subjecting your own—and your allies'—experience to the same hard look that you demand for adversaries. It is to ask what you might have missed or excused in your work, or in what you observed around you, which can illuminate the larger problems with the way politics is practiced. It might come about in deciding what is necessary to win an election—and appreciating that it really does matter how, not just whether, it was won. Or in using the law to harass or hound political opponents. Or making questionable legal arguments, and sowing mistrust of the legal system, in the belief that the best political lawyers are the ones who will say whatever works, who reliably "do whatever it takes" to win.

In telling the story of the bad state of ethics in government and politics, I will tell my own; I will tell it *through* my own. In relating my experience, mustering as much honesty as possible about successes and failures, I might be able to say something of use about the unreliable moral compass of the political class, on the central importance of ethics in public life, of individual choice in "doing the right thing." Now in my seventies, I am trying to better grasp what has gone wrong here, around the time that I have been looking back on my years in politics to understand what shaped my own decisions and actions.

This is the hard part—when a fellow citizen terrified by the state of the democracy is asked to keep an eye on their ethical responses to the danger. After all, if the democracy confronts an assault that is conducted without concern for limits, how can a defense succeed if it is hobbled by worries about ethics? How, such a troubled citizen might ask, could any suggestion be less timely, more self-destructive?

The choice is a false one. Nothing in my recollections and observations suggests ethics as a kind of fatal weakness of will. A tough response to attacks on the democracy is not alien to ethics in the practice of everyday politics. Calling attention to that ethical challenge is simply to recognize that it is in the details of routine political action that fundamental democratic principles and norms are honored—or, if disregarded, weakened. It seems hard to imagine that the defense of democracy can succeed in the long run if those conducting it also trash those principles and norms.

This is not just an appeal to the aphorism "when they go low, we go high," betting on a winning contrast between democracy's foes and its friends. It does not require the lazy supposition that "we" are "better" than they are. It is a belief in democratic politics, which relies for the defense of democracy on the very institutions and norms it is defending: free elections, a free press and untrammeled debate, meaningful constraints on the abuse of government power, and respect for voters who are not assumed to be easy marks for propaganda. A politics in which all these norms and institutions have been discredited becomes the antipolitics—anti-democratic politics—that democracy's assailants are counting on for their success. An ethical politics is one that faces up to the hard choices that vying for political power often poses.

The experiences I recount here are meant to draw attention to those choices. Sometimes I am OK with the advice given and choices made; sometimes, looking back, I am less so. This book is not prompted by any need to confess sins or point fingers, but a desire in our current circumstances to reflect on experience. Because if a commitment to ethics means anything, it starts with taking it seriously, discussing it honestly, and holding onto some hope for improvement.

Family history is one key to how I understand the ethical dimension of politics. My father was an ardent Democrat, a refugee from Nazi-occupied Austria who was passionately grateful for the home and career that America afforded him once he was off the boat from Portugal after a hazardous flight through Czechoslovakia and France. He took politics seriously; it always remained for him a matter of life and death. He survived the corruption of his country's politics and its eventual invasion. His mother who had raised him alone, having lost her husband in World War I, did not survive. The Germans shipped her to a death camp in Belarus, where she was shot on the day of arrival, as was her sister.

From this background, I absorbed powerful and sometimes but not always compatible commitments. One was a highly partisan outlook on politics—Democratic party politics, mostly in line with its progressive wing. Another was a concern with the requirements of basic civility in political speech and behavior. My father was a Democrat through and through: he did not demonize all Republicans, though he had a lifelong and passionate aversion to Richard Nixon. But in politics, as he saw it, there was a right and a wrong, a wise and a foolish, even a good and a bad, and he was sure that Democrats mostly got it right—and Republicans got it very wrong. For all the importance to him of party labels, attachments, and convictions, he was still civil in manner and decent in his treatment of others. For him, the treatment of others, especially those with whom we disagree, was as fundamental to democracy as voting.

As a young man, son of a Catholic father and Jewish mother who converted upon marriage, he was raised in the church, and it was always very much part of him. But he was horrified by the Austrian Catholic hierarchy's failure to stand against Nazism, and he left the church, never to return. For him it was a question not so much of ideology or doctrine, but of basic decency toward others. It was a matter of ethical choice.

I was also deeply affected by my father's commitment to institutions. He was born into the Austro-Hungarian monarchy and baptized into the Catholic Church, and while he understood that institutions could be corrupted, as he painfully observed in this church's scandalous behavior, he could not fathom the political order without institutions, even if these were imperfect and might always require criticism and reform. He watched as the fragile democratic institutions and norms of interwar Austria came apart. When his despised Richard Nixon resigned in the Watergate scandal in August 1974, I sat with him as he watched Gerald Ford's first words as president from the East Room of the White House. My father wept quietly, moved that in this moment the battered institutions of American democracy had proven their resilience, their durability.

This family history imprinted on me these commitments and left me to resolve the occasional tension between them. Partisanship in a no-holds-barred politics has been hardest to keep under control, especially when the consequences of losing have seemed inconceivable. I remain very much a Democrat in my formal commitments and voting patterns, but I now find it increasingly unhelpful to think "like a Democrat" in reflecting on contemporary small *d* democratic problems.

The purest partisanship, or what the public takes it to be, is childish: my party, right or wrong. Gradually, under group and political pressures, it can degenerate into something far worse. A political commitment at its best can be joyous, an inspiration, a reason to rise in the morning with a sense of purpose. Once a certain uglier form of partisanship takes hold, that sense of purpose can become a dark obsession with an enemy—the other side—and the martial discipline believed necessary for mortal combat sucks the joy out of it. Certain topics cannot be discussed, certain questions cannot be raised, certain doubts cannot be expressed, because these would sow discord in the ranks when unity is deemed indispensable in vanquishing the enemy. And winning becomes everything.

Other veterans of government and politics have been moved to consider the question of ethical choice in politics, and yet often what they offer is simply one version or the other of answering to their own consciences. Jim Comey, former director of the FBI, chose to operate outside normal government processes in addressing allegations of senior government wrongdoing, drawing fire from both Democrats and Republicans. His answer has been that those in politics and government have a "higher loyalty" that compels them to answer to a moral law, generally defined as "the values that sustain us," and his list is "restraint and integrity and balance and transparency and truth."[1] Tim Miller, a former Republican operative and consultant who has repented his work on behalf of the Trump Republican party, now appeals to the "desire within us to be seen by those we care about as righteous and good."[2]

Well, sure, there are moments when the overriding need is to identify what it is you can live with, and what you can't. But ethical conduct in politics is not at bottom about conscience and the limits of any one political actor's personal tolerance for particular tactics. The call for ethical action comes from the *outside*, from considerations connected to what a healthy politics requires. These are the considerations that distinguish relatively harmless, obvious political lying or puffery—"I am delighted to be here with our great [in truth, detested] Governor Jones"—from democratically corrosive deceit. Or the difference between political "hardball" and outright thuggery in which any limits in the pursuit of victory are swept aside. Or the difference between reform to strengthen democratic institutions and processes and "reform" as the cover story for what is in fact a strategy to enact into law special competitive advantages for one party over the other.

The concern of ethical politics is the health of democratic institutions, norms, and processes that define civic engagement and life. The Trump years brought on much discussion of "norms"—those practices and understandings that bind a democracy together, filling in the spaces left open by constitutional arrangements and law. In a well-known formulation, the political scientists Steven Levitsky and Daniel Ziblatt stressed two norms of central importance: "mutual toleration, the understanding that competing parties accept one another as legitimate rivals," and "forbearance," which requires restraint in the exercise of power.[3] And these norms, like others, reinforce each other. A government may have the capacity to deploy its authority in the most political of ways, to intimidate or marginalize its opposition; but this absence of forbearance is also an offense against the norm of "mutual toleration."[4] We may disagree violently with others, but we may not resort to violence to express that disagreement; we may find it hard to accept what our political opponents say, but we accept their right to say it.

Political ethics are the decisions that political actors must make in concrete circumstances to give life to these democratic norms or violate them. An unethical choice can occur by action or speech—by calling out political opponents as "enemies of the people," or by joining these words with a refusal to concede a lost election and support the peaceful transfer of power. Those who occupy positions of both high responsibility and great power have choices to make all the time about how to use that power, and it is sometimes, maybe even often, possible to use that authority to make it harder for the opposition party to be heard and to compete.

Many notable failures of politics come about because of blindness to ethics in this very particular sense. While a highly individualized ethics—say a public official's taking care not to make questionable commitments to donors in return for their contributions—is certainly better than no ethics at all, it is not enough. It is the least we might expect. It is insufficient to pass on to the next generation any richer sense of the standards for the conduct of public life in a democracy.

In my teaching and writing in the legal academy, at the New York University School of Law, I have been working on these issues of ethics in politics and government. I developed a professional responsibility course for students, titled the Role of the Lawyer in Public Life, to examine the sources of ethical guidance for responsible public officials and other political actors. Our focus is the American Bar Association Model Rules of Professional Responsibility, and one of particular interest, which all lawyers are called upon to consider as they go about the business of representing clients, is Rule 2.1:

> In representing a client, a lawyer shall exercise independent professional judgment and render candid advice. In rendering advice, a lawyer may refer not only to law but to other considerations such as moral, economic, social and political factors, that may be relevant to the client's situation.[5]

The commentary accompanying the rule notes that "advice couched in narrow legal terms may be of little value to a client, especially where practical considerations, such as cost or effects on other people, are predominant." It may not be enough to give "purely technical legal advice," and it is "proper for a lawyer to refer to relevant moral and ethical considerations in giving advice," because these "considerations impinge upon most legal questions and may decisively influence how the law will be applied."

My hope is to bring home to my students, many of whose careers will include significant positions in the public life of the nation, that ethical considerations—the choice to take or not take an action because it is the right thing to do, or not do—are vitally important in the performance of their professional responsibilities. Being the smartest or cleverest adviser in the room is not all there is to it.

In our class's discussion of ethical issues, we touch on the virtual absence from public life of resignations tendered for the right ethical reasons as evidence of the degraded state of ethics in public life. Disgraced politicians or officials in the United States do not typically resign in true disgrace and because of it; they give other reasons, such as wishing to avoid distractions or needing to spend healing time with families they happily ignored for years as they pursued greater glory. They resign only when the jig is up: their political support has collapsed, or the law is at the door. Graceful departures from the public stage prompted by ethical misconduct—by the exposure of outright lies or of policies dictated by naked self-interest—are virtually unheard of. And this insistence on clinging to power and position is itself a glaring ethical failing.

But what I have to say about all this will emerge from my own experiences: this is not a book of law or policy, nor a manifesto for reform. It is a story about one person's involvement in American politics, in the course of which ethical questions kept coming up, and now, at this time, seem to me of central importance.

CHAPTER 2

Getting into the Business

In the 1970s the United States begins to pass laws to regulate politics, and I jump at the opportunity to become a political lawyer and help politicians navigate these new rules. There are complications: politics costs me a job at a law firm, I have no clear idea what I am doing, lost elections mean lost clients, and my law practice becomes very personal for me.

I graduated from law school in 1976, a year after a disgraced Richard Nixon resigned the presidency following the Watergate scandal. I had hoped to use my law degree in politics, and Watergate presented the opportunity. A president who refused to leave his reelection to fair competition under the law had committed crimes to improve his chances and damage his opponent's. The scheme began to unravel when a team of burglars operating on his behalf botched a break-in of opposition headquarters. Soon it all came out: a range of abuses of power, political dirty tricks, sketchy campaign money practices, and a cover-up of crimes as inept as the felonies it was designed to conceal. The entire episode led to calls for reform—legal reform—which meant that politicians needed lawyers more than ever before.

Until the post-Watergate 1970s, the United States did not have a highly regulated electoral process. In 1907, Congress banned direct corporate contributions to candidates. In the early 1920s, Congress had passed a campaign finance law ostensibly establishing limits on the contributions candidates could receive and public disclosure requirements for their campaign organizations. These measures languished on the books for decades, largely ignored and without effect. There was another of these passes at reform in the 1940s, aimed at political spending by unions, but this, too, lacked any real bite.

The Watergate reforms changed all that. They included laws passed to fill the gaping holes in coverage and compliance in federal campaign finance laws. A new enforcement agency, the Federal Election Commission, began issuing rules and interpretations. Campaign money had to be tracked; some contributions had to be kept within limits, and others, like those a corporation might offer, turned away altogether. Even a party's support for its own candidates was subject to new controls. Politicians raising and spending money in their campaigns had to have lawyers on hand.

Beyond that, there was even more for lawyers to do. Congress also toughened up its code of ethics, a body of disciplinary rules its members would have to observe, such as limits on gifts they could receive from those with business before Congress. The executive branch did the same for its employees. Both members of Congress and senior executive branch employees had to file personal financial disclosure reports of their income sources, assets, and holdings, which allowed for public inspection of possible sources of conflict of interest. In this same period, federal prosecutors tried out new theories on which to base charges of public corruption. In a few years, Congress would also turn its attention to regulating lobbying, which it had never had much appetite for: the last lobbying law it passed decades before was supposed to produce reliable reports of money spent by interests to advance, stop, or modify legislation, but it was useless, all too easily evaded.

Worrying about the law was now part of the routine business of politics in this new era. If a political party organization did research for one of its candidates, would that count as a contribution, such that its market value had to be estimated and it could be given only within the lawful dollar limits (at the time $1,000 per election)? Could a corporate executive who was active as a political donor use her office staff to research the candidates and help send out the money—or was this use of the company personnel and office space an illegal corporate contribution?

Did campaign volunteers make a reportable, regulated contribution to the candidate by renting a car, paid out of their own pocket, to travel around a congressional district? Mistakes could result in government enforcement and penalties.

These laws and rules could interact in still more dangerous ways for politicians. All these requirements were criminally enforceable if there was evidence that they were ignored or intentionally violated. And there were hard questions, not really resolved to this day. When did a campaign contribution become a bribe—the potential subject of criminal prosecution—and not just the support that a donor would naturally provide to a politician whose record and public commitments aligned with the giver's political views or a constituent's legitimate expectations? What were the criminal legal consequences of inviting a politician to give a speech at a trade association convention at a sunny resort location, and reimbursing travel and lodging expenses, around the time that a vote was scheduled in which the association was vitally interested? More generally, when did all the ways of buttering up a politician—"building a relationship" to smooth the path to successful influence peddling or lobbying—become a serious legal problem?

Among the notable signs of this post-Watergate period was a federal law enforcement sting operation named ABSCAM. Members of Congress were invited to take official action in immigration matters in exchange for cash provided by FBI agents posing as wealthy Arab sheiks. The government could not know that these elected officials would reveal themselves to be corrupt. It was a test. As a court later described the mission, in one of the many appeals filed by defendant members of Congress: "The Executive Branch of the United States has carried out a plan to determine whether members of the Legislative Branch and others would commit bribery offenses, if presented with the opportunity to do so."[1] A few of the targeted members gladly took the bribes. A couple resisted, and the agent-sheiks persisted with their offer and eventually got them to take suitcases with cash. All the public officials who were tried were found guilty.

It was clear to me at the time, as it was soon enough to the parties and politicians: there was a need for political lawyers.

My practice had to start somewhere, as in having a client, and one showed up almost immediately after I left law school. I had been an unpaid intern at a Democratic Party organization, Nordy Hoffman's Democratic Senatorial Campaign Committee, and there I met and worked under the supervision of a member of the staff, Bob Thomson, who later took his law degree to a firm to which he brought the DSCC as a client. Bob and I got along well, which was not what I had any reason to predict or expect. A former marine and Vietnam War veteran, he was highly organized, retained a sharp focus, and "read the room" very well. I was full of energy, but sort of all over the place. I had the tendency, youthful but also temperamental, to bring a certain excitability to stressful situations. Bob seemed to think I had the makings of a good lawyer and a chance to get my impulsiveness under control. He was a true mentor.

When Bob left his law practice for a position in the Carter administration, he invited me to take his place at the firm. I inherited the DSCC as a client, and it was unusually valuable for a lawyer starting out, only twenty-five years old. Not only was the DSCC one of only six national political party organizations, but it was also run by Democratic members of the U.S. Senate; and so now I could counsel the committee as well as the senators who ran for reelection every six years and recruited other Senate aspirants to challenge Republican incumbents. I steadily added more Democratic Party organizations and candidates. Soon other clients adapting to the radically transformed legal environment sought help: trade associations and corporations seeking to encourage their executives to make personal contributions because the companies could not, lobbyists, wealthy political activists, and political organizations formed to support candidates or appeal to the public for the adoption of particular public policies.

This was the base of the early practice. It was a Democratic practice: most of the then-meager revenue flowed from that source, and I would not accept clients whose interests were adverse to the Democratic Party. By 1980, I was able to keep myself more or less busy full-time with this work in the D.C. office of the Philadelphia-based firm of Dechert, Price and Rhoads (now the Dechert firm).

Then a bit of politics shook up my political practice, forcing me out of the law firm. One of the firm partners, Arlen Specter, a Republican and nationally prominent former district attorney of Philadelphia, had decided to run for the U.S. Senate. He had earlier let the firm know that he had no plans for a 1980 campaign, then changed his mind and concluded that it was unhelpful to him to have within the firm a lawyer, a young associate attorney no less, who was working with Democrats to retain control of the Senate. He wanted me out. The firm management was embarrassed by this turn of events, but explained to me that I had to go, and offered me a loan to open up my own office for the duration of the election year. If Specter lost, I was told, the problem would disappear—as it would if he won (which he did) and left the firm for the Senate. In the meantime, I could keep my practice going, maintaining my roster of Democratic clients, but somewhere else.

And off I went. For a few months, I practiced on my own, with one assistant, as I waited out the election and the resolution of the Specter problem. I did not, however, return to Dechert. In the fall of 1980, I joined the firm of Perkins Coie, which came knocking on my door with the commitment that I would be well supported in practice-building and not shown the door because of political conflicts. They were true to their word, and I stayed for thirty-eight years, with a few departures in between to be counsel to the Senate Democratic Caucus in the Clinton impeachment trial and then White House counsel to President Obama.

Over those decades, the field of political law came into its own. I began hiring additional lawyers to help with the growing client list. We managed to establish ourselves as the leading legal team for Senate and House Democrats, representing their party organizations and many of them in their campaigns. It is because of this presence in the party that for years I handled political law issues for Democratic leaders Senator Tom Daschle and Representative Dick Gephardt. Allied groups outside Capitol Hill called on us to advise them on building or expanding their political organizations and programs. Not all our work was party-connected, as we advised a range of organizations and individuals on legal channels for achieving political goals and influence, but the reputation we developed, and the vast majority of work I did in a given year, was for Democratic interests. It was through this work that I became involved in the Clinton impeachment trial, and later met Barack Obama and Joe Biden.

The circumstances in which I came to adopt political law as a career path strike me now as having had consequences for how I approached the practice and appreciated, or did not, the demands, including ethical demands, of doing this kind of work.

Because it was a new field, I was largely on my own. Bob Thomson did what he could to prepare me for private law practice, but the transition, before he went to take up his White House position, was brief. No one else in the firm where I practiced was a political lawyer. At a very young age I had both the advantage of developing a special expertise and the opportunity to establish a practice of my own, but the disadvantage of lacking any practice or role model. The period on my own before I joined Perkins added to a false sense of myself as a lawyer already well-equipped for prime time in political law.

This didn't bother me a bit. What young lawyer would not treasure this level of independence?

But independence from supervision did not mean distance from my clients, and of that I had little. I kept close company with the political clients I represented. It is generally to the advantage of client and lawyer that they do not grow too close, that the lawyer not overidentify with those they owe the duty of dispassionate legal advice. I did not grasp that at the outset; I was happy to be a member of the campaign team. Taken altogether, my youth, intense political commitments, and not much of a professional model to guide me, shaped, and in some respects limited, the guidance I could offer my clients in the early years. I could certainly practice the basic craft of law—read and understand the statutes and case law, lay out options, evaluate legal risks. I was far less equipped to season my technical legal analysis with sound judgment. I was drawn to doing what they most valued, which was demonstrating zeal in our shared commitment to the cause.

I also shared with my clients the instability of political life. For many years, my practice rose and fell with the fortunes of the party. When we won elections, campaign funding flowed, and there were resources available all around, including fees for legal work. Elections that turned out badly, like the 1980 elections, left the party gasping for funding to pay off debts and rebuild what lay in ruins before for the next cycle. Clients I represented who lost elections disappeared from the lists, often leaving behind unpaid legal bills. I had to effectively start all over again. This happened when I joined Perkins in October of 1980 with a solid list of clients who, within a month, were swept away in the Reagan landslide and Republican gains in Congress—control of the Senate and a thirty-four-seat pickup in the House.

I was left trying to put the practice together again while doing other work as assigned by the firm to make myself useful and not be a complete financial loss. I would find myself on projects unrelated to political law, such as one involving advising a natural gas company on an energy regulatory matter. Not what I had in mind for that stage of my career, but politics was not then paying the bills.

This problem improved as the practice expanded and the Political Law Group I established at Perkins was buffered against the boom-and-bust cycle; but still the reversal of the party's political fortunes remained a continuous risk for the practice. A bad election cycle for Democrats was a very personal and not just professional setback for me. I took my clients' losses hard. This was another reason why it was easy for me to see things from the narrowest, most intensely partisan perspective—to have a warrior mentality.

CHAPTER 3

Politics and the Warrior Mentality

Political lawyering can mean making sure there is water and air condition-
ing in a presidential campaign headquarters, but also that you would share
your client's total commitment to winning. I go all out, a partisan warrior
suing a House Republican leader for "racketeering," warning Republican
donors that they should also watch their step or find themselves on the wrong
side of the law, and gaining some press attention for rough if "innovative"
strategies in the defense of my clients' interests.

For candidates and their parties, campaigns are all about winning, of
course: what else would they be about? Candidates compete for voter
favor, and eventually one succeeds and the other fails. The one in the
winner's circle is entitled on Election Night to the roar of the crowd, the
blast of celebratory music, and a colorful shower of balloons and confetti.
A concession is a gloomy affair. Occasionally the failed candidate strikes
a graceful note, but the mournful family arrayed around them on the
stage tells the tale of dismal loss. The news cameras scan the dejected
crowd and zero in, for maximum effect, on the tearful young volunteers.

It is also rare that a losing campaign leaves much of a mark. The
public may applaud the good college try—but the loser is then carted off
to political oblivion while every decision or statement they made on the
way to defeat is gleefully second-guessed by opposition and pundit alike.
In campaigns, there is no tomorrow, no participation trophy (except for
presidential candidates who can finagle their way onto the debate stage

with no chance of winning anything but a shot at national attention that will garner a book deal or speaking engagements or a cable TV gig. And even that may not last).

The political lawyers and the other campaign consultants are charged first, foremost, and almost entirely with the all-consuming business of ending up in first place and avoiding the catastrophic second-place finish. It may seem that they have other responsibilities, but not really. Ensuring that the campaign complies with all the rules and regulations may seem like nuts and bolts legal work, and it is, but "staying out of trouble" is also a requirement of staying out of bad headlines. A campaign with legal troubles is one with political troubles. Good lawyering is good politics— up to a point.

The point is always to win.

The work is not all, in every detail, high drama. A campaign is a medium-sized business, certainly at the federal level. Presidential campaigns, the ones that have a shot at the finish line, are massive enterprises. There is a routine "corporate" side to the work. Campaigns hire vendors and employees, prepare staff manuals, enter into lease arrangements, and file tax and regulatory forms. In 2006, when then-Senator Obama returned from a Hawai'i vacation and relayed to the staff and political team his decision to run for president, the campaign manager–designate David Plouffe and I sat in my law firm's conference room and tried to figure out where to begin. We had about a year to stand up a campaign that would eventually raise and spend well over three quarters of a billion dollars and employ directly, or indirectly through the state political parties, thousands of employees.

But even on the corporate side, politics is not far away. It lurks behind every issue and colors every choice. The Obama campaign was set up in a downtown Chicago high-rise, a good many stories up into the city sky. Chicago does have summers and very hot days and suddenly the HR department and the political team were battling over the question of whether free water would be stored in the headquarters and the air conditioning kept on beyond 6 p.m. The political people were worried about money; the HR people could not accept that the staff would be dispatched to elevators, down to the street, for water, or would have to work in sweltering conditions after normal business hours. I was called upon to express an opinion, though it was far from clear that the decisive consideration was legal.

My advice was simple and did not require me to showcase my finest legal analytical abilities. Who in a smart political world would want a disgruntled employee of the campaign to tell the press that they were denied ready access to water and forced to work the long hours so typical of a campaign in the smothering heat of an office building whose windows could not be opened? Not a good look. I joined forces in support of a well-hydrated, comfortably cooled workforce, and the political people swallowed the defeat with grace—eventually discovering that we could raise so much money that we had a surplus at the end of the campaign.

Of course, I had won the argument on politics, when really the issue was the decent treatment of employees. I have always suspected that it was decency that won the day, even if the argument had to be couched in political terms.

The issue in the Case of Cool Air and Free Bottled Water was straightforward. More often the lawyer is asked to chart a path through the law to the best, most winning ways of raising money, or make it harder for the opponent to compete financially, or help clear an attack on the other side in the "opposition research" program, or work the press to ward off a damaging story. In this competitive setting the lawyer whose "nos" to a proposed course of action exceed in number their "yeses" is going to have a hard time of it. The clients expect the lawyers, as they demand of all advisers, to find a way.

But someone might reply: who hires any lawyer except to win—win a big jury award or stave off a disastrous one? The pressures seem different in politics if only because the losers often feel effectively erased from the political landscape, unsure that they will have a second chance, and they share this pain with the pool of distraught supporters who invested time, energy, and even money in their hope of victory. The lawyer anticipating a loss cannot "settle" it and hope to come away with something, anything. Unlike a jury or court of law, the voters have only one choice to make— yea or nay, in or out—and cannot settle on some charges while acquitting or deadlocking on others. It's all or nothing, and the entire campaign is waged on the claim that the outcome *really matters* to so many, not just to the candidate on whom the verdict is rendered.

If winning is everything, the lawyer, like the other senior political staff, has to "get it." Early on, now many years ago, I did not—not fully. I was committed to the clients, but I somehow thought that a demonstrated mastery of the legal material would impress, and if my answer had to be "no, you can't," the client would come away perhaps disappointed but staggered by the high-quality counsel I was pleased to believe I had provided. Now why would I have thought that? "Yes" is the legal advice most coveted in the campaign.

And a no is often met with disbelief. Very early in my career, the late Senator Daniel Inouye of Hawai'i once summoned me to explain, in person, why I had given an unwelcome bit of advice that some proposed action, nothing scandalous, still faced legal hurdles. I was thrilled for the chance to display my professional wares and explained how my answer rested on a sharp reading of the law. "I *never* voted for any law like that," Inouye growled in reply. I might know the law, but he knew his voting record—wouldn't he? He glowered at me; I smiled wanly back in his direction. What was there to say? If from his recollection, there was no law to deal with, then no unwelcome answer was necessary, and all that remained was a clear, unfavorable verdict on my legal abilities. I nervously stood my ground, then slunk away without the warm appreciation for my legal talents I had hoped for. I cannot recall whether he followed my advice or turned to another lawyer for a second opinion.

There is another, psychological dimension to these pressures on the campaign team. The candidate values in their lawyers and senior advisers basic skills but also a kind of warrior mentality, a taste for combat and the guts to do what is necessary to win. Popular synonyms for defeating the opposition are to "destroy" or "crush" them—or one of my favorites, to "croak" them. The lawyer's advice on any matter important to the campaign is expected to show an appreciation for this end goal of "croaking" the other side.

I never observed anyone planning to actually croak the other side. But early on, I was witness to a remarkably aggressive attack on the state of mind of an especially vulnerable political candidate. In 1980, three years into my practice, I was invited to attend a meeting, one of a series, of aides to Democratic senators facing difficult reelections. They met in the Capitol, largely to keep up their morale, but also to share information about what they were seeing from their opposition, in their states, which their colleagues might need to prepare for in their own. One of them, an aide to Democrat Senator George McGovern, held the room in thrall with the tale of how he had assisted his candidate in winning a debate with his last reelection opponent six years before. The Republican challenger, Leo Thorsness, was running on his distinguished record as a combat veteran of the Vietnam War and Congressional Medal of Honor winner. He had been shot down, captured, and then tortured over a period of four years of captivity.

In the course of researching Thorsness's record, the McGovern campaign had learned from accounts of his capture the terror he experienced when, as his sadistic jailer approached the cell, he would jingle a collection of keys. So during their debate, this McGovern aide claimed, he stationed himself backstage, within hearing distance of the two candidates, and softly but audibly rattled a collection of keys. "His face turned white," the adviser told the rest of the room, who chortled in only slightly embarrassed admiration at this move to shake Thorsness up, throw him off his stride, in mid-debate. I should note that the McGovern campaign aide did not suggest that his candidate, the senator, knew about this dirty trick.

Campaigns can be a violent affair. The candidates, the lawyers, the staff, the consultants, are all in a war. Electoral conflict is always rough: only more or less so, depending on the weapons used and the stakes of the battle. In the 1890s, a senator from Kansas, John Ingalls, expressed this martial perspective with beautiful candor: "Government is force. Politics is a battle for supremacy. Parties are the armies. The Decalogue and the Golden Rule have no place in a political campaign. The object is success. To defeat the antagonist and expel the party in power is the purpose."[1]

The opposition as enemy: this can go too far. In the Watergate scandal that forced the resignation of Richard Nixon, the White House and their political team saw the 1972 reelection campaign as a war and the Democrats as the enemy. In a memorandum from August of 1971, Nixon's White House counsel, John Dean, agreed to develop a plan for "Dealing with Our Political Enemies." But he chose his words with care. He did not suggest that the administration "deal with" or "undermine" or "help defeat" the opposition, but instead "use the available federal machinery to *screw* our political enemies" [emphasis mine].[2]

Dean later testified to the Senate that he prepared the memorandum reluctantly—that "it took a good bit of push before I would even prepare a document like that. I had request after request to prepare this."[3] But the memo reads as if written by someone with no small enthusiasm for the project—the choice of the verb "screw" does not suggest that he was writing a CYA (cover your ass) memo or looking to soften the description of the project so that it would come off as less thuggish. And the same John Dean wrote a memo on the use of the IRS in particular to harass political opponents.

This is what he thought at the time a first-rate lawyer on the political team should be proposing and prepared to do—be a true warrior in his political army.

I have never fallen to these depths, nor, until the 2020 presidential election, known others in the army of political lawyers who have done so or come close. But I have taken some pride in the fact that I've found other ways to exhibit the warrior mentality. My clients appreciated it, others less so. In 2008, as general counsel to the Obama campaign, I deployed various weapons—I use the term "weapons" advisedly—to challenge the money behind attacks on my candidate.

In that day and age, now seemingly long ago, the campaign finance regulatory system had not completely collapsed. Contributions were meaningfully limited and publicly accounted for. Limits of this kind, of all kinds, are anathema to campaigns, and so campaigns and their allies are always searching for new ways around these finance restrictions. Campaigns can never gorge enough on money: they are always foraging for additional cash to pump into TV ads and other needs. In 2008, one move was for a campaign's allies to establish an entity known as a 527, which, for technical legal reasons, could claim the right to accept contributions of any amount they could then spend to benefit their favored candidate.

One such organization appeared on behalf of Senator Obama's primary opponent, former Secretary of State Hillary Clinton, and another popped up to support another of his competitors, former senator and 2004 vice presidential nominee John Edwards.

And so I went after them. On behalf of my client, but with enthusiasm, I charged them with illegally evading campaign finance laws and, in so doing, committing criminal, not only civil, offenses. I called for the Federal Election Commission and the Department of Justice to investigate them, subjecting the political coconspirators to the threat of fines and even jail time. Moreover, I took the position that the investigation I was demanding should be directed at the entities' donors, not only their officers and staff.

In a book devoted to castigating the left for censorship of free speech, *Wall Street Journal* columnist Kimberley Strassel assailed me for playing the "intimidation game." I had, she claimed, "laid the groundwork for an entire political movement" built around "using government—even if only the threat of it—to silence political opponents." In this respect, I was "a modern innovator." But one to be denounced, not admired.[4]

Now I don't credit much of the writing of Kimberley Strassel, who exhibits a warrior mentality of her own in columns that predictably uphold the conservative Republican cause and damn the Democrats. But she could not be faulted in this instance for her basic premise. The strategy we pursued in trying to shut down these anti-Obama (or pro-Clinton and pro-Edwards) 527s involved weaponizing the law. We hoped to saddle the organization with bad press and to spook the donors. We were quite convinced that we were doing what any sensible campaign would do to defend itself against sleazy cheating.

Strassel insisted that, at least in the Clinton 527 case, I was successful—that because "donors had no interest in an FBI knock on the door or in [being named] publicly by Mr. Bauer in his next national press conference," the stream of money for this enterprise "dried up." She cited the political news publication *Politico*'s reporting that my legal attack had "the effect of scaring . . . donors and consultants," even if the basis for threatening them with legal action was (in their view) entirely lacking.

My pursuit of this strategy in 2008 was a still distant second in aggressiveness to my assault eight years earlier on the fundraising practices of a member of the Republican House leadership, Tom DeLay—otherwise known as the Hammer. The Hammer made no bones about his bare-knuckled tactics in what was a war on Democrats. I don't know who came up with the name Hammer, but I assume he embraced it at the time. Later, he ran into all sorts of trouble, with the House Ethics Committee and with the law. He was convicted for criminal violations of state campaign finance laws, which were later reversed on appeal. His House career ended with a resignation. (After public service, he was a featured performer on *Dancing with the Stars*. He stated his artistic ambitions in characteristically if weirdly pugilistic terms: "I'm going to go after the American people, show them that I can dance," he declared.[5] *Go after them?*)

I cannot say much good about Tom DeLay's politics, but I also cannot take responsibility for his actions, only for mine. My direct engagement with him arose over his announcement that he, too, had found a way around the campaign finance limits. He would use his fundraising muscle to fund in the millions of dollars a series of organizations of the mostly unregulated 527 type to be run by his associates.

I suggest "muscle" intentionally, since the Hammer would slam down hard on organizations with interests before Congress who were led to understand that good relations with the Republican halls of power depended on doing his bidding. He and other House Republicans thought too many lobbying firms and trade associations hired Democrats. He spread the word that any organization aspiring to have access to the House Republican leadership should think hard about the political affiliations of their executive suites. Showing that he meant business, DeLay retaliated against a trade association that was preparing to appoint as its president a former Democratic House member of Congress—not a retiring Republican that DeLay and his congressional leadership team wanted in the post. They sent their message by delaying votes on an international treaty important to the association. DeLay had the unusual distinction of provoking the House into adopting a new rule prohibiting this kind of behavior—a clear abuse of power that his colleagues simply could not ignore.

Against this background, the party committee I represented responded to his multi-million-dollar campaign finance work-around by filing a "racketeering" suit against him and his allies. In effect, the suit alleged that they were engaged in money laundering and extortion. A statute deployed most notably against mobsters was now being directed at an elected official and party leader. We had cast DeLay as a partisan John Gotti. The press took immediate note of what the *Wall Street Journal* referred to as "an extraordinary escalation in the fight between the two parties for control of the narrowly divided House."[6] And so it was.

The press and commentariat responses were highly agitated and critical. The *New York Times* editorial board expressed reservations; the *Washington Post* went the next step to registering disapproval. The well-regarded *Post* columnist Michael Kelly denounced the suit as "the criminalization of politics" in a precedent-shattering form. "If this goes forward," he wrote, "party politics enters a new and quite possibly terminal phase, the era of mutual assured destruction."[7] My father, a close reader of *Post* opinion, abandoned his normally intense support for my professional endeavors and nervously asked me whether I knew what I was doing.

This all seemed overwrought to me: DeLay was the one, I reasoned, who was shattering precedents—for the behavior of elected officials in making extreme use of official power. In any event, the Democrats could not abide an audacious scheme of cheating in the competition for control of the House. The suit was eventually settled, and DeLay and his lawyers agreed that as a result of "changed circumstances," the complaint we had filed did not "reflect [the Republicans'] current actions, intentions or expectations" for the coming election. In other words, they were standing down. The program we were suing to stop was not in their "current plans."[8]

We were joyous: we believed we had gotten the job done. I could not have been more pleased when I read that the chair of one of the groups named in the suit acknowledged that our legal action "did scare away potential corporate donors."[9]

In retrospect, I have mixed feelings about the DeLay suit. On the one hand, one might say that DeLay had little to complain about. He was a free-swinging partisan brawler and we decided to respond with upgraded intensity and innovation in our defense. We had laid down a marker that the Hammer and those who might imitate him should not assume that they could act recklessly with impunity. But while we were all aware, both client and lawyer, that we were breaking new ground with a racketeering claim against a House Republican leader, the conversation we had about the impact and consequences of this course of action was not especially thoughtful. The criticism we faced, for a major escalation in the partisan political conflict, had merit, and we did not have the most convincing response. On the law of the case, yes; but on the wisdom of bringing it, less so.

This became clear to me when Michigan Senator Carl Levin called me to his office after the filing of the suit to raise his concerns. Spread before him on a conference table were photocopies of statutes and case law. Levin was always thoughtful and well-prepared in any conversation I had with him as a party lawyer. During the 1999 Clinton impeachment trial, when I represented the Democratic Senate Caucus, he would stop me in the hall and ask detailed questions about the facts of the case, questioning apparent discrepancies in witness testimony and the like. He had thrown himself into the minutiae like no other member. Now he wanted to know whether there was a supportable legal foundation for the racketeering suit against DeLay. Peering at me searchingly over his bifocals, he pressed me for the legal authority I had relied on. An aide seated to his right stared hard at me—as close to a glare as a stare can be.

I had plenty of legal answers and I came away from the meeting well-satisfied with the lawyering I had displayed. We had assumed in the conversation that the legal answer would be the answer, in full, to the question about the lawsuit. Of course, there had to be a legal answer; the discussion had to start there.

Then came the more difficult questions, more briefly discussed, which could not be settled by law. Was this DeLay fundraising scheme so competitively significant that it justified this escalated legal attack? Campaigns can overestimate the effects of money. And if a legal response was warranted, was the one we fashioned responsibly drawn? What DeLay was planning seemed legally sketchy—but in the sad state of campaign finance, it might have been judged to occupy the shadowy border between the plausibly legal and the surely illegal. And could we say that we would not under any circumstances consider a similar strategy with the help of our allies and donors?

There is a basic defense of what we did—that in any regulated industry, each competitor has a clear interest in ensuring that all are playing by the same rules. DeLay, and then later supporters of Clinton and Edwards, at least played games with the rules to my client's competitive disadvantage. We turned to the legal process and to the press to make our case, and we certainly understood that the noise we made would reach the ears of potentially skittish operatives and donors, inviting them to have second thoughts about continuing on this course. Nothing in the tactics as we employed them was illegal. Nor was my legal argument entirely without merit, though I will be the first to admit I was not confident of ultimate success. I certainly don't believe that I "laid the groundwork for an entire political movement" of political intimidation.

And yet . . . it is not unreasonable to worry about all-out combat in which donors to campaigns become targets or collateral damage. In the thick of political struggle, the worry may not come all that easily. After all, very wealthy donors have the resources and real-world experience to evaluate and then take the risks of putting vast sums into controversial political projects. They often have outsized influence; it may not be unfair to expect that there is some risk to go along with it, and they certainly have the means to evaluate the risk before deciding to take it on. But while well-heeled donors giving within the lawful limits might have to live with some degree of exposure (this goes with the regulatory territory, which requires some degree of transparency), it does not follow that it is somehow good for democracy that they be publicly hounded into hiring lawyers to defend themselves.

Now, in the savage era of internet politics, the donors have much more to fear. In 2019, a Democratic congressman decided to tweet out the names of donors to the Trump campaign from the district he represented. "Who's Funding Trump?" he asked the social media world, and he then listed the names and occupations of forty-four donors who had "contributed the most allowable by federal law." He wanted the world to know that these donors were financing "a campaign of hate."[10] There was much agitation in the press. He denied that he was seeking to put them in danger, that he would want "anyone to be harassed," but observers could not see any other point to his message. He wanted them to be shamed, and he presumably hoped that the shaming would end or chill the giving.

Moreover, once campaigns go after one class of donors, there is no reason to expect that they will stop there. In the age of internet fundraising, which has greatly expanded the clout of the smaller giver, campaigns might also have the incentive to suppress that stream of revenue for the opposing side. As the Supreme Court had occasion to note in a case about political speech, the risks of donor harassment "are heightened in the 21st century and seem to grow with each passing year" as the internet affords anyone the opportunity to chase down their targets' personal details, such as home addresses or the schools attended by their children.[11]

Another consideration deserving more weight in the final decision on the suit was the basic move of suing DeLay himself, a member of the congressional leadership. The legal theory and public messaging seemed to require it. We might have just challenged the legal conduct of the 527s, subjecting them to sundry allegations of campaign finance law violations. The Hammer's orchestration of this scheme added the compelling plot point that the success of this seedy enterprise depended on the abuse of power in the form of extortionate fundraising. This made good sense: it struck at the heart of what was unique about DeLay's role.

On the other side of the argument was the escalation of a campaign finance dispute into a lawsuit by the House Democratic leadership against the House Republican leadership. My client was technically a private organization, the Democratic Congressional Campaign Committee, but its chair is always a Democratic member of the House elected to the position by the House Democratic Caucus, and no suit of this kind could proceed without the express consent of the Democratic leader. While it was not uncommon for parties to file suits against candidates of the other party in the course of a campaign, citing one alleged irregularity or the other, the racketeering suit was a major step beyond these garden variety skirmishes. The lawsuit pushed the electoral conflict into the House. The two parties were already at each other's throats, and while it may be hard to show that the racketeering charge worsened already wretched institutional relationships, it was at least a serious question.

If I have any regrets at all in this purportedly mailed fist move to scare off donors and, putting him on the defensive, stymie DeLay's spending plan, it is that none of these considerations especially concerned me. All that mattered was that we could plausibly make the argument, grab press attention with it, and perhaps successfully drive donors away from these committees. It was political law in the true sense of the word: politics and law all wrapped together, virtually indistinguishable. Still, a more probing conversation about whether we needed to do this, balancing the short-term advantage against the longer-term costs to the democratic process, might in hindsight have been what I should have urged on the client.

These costs are always routinely minimized. It is possible to argue those costs a different way in a case like DeLay's, by looking to the longer-term cost of *not* challenging Hammer-style politics. Letting it go, contributing by inaction to its "normalization," could add wear and tear to a healthy democratic politics. I am tempted to take this argument seriously, but it does not seem to answer the basic objection to how the challenge to DeLay was designed: the use of racketeering statutes in a context for which they were not intended, which created the risk of an escalation of the conflict between the parties that entailed long-term costs.

As this book was being prepared, a racketeering charge, one of even greater consequence, joined the list of prosecutions related to Donald Trump's refusal to accept, and maneuvers to reverse, the outcome of the 2020 presidential election. The district attorney of Fulton County filed this case against both the former president and those who aided him in the alleged criminal enterprise. The legal jousting over this case will be intense, and no doubt it will involve a challenge to the use of the racketeering law in this context. It also featured in the early-going attempts by several defendants to move the case to federal court. Whatever the outcome, my use of the racketeering laws presented, as I see it, a very different set of choices and issues. In my case, one party was deploying this theory against another, in a civil rather than a criminal context, but it would not have the benefit, available to a law enforcement officer, of months of investigation, including the acquisition through grand jury subpoenas of documents and testimony. The DeLay suit was fashioned to win a fight between the parties over the legal access to resources, and there was a chance, eventually realized, that it could succeed just by virtue of being filed. In the Trump case in Georgia, the prosecutor, like any prosecutor, must answer to the public and the system for bringing cases on the law and facts and seeing them through to a fully tested conclusion, after a full trial (or in this instance, multiple trials of multiple defendants) and the likely series of appeals both before trial and in the event of a conviction.

So while each of these cases may be controversial, they are fundamentally different. There are checks in the latter case, brought by law enforcement officials, which do not apply to ones like the Democratic DeLay suit, brought by a political party. In assessing the significance of these cases, no one should confuse one chapter in the running conflict between the parties over campaign finance with the legal system's response to an unprecedented attack by a losing presidential candidate on the outcome of the election.

To the public, it may all seem the same: just more of the sordid politics and bruising campaigns. Perhaps, as some believe, once the violence of the campaign subsides, the questionable conduct accepted in politicians and those who serve them will change. There is some consolation in the thought that, with a few exceptions, the winning candidate will behave better in office than on the campaign trial. They will "grow." They will appreciate the difference between the largely privatized world of campaigns, where the First Amendment protects a lot of what passes for sleazy behavior and "dirty tricks," and the high honor of public office that should inspire their occupants to behave as called for by their new station in life. Plus, the public corruption laws that kick in when the prize of office is theirs may help keep them honest if their personal growth is slow or stunted.

Not much comfort should be taken in this "privatized" view of campaigns. The candidate who pushes the limits to gain power becomes the official who may be entirely comfortable doing the same to preserve their hard-fought gain of power and glory. It is hardly surprising that out of four presidential impeachment proceedings in the last fifty years, three have involved alleged misconduct in office to win an election, or to reverse a loss. Nixon's burglaries and cover-up were all strategies to win reelection. Both of the Trump impeachments involved charges that he abused his office in his quest for another term: in the first, by attempting to bully the government of Ukraine to investigate his likely (and in the end actual) 2020 reelection opponent, Joe Biden, and then again in his attempts to overturn the outcome of the election he lost.

The campaigners are always shadowing their official selves, whispering or sometimes shouting in their ears. The unethical campaigner is the unethical, impeachable president (or unethical, indictable federal elected official). Senator Ingalls's late nineteenth-century avowal of the amorality of politics connects governments with campaigns: he opens with the declaration that "government is force," but he bundles it together with an immediate reference to politics as "a battle for supremacy." He rightly understood that the political campaign is integral to the governing process and the ethics of one cannot be divorced from the other.

A problem at any time, it is even more of one in the deeply polarized politics of today, when victory may seem so imperative that ethical, even legal, considerations will factor even less into campaign strategic deliberations. The imperative is to emerge on top, to vanquish the enemy.

The staggering expense of competitive races—millions for House races, millions and even hundreds of millions for Senate races, and two billion dollars or more for presidential campaigns—also squeeze ethical considerations to the margins. The campaigns and candidates have invested too much money to worry about much other than winning, and advisers and vendors who earn handsome livings in this line of work have little incentive to bring ethical considerations into strategic decision making.

A toxic politics selects politicians indifferent to ethical concerns, as influential segments of the parties' "base" reward them as fighters whose slash-and-burn tactics confirm their commitment to the cause. Donald Trump's campaign in 2016 demonstrated to shocked rivals that far from a liability, he could make an asset of his open contempt for limits on what he was willing to do or say. He brought his business ethics to politics, which made for a grievously bad turn in the civic life and political affairs of the country.

I would like to believe that, among a candidate's senior advisers, the lawyers are the ones who most reliably will act to prevent the warriors from losing control of themselves. Yet as in Watergate, in 2020 that was not the case. Donald Trump found lawyers willing to advise courses of action and make public statements well outside legal and ethical boundaries. To be fair, other lawyers in the government took a more sober view of their professional obligations and acted honorably to reject fabricated claims of fraud and refuse participation in illegal schemes to keep Trump in office. But there were no shortage of lawyers selling out or revealing that they seemingly had no ethics to sell in the first place.

Their offenses were more dangerous than those committed by lawyers in Watergate. Nixon's legal advisers were crooks who authorized illegal break-ins and the payment of hush money to the burglars; they happened to be lawyers who might have been expected to respect the law, but there was nothing about being lawyers—nothing in the nature of their crimes—which had anything to do with their legal training. Lawyers are not more or less skilled at conspiracies to break in and enter an opposition campaign's headquarters, as evident in the clumsiness of the Nixon conspirators' execution and their rapid apprehension. The Trump lawyers did their Watergate ancestors one better: their part in the criminal acts planned by Donald Trump consisted of bad, dishonest lawyering. It was in their role as lawyers that they aided and abetted the scheme to cast aside the results of the 2020 election.

This strikes me as something altogether new. A lawyer infected by the warrior mentality may contrive or fail to resist a course of action which, while arguably legal, is inarguably inadvisable, an escalation of conflict into potentially dangerous directions for the democracy. Then

34

there is this development of a warrior mentality run wild, when the lawyer begins with an outlandish objective—refusing to accept an election—and invents a case or claim to support this illegitimate cause. In a polarized politics, it is a mistake to assume too readily that lawyers, the ones who love the "game" and care deeply about being on the winning team, will distinguish themselves from other advisers and strategists.

CHAPTER 4

The Weapon of Political Power

I understand early on the uses of government and political power in waging the partisan wars. I argue for tax rules to discourage political ads my clients dislike, file complaints with the Federal Election Commission to put opponents under a cloud of suspicion, and watch as political adversaries use "ethics" requirements as standard ammunition to generate scandal. I begin to have second thoughts about scandal politics, write an article to express them, and pull it when a client objects that I should not be saying such things in public. I become involved in a controversial election contest in which the House Democratic majority rejects the state-certified results of a congressional election and conduct their own vote count, resulting in the election and seating of the Democratic candidate.

The DeLay suit was a battle between competitors who tussled to a resolution in the courts. Not pretty, but a familiar sight in this country: a dispute becomes "legal," and the lawyers are called in to make their case to the judge. There are whole other, more intense hostilities waged with more lethal weapons and more vulnerable targets.

First, there is the use of the government *as weapon*, the brazen deployment of state power to win elections. Calling out your adversaries and trying to turn the electorate against them: this is public debate, not all of it very honorable or elevated, but still an appeal to the voters to make a political judgment. It's all up to the voters. To call in the government, demanding that it launch investigations and get its powerful machinery entangled with politics, is not a step to be taken lightly. Yet many partisans cannot resist turning the government power or authority into a weapon.

Examples come in large and small sizes. None comes close to the abuse of power championed by Donald Trump, unprecedented in its brazenness and disregard of law and basic norms. Period. Thinking about ethics in politics does not mean conflating the extreme case with others, treating all the same. The extreme case cannot define the ethical limits. By the time those limits are reached, the crisis has gone from the ethical to the constitutional.

One early case of misguided warrior mentality on my side of the political fence brings out some of what may seem ordinary "hardball" but, judged by the basic principle, was misguided.

In 1981, the Democrats were reeling from the Reagan landslide election the year before, the loss of the Senate majority, and extensive losses in the House. We had been a party in denial, and rather than come to terms with the reasons for voter rejection, many Democrats decided to look elsewhere for suitably consoling targets to blame. High on the list was the money spent by Republican allies, working through "independent committees," to conduct effective "negative campaigns" against our incumbents. The question then was: how do we make it harder for the other side to get out this negative message about Democrats—their characters and policies—which took this electoral toll?

The IRS, of all places, presented one opportunity, when it ruled that a tax credit then available for political contributions be denied to any monies donated to negative campaign activity. The Senate held hearings to consider whether the nation would really want its tax bureaucrats to decide which political messages were negative and which positive and extend tax benefits accordingly. On behalf of the party, I testified shamelessly and with no small measure of professional satisfaction that, of course, the IRS was on strong ground. It had correctly read its authority, and after all, I informed the senators: "The government is not bound . . . constitutionally or otherwise . . . to support with tax dollars scurrilous campaigns of this kind which are totally at odds with the best political traditions of our country."[1]

To their credit, not mine, the Committee Republicans, and even some of the Democrats, were skeptical. But I got points for trying. Senator Russell Long opened his line of questioning me with this statement: "First, let me commend you for intellectual fortitude, coming up here to explain your position on this matter, in view of the parade of witnesses on the other side of the issue."[2]

And, looking back, my thought is: good for that parade of witnesses on the other side. They were right on the law and on the policy, and on the basic principle that we would not even want to empower government to make these kinds of decisions. I could not have been more wrong.

Of course, I was a lawyer representing a client, and the client took the position I was charged with defending. But I do not recall having qualms, expressed to the client or kept to myself, about going before Congress to argue for the government to manipulate the tax code to favor one political interest over another. We did not discuss whether we should even suggest that the IRS should involve itself in this way in politics. Remarkably, we rushed to defend the IRS's political intervention less than a decade after Richard Nixon was driven from office for, among other impeachable offenses, attempting to use the IRS to harass and punish political opponents.

To be sure, we did not argue for Nixon-level political interference with the IRS. We did, however, take a position that would have put the tax bureaucracy in the middle of politics, which could have only encouraged pressures from the White House and parties to use that authority to expand or contract what was deemed negative, as partisan political interests dictated. Our position was driven only by those interests. Troubled as we were by the negativism of the campaigns that took a heavy toll on Democrats in 1980, any sliver of honesty with ourselves would have compelled this admission: we disliked their negativity because it moved votes against us, but we were ready without question to deploy our own negativity if it turned voters in our direction.

I wish I had had reservations about the party's defense of this poorly judged IRS policy or had encouraged that discussion. Partisan warrior that I was, I did not. Campaigns don't generally have conversations like this, about whether the IRS's negative campaign tax credit policy would have built politics into the way that the tax agency did its business. They leave the responsibility for the "system" or the "process" to a later day, to others who will debate these questions long after the campaign has closed its doors. If campaigns embrace an ethical vision, it is often showmanship: good politics and not much else to it.

The government gets mixed up in the political business in other ways, sometimes as a result of reforms passed with the best of intention, but which backfire badly. Federal campaign finance laws allow private citizens to bring complaints against persons for alleged wrongdoing. As a general rule, next-door neighbors, or the average person on the street, don't trouble themselves to police politicians and their supporters' use of campaign funds. For the politicians and activists and parties, the temptation to play cop is irresistible—to plague the opposition with charges of wrongdoing and calls for investigations. A standard game for years was to spot a violation of no particular consequence—an apparent transgression against some fundraising rule—and spin it into a legal yarn of intolerable corruption the government should not delay looking into.

The Federal Election Commission (FEC) charged with considering these complaints is split between Democratic and Republican commissioners whose political allegiances are always being tested. On major issues that divide the parties, it is not uncommon for the Democrats and the Republicans to deadlock, or to delay acting. No matter: the party filing the complaint has had the opportunity to turn it into a press talking point about the opponent who "is under investigation."

I did this more times than I can count, with complaints that concluded with a warning that unless the government took action, the very walls of the democracy would crumble to the ground. In one Senate race in Nebraska, I travelled to Omaha to make a fuss, complete with the announced filing of a complaint, over supposed illegal corporate contributions to the Republican Senate candidate. What were these contributions? Campaign staff had briefly used the offices of the finance director, a lawyer whose firm was a professional corporation, and we alleged that the campaign had not paid for this use of space. It turned out that it all boiled down to a few unreimbursed long-distance calls: not much of a "there" there. I held a press conference at the Omaha Press Club, expressed outrage at this offense to the campaign finance law, and by the time our complaint died at the agency, we had the benefit of some bad press for the opponent.

It's all in the game, yes, and some might say that this game is on the whole harmless enough, since everyone is in on it. But the government should not structure law enforcement regimes that lend themselves to this kind of political intervention and theater. Even if a complaint is eventually dismissed, it has to be defended, which costs time and money. And before the dismissal, the accusation hangs in the air.

It is rarely the big players who are hampered by these tactics in their various campaign fundraising and spending schemes. They do just fine in the end. They have the lawyers, the money, and the skill to manage the legal challenge and the bad press. The agency still has to show that it is not utterly useless, so it beats up on the more defenseless—the losing candidate with no funds, or some hapless business that failed to follow the complex rules in renting out its space for a fundraising event.

The enlistment of government power to advance political goals is not just part of the sideshow that enforcement of the federal campaign finance laws has become. As the FEC becomes less useful as a platform for attack, the political actors and activists have to look elsewhere to get attention for their grievances. One alternative: demand that the Department of Justice ride in with criminal investigations. This has been the occasion, too, for disastrous experiments with independent counsels or special prosecutors who ostensibly carry on the investigations at a remove from any political interference from the executive branch or Congress. In practice, as both Democrats and Republicans discover, a prosecutor with limited accountability can take a criminalized political complaint and investigate it forever and a day, with what is a more or less unlimited budget. In calling for the criminal investigation of 527 activity in 2008, I would have been all too glad to have these committees paralyzed by the requirement of fending off criminal prosecution.

The ethical problem of weaponized law has spread even to the rules that the government has laid down to prevent . . . ethical misconduct. With no small irony, but to considerable effect, partisans have added ethics charges to their arsenal. The federal government has promulgated such rules, as has each chamber of Congress, and there are variations and extensions that individual departments and agencies have adopted. Some are very specific, such as the limitations on gifts government officials or legislators may receive. Others are entirely malleable, meant for adaptation to particular cases as the regulators see fit. An example is Congress's command that members should not act in a fashion that "reflects discredit" on the institution. It is a cousin of the "appearances" standard of ethics regulation, which prohibits behavior that, even if not expressly banned, does not look good. There is a lot in this material for weaponizing partisans to work with.

Former Republican Speaker Newt Gingrich rose to power by charging the Democrats in control of the House with corruption, and he successfully made an example of Democratic Speaker Jim Wright, lodging accusations of ethical misdeeds that eventually drove Wright out of office. Gingrich fashioned his case out of various ways Wright looked to make money on the side. Most famously, the Speaker had assembled *Reflections of a Public Man*, a thin compendium of speeches and sayings self-published with the help of a printer who also worked for the Wright campaign organization. Wright's royalties were set at 55 percent of each purchase, far higher than the market standard. Friends of Wright bought a lot of copies: a bad odor. But the ethics rules did not clearly prohibit this arrangement, as they allowed members to earn extra income from book publication royalties.

Wright did not become rich, and there was no credible allegation that he sold his votes or policy positions. All the same, Gingrich's charge had staying power, and the House Ethics Committee took up this claim and others concerned with Wright's small-bore pursuit of more money to supplement his House salary.

Why? Scandals have a way of feeding off other vulnerabilities, sprouting from small beginnings to grip the Capitol, because they supply a powerful metaphor for an emerging political story. The lawyers defending clients in the wrong place and at the wrong time can be taken by surprise by how little space is then left for their craft, for a defense on the merits. They wave around this piece of evidence or the other; they hold up triumphantly a fine bit of argument; they try to show that the press is overheated and missing key context: none of it seems to take. The law is not wholly beside the point, but it is easily swamped by a sense that the lawyers are just muddying up what is meaningful in the tale of wrongdoing. And typically, there is a fair charge of questionable behavior, enough to get it all going. If the narrative structured around these offenses comes together at the right time—if it seems to illuminate a systemic failing or offer an outlet for voter frustration—it takes on a life of its own, and the lawyers are left to catch up. Whatever might be the merits of the strictly legal case, the politics take over.

The Wright narrative was built to achieve escape velocity. There was legitimately reportable material in Wright's clumsy moneymaking ventures, but as corruption, it did not amount to much. Yet Republicans despised Wright, whom they accused, with some justification, of ruling the House with little regard for the rights of the minority, and Democrats were also not uniformly happy with his high-handed rule. It never helps that the figure at the center of the scandal is not especially well-liked and cannot count on fellow partisans to keep up the fight.

More dangerous to Wright was the potential that these institutional tensions and personal animosities would be swept up in wider political conflict and give meaning to it. His heavy use of his gavel connected to the larger context of forty years of unbroken Democratic control of the House, which gave Gingrich leeway to use Wright and his rule to great effect in making his case for change. The storyline was irresistible. Wright was the past; Gingrich was fresh copy, the future.

It did not help Wright that, as this narrative took shape, his majority whip, Tony Coelho of California, resigned his leadership post and seat after allegations that he had exploited his standing and influence to obtain a personal loan on favorable terms. Gingrich now had an "Exhibit A" to illustrate his argument that Democrats' long tenure in the House majority had made them clubby, arrogant, and corrupt. (I represented Coelho in his defense against these charges, which I take up in chapter 7.)

The Ethics Committee hired a special outside counsel and eventually found that Wright had violated various provisions of the House ethics code. Wright delivered a defense of his actions on the House floor—he thought it all came down to a story of "petty personal finances."[3] And he resigned.

By 1994, Gingrich had become the Speaker. And by 1995, he too faced an ethics charge and a special counsel investigation, and then, in 1997, the inquiry concluded with a reprimand and a $300,000 penalty—the first of its kind against a House Speaker. In the main, Gingrich's offense was the abuse of tax-exempt entities, barred by law from engaging in politics, to pay for the development and dissemination of his partisan and ideological program. A political organization he controlled had helped him finance a college course he taught, Renewing American Civilization. The Ethics Committee also found that he had not been straightforward in responses to its requests for information.

Democrats had worked hard to put together and press the ethics case against Gingrich. Like Wright's, it had merit—to a point. Like Wright's, it was not made of shocking stuff. What goes around, later comes around, as far as Democrats were concerned. Gingrich had thundered away at Democratic corruption and now had, with justification and much political profit to the Democrats, to account for a version of his own. There was much I actively disliked about Gingrich, and my objections ranged well beyond a Republican politics that I, as a Democrat, rejected. He was narcissistic and a bully who had mastered only the politics of attack. I detected little to support his pretensions to the status of visionary and public intellectual. Far down the list of my concerns about Gingrich was his machinations in the funding and function of a college course.

The ethics charges weakened Gingrich, and in the following year Republican losses in the 1998 midterms added to his political woes. Republicans concluded that he was a liability and turned on him. He faced a challenge to his reelection as Speaker and resigned.

Before Gingrich's House leadership came to an end, the cycle of ethics charges and countercharges in that time had continued with the launch of a counterattack on Democratic leader Richard A. Gephardt of Missouri. It was a telling experience in the weaponization of the ethics process. House Republican leadership sent word to Gephardt that they had had enough of Democratic assaults on Gingrich's ethics. Put a stop to it, Gephardt was warned, or we will make sure you face some of the same music. I had been Gephardt's lawyer for years, having represented him a decade before in his presidential campaign, and the threat was reported to me. It was agreed that Gephardt would decline to respond. He had not initiated the ethics controversy enveloping Gingrich, had no way of ordering it to end, and could not at any rate give in to threats.

In short order, the House majority whip, Jennifer Dunn of Washington State, cooked up a complaint that Gephardt had manipulated the tax code in the purchase and later exchange of a vacation property in North Carolina and, in so doing, had filed false personal finance disclosures. The details of what passed for an ethics charge are not worth recounting. It was not a hard case for me to defend. It was a purely political ploy, useful only as a press play and act of revenge. The Ethics Committee dismissed it, though it criticized Gephardt for his reporting practices and, for reasons I cannot recall or fathom, his lawyer (me!) for unnecessarily delaying the resolution of the matter.

I doubt Gingrich and the Republicans were surprised that their charges failed. They wanted to punish the Democrats for their ethics vendetta against Gingrich, and they retaliated in kind. The Gingrich rise in American politics marked a "nearly decade-long conflict in which ethics charges were the primary weapon" in what he had proclaimed to be a "civil war" with Democrats.[4]

Of course, there have to be some laws to constrain corrupt campaign behavior or ethical misconduct in office, and with the law comes the necessity of enforcement. This is where the ethical judgment of the responsible actors—candidates, lawyers, and advisers—becomes the check of first resort against the abuse of government power. And it falls to the government to design schemes for law enforcement that minimize the potential for abuse. An open invitation for anyone to file complaints with a federal agency or Congress in matters so political in nature—the financing of campaigns or the enforcement of ethical constraints on officeholders—is a poor design feature.

By the 1990s, I had begun to second-guess myself on some of these questions, becoming steadily less sure that all-out war with legal weapons, as much as I enjoyed the free-for-all, was good for the civic life of the nation. It had gotten out of hand. As Democrats called for various investigations of the Reagan administration, I drafted an opinion piece suggesting that the costs of this brand of politics be more carefully considered, for the good of both parties and the country at large. I was a party lawyer, and the position I was taking, I knew, would not go unnoticed. I submitted the piece to the *Washington Post*, and it was accepted immediately.

It then occurred to me that I should let my major institutional party clients know I had written the piece and it would appear in the coming weeks. Only one member of the House leadership had reservations, but they were strongly held and expressed. Hold the piece for the time being, he said: it is too controversial for the moment. The *Post* called for last edits, I advised the paper I needed time to make major changes, and the editors were displeased.

I pulled the piece. I learned my lesson though—if you write material like this, which I did in the coming years, and quite a bit of it—make sure to ask clients for forgiveness, not permission. I also learned that the line of argument in my *Post* submission was not an appealing one on my side of the political divide, and I had no reason to think it would find an audience on the other. The cycle of political violence I warned about in my unpublished piece might well have left some observers cold, those who could not muster much concern about candidate or political parties or rich people who get scarred by these processes.

In a period of angry, politicized politics, the weapons may be turned in fresh, expanded directions. For once the fire is trained on a candidate's supporters, weapons can be turned on *voters*. This is not "collateral damage": this is an emergency for American democracy, as has become plain for all to see in just the last few years.

The attack on voters has become a staple of the partisan wars now underway, and the Republican Party at the national, state, and local levels has to answer for it. It starts with state legislatures enacting laws to restrict the vote by burdening voters with the expectation that some will be deterred from voting and others will make errors that disqualify their ballots. The intention is clear: making it harder for certain communities of voters who, not at all coincidentally, are more likely to support the opposing party. So partisan lawmakers try to limit voting by mail or

restrict ready access to locations for the casting of ballots; they complicate the signature and witnessing requirements for casting a ballot; they
restrict the assistance voters can receive from parties and voting rights
organizations; and they refuse requests from election officials for more
funding to enable them to run more efficient, well-staffed polling places.
Thee are ways that government power is used to terrorize civilians and
enhance the chances of battlefield victory.

Sometimes, but far from always, these restrictive measures targeted
at voters are successfully challenged in court. Many of them—most of
them—survive legal attack, because legislatures can assert broad power to
regulate the terms and conditions of participating in the voting process.
This power includes putting great weight on "secure" voting to protect
against "fraud," and far less on making voting more accessible. Now we
see the rapid pace of escalation of this attack into the use of criminal laws
to intimidate voters in the name of guarding against fraud. Yet there is no
reasonable disagreement, among Democratic or Republican experts, that
fraud in U.S. elections is exceedingly rare.

In 2013 and 2014, when I was Co-Chair of President Obama's Presidential Commission on Election Administration, our bipartisan group
of commissioners took testimony, held hearings around the country, and
met with election administrators at all levels of government. Our report
to the president contained a number of findings and recommendations
to strengthen our system of elections, and we took seriously, as we should
have, that the systems required protections against fraud. But we also
noted without dissent that fraud was a rarity.

Today, however, state legislatures are experimenting with a host of
new ostensible "law enforcement" mechanisms for ferreting out and
punishing the nonexistent threat of fraudulent voting. These laws include
establishing new investigative agencies dedicated to criminal voting
offenses and measures to pressure election officials to collaborate in voter
witch hunts or themselves face legal consequences.

In Florida in 2022, the governor called for and the legislature established an Office of Election Crimes and Security. The very purpose of
this operation was to cast a shadow over the voting process and to put
voters—especially the ones with every reason to distrust treatment at

the hands of the state—in fear of a corps of voting police roaming the registration rolls and polling places. The office promptly chased after felons accused of illegal voting after the end of their incarceration. These prosecutions charged ahead despite the fact that many of the targets were simply confused about their rights and cast ballots without any illegal intent. Even worse, in some cases, these Floridians had received voter registration cards from the state itself. Most of these cases were dismissed.

This program of instilling terror among voters and election officials puts a special responsibility on candidates, aides, and lawyers to resist it at every turn. And to recognize that there are less dramatic but still serious attacks on voters and the process that must be met with a vigorous defense.

One popular concern of recent years is that candidates who lose an election should concede it. When it's over, it is over. But another is the ethical conduct of fully legal processes for ensuring that a vote count is accurate. In every election recount or contest, the hunt is on for voters whose lawful ballots were not counted, and for others whose ballots failed to meet lawful requirements and were improperly included in the tally. Perhaps the voter neglected to sign or date their mail-in ballot, or they marked the ballot in such a way that made it impossible to know for sure which candidate they selected. Lawyers in a recount take it as their special mission to protect their votes, the ones cast for their candidates, and challenge the votes cast for the opponents.

To a point this is fair enough: the law is the law, and only the lawful votes of eligible voters should decide the election. But in the competitive world of recounts, when the outcome produces a winner and a loser, the temptation for cynical challenges is just another means of victimizing voters.

I am aware that there are Republicans who stand firmly behind their party's long-time preoccupation with voting fraud but draw the line at Trump-level election denialism. And in conversations with me, some with long memories question whether Democrats have full moral authority to position themselves as faultless champions of a free and fair voting system. These critics do not hail from the Trump wing of the party, and they do not suggest the Democrats have behaved in a way that resembles or justifies the Republican party "election denialism" of 2020 and beyond. They do seek some recognition that over the time that American political polarization has generated intensifying conflict over the results of elections, Democrats have played their part. They cite the case of the Democratic House majority's refusal in 1985 to accept a Republican victory in Indiana's Eighth Congressional District.

I was involved in that conflict. It is fairly considered as an example of how partisan passions once unleashed might overcome better judgment.

In 1984, the Democrats were staggered by Reagan's forty-nine-state landslide, but they had managed to retain their majority in the House. On election night, it appeared that the Indiana Eighth Congressional District incumbent, Frank McCloskey, had won, if by only 72 votes. A tabulation error in one county was discovered and the lead switched back to the Republican Rick McIntyre, who now led by 34 votes. A state-ordered recount took his margin up to 418, and the state certified the election, sending McIntyre off to claim his House seat.

The full story is complicated. Without a doubt, the election was close. The battle over voting rules, the vagaries of recounts and contests, errors by voters and election officials, leave in their wake the unsettled question: if every close election ran exactly as it should have, who would have emerged victorious? There remains the imperative of identifying a winner, which means that, in these circumstances, one of the candidates walks away with the prize and takes the contested seat. The only hope is that the process by which the determination is made seems fair enough, defensible to a reasonable observer, and not so outside the historical precedents for resolving election contests that it provides new opportunities and arguments that partisans can exploit to make mischief in the future.

In the McCloskey election, the state process got tangled up from the beginning, when it was clear that one county had committed a counting error, the correction of which would swing the election to the Republican McIntyre. The Republicans insisted that the error be corrected before any check for other errors in that county, with the expectation and result that McIntyre would be the state-certified winner, whose certificate of election would go to Washington and normally entitle him to be seated.

Certification heavily favors the certificate-holder in subsequent legal challenges. (There was a similar struggle over certification in the early stage of the Bush-Gore Florida presidential recount in 2000.) The state eventually certified McIntyre, and the fight progressed from there.

Democrats had options for the continuing challenge, but chose to exercise one that is rare: ignoring the state certification of McIntyre's narrow victory, refusing to seat him and leaving the seat vacant, and conducting their own recount. They believed that they had good reasons, including questions about a state recount process that resulted in the exclusion in one county of a significant number of African American voters. The House established a task force with a majority of Democrats to conduct the recount. Issues that arose during this process were repeatedly decided by party-line votes.

Thirteen months later, McCloskey was returned to the winner's circle, with a margin of victory of 4 votes. Republicans went berserk. Wearing black arm bands, Republican members walked out of the House in protest on the day that McCloskey was sworn in. They pledged to not forget.

There was blame to go around, but once the state process had become messy, controversial, and sure to arouse Democratic distrust, partisan pressures were likely to become overwhelming, and they did. The Democrats dug in, rejecting, among other options, a new election to resolve the conflict. As the historian Julian Zelizer reflected years later, "Democrats won the seat, but lost the larger narrative," as Republicans dined out politically on a charge that after decades in the House majority, Democrats had become corrupt and autocratic to the point of casting aside state electoral processes to add one more seat to their already substantial House majority.[5]

As a counsel to the Democratic leadership, I observed how this House controversy became the mess that, in hindsight, I believe it was. Early on, Speaker Tip O'Neil took an institutional view of the matter. The House had the constitutional authority to intervene in a contested election and conduct the decisive recount: about that, there was no question. The harder issue was when a majority in control of the House should set aside the state's legal process, from Election Day through a recount and official certification of the winning candidate, and make its own determination.

At a meeting shortly after the election that I attended with O'Neil and McCloskey, the Speaker committed to consider House action, but he warned the agitated candidate, who sincerely believed that he had been duly elected, that the House majority would not intervene unless there were clear grounds—exceptional circumstances—to justify the House's displacement of the State of Indiana as the decisive vote counter.

Not too long afterward, I received a call from a member of the House leadership who told me how important it was that "we" win this seat. Full stop: end of story. Ah, game on, I thought, already mentally suiting up for battle, and I replied that I could not have heard the instruction more clearly.

What had changed from the Speaker's cautionary note about institutional restraint to a full-steam-ahead edict issued by a member of his leadership team? Fleetingly, at the beginning, it was an institutional issue, but very soon, it was just another election. Parties are committed to winning elections. Lawyers for parties help them to win. The longer-term "narrative" becomes a distinctly secondary consideration, if it remains a consideration at all.

Not all of this can be blamed, as lawyers like to do, on the client who makes himself perfectly clear about his expectations. Lawyers and other senior political advisers have an obligation to speak up, but it is also true that when they don't, it is not only because the client has made their wishes known and is deaf to contrary views. Those who do this work are normally fascinated by politics and may have, whether they admit it, their own political ambitions or fantasies, or a passion for being close to the action. They like being around elected officials and candidates and aspire to join the club. For the lawyers, no handicapping of races, or dissection of polling results, or conversation about high strategy, fails to hold their interest. It is far from attractive to be the naysayer, the softie, who shrinks from the hard hand-to-hand conflict that victory is believed to require.

And it is delightful for lawyers when the client ladles out praise for their tough-mindedness. Politicians know well that a little flattery goes a very long way. I speak here, again, from experience: mine and what I have observed in others who fall hard for the seductive ego stroke. The politician beams at the lawyer ready to dirty his hands in the service of a win. The lawyer has earned admission to the cool kids' club and wants to remain a member in good standing. They pay out their dues in the coin of accommodation. "Can you get this done?" And the response goes something like this: "Yes, sir, we'll get there. You can count on me."

None of my own regretted behavior includes behavior like this, or so I like to believe. But you have to worry about it. Always.

CHAPTER 5

Lying, Manipulation, and Debates

Political lawyers defending their clients against lies appreciate that law is little help and have to explain to politicians why they normally should not sue for libel. I work through these issues as I lobby media stations against running false political advertising, which lands me in a lawsuit and a luxury suite in Vegas. Voter manipulation becomes a popular and effective strategy, which is not a good development. I see how lies in debates can swing an election and fall into a swimming pool while playing the ever-dishonest Trump in mock debates with Joe Biden.

It is pointless in any discussion of campaign ethics to argue that "politicians should not lie." Politicians shade the truth or leave out material information in claims they make or defenses they offer for their actions. They certainly indulge in the political white lie, a modest example among many being statements such as "I am so delighted to be here today and to have at my side one of America's finest public servants, your Mayor So-and-So." Or: "You the people of [town, city, state] have been a model for the nation [give reason], and I am delighted to be here today." For a variety of reasons, politicians must do some of this, some of the time: it is essential to their craft. They are in the business of persuasion, bringing people to their side for one purpose or another. They are always selling, and salesmanship does not usually thrive on candid admissions about flaws in the featured product—which include themselves.

Not all lies are the same: not all are offenses against the political pro-cess and a betrayal of their ethical obligations. The whole subject of lying in campaigns has also gotten seriously confused when it is connected to a related, but quite separate concern: negative campaigning. Political reformers and editorial boards anguish about "negative" campaigns. But what is expressed in negative terms need not by any means be false. Each party rails against the other for smears and negative campaigning when it suits them, and then gladly resort to the same tactics when the opportunity arises and there is political advantage to be had. Democrats were negative toward Donald Trump ceaselessly, and without drawing a breath, and I thought it all quite merited. There was a lot to be negative about the 45th president, both as an officeholder and as a candidate, and it needed to be brought out and presented persuasively and urgently to the voters and general public.

Moreover, not all lies are negative wielded against an opponent; some are meant to deceive the voters about the mendacious candidate's attributes and achievements. The House of Representatives found itself in 2023 with a newly elected, compulsive liar in its midst, George Santos of New York, whose personal story held up for his voters' admiration was pure invention, from business successes he did not have, to faked employ-ment histories, all the way to tragic family narratives full of falsehoods and contradictions. The voters elected an impostor.

The focus has to remain with lying—outright falsehoods. The context in which the lie is told is all important. It calls for attention to the reasons for the lie, the audience for the lie, and the potential consequences, both intended and unintended. Some lies are commendable. A politician who is celebrating success on a legislative initiative may pass around healthy helpings of credit to colleagues, some of whom did nothing to deserve it. She tells the public she could never have gotten the job done without her colleague Jones, although everyone modestly informed about the matter knows Jones is lazy and useless. But Jones is a vote she will need in the future and other colleagues will also take note and be impressed with the credit-sharing. This is smart politics. It is good for the institution.

This unfounded generosity to others can be offered up to larger or smaller gatherings, and one of my favorite examples was provided by the irreplaceable late Senator Daniel Patrick Moynihan of New York. As he walked toward his office in the Senate, tourists who recognized him approached for a handshake and announced their state of origin and the Democratic senator representing them, of whom they were proud. "Senator [so-and-so]!" exclaimed Moynihan, who then proceeded to extol his colleague for exceptional service to state and country. The tourists and he then parted ways, and as he resumed his trek to his office, Moynihan mused aloud to an aide in his company: "Senator [so-and-so]—such a dim bulb."

Political lawyers don't advise on those harmless, even salutary, adventures in political mendacity. They do advise on other questions of truth and falsity, such as when screening ads or campaign communications to weed out claims so reckless in their disregard for the facts that the victims could sue for the damage to their reputations.

Normally, the concern is not about candidates committing libel against their opponents. Plenty of room is available under the law to say horrible things about an adversary. Any clever campaign can go right up to the legal limit and escape a lawsuit. Over the course of my career, I counseled every candidate and officeholder roused to fury by any such personal attack that the answer did not lie in a libel action.

It often took me a few tries to explain why I, a lawyer, was counseling against going to court and foregoing the fees and excitement I would enjoy every step of the way. This is one instance in which I could have come across as lacking the mettle of a hard-charging lawyer fit for political strife. Eventually, in advising restraint, I would prevail. Of course, the estimate of likely legal fees did not hurt my cause.

Perhaps more persuasive than anything else is the opening a libel suit provides to the defendant to use the legal process to explore various dark corners of the plaintiff's past. *Ah, so you say I have tarnished your reputation for probity? OK, let's spend some time checking out how much of that reputation there is to be harmed.*

Moreover, a libel suit cannot settle matters during the campaign: years are required for them to be resolved. The most it can achieve is showing the public that the candidate is really, really outraged and ready to prove that the lie was really, really a lie. But then the lawsuit just sits there.

Possible vindication is far away. There is a good chance that it never comes. The candidate loses in court, and having lavished time and money on a lawsuit, now has to live with the inference some may draw that if the suit failed, the lie that prompted it may not have been a lie after all. Why else would the candidate have failed to win vindication in the courts?

Then there are the lies told for the benefit of a candidate by their allies, which are also difficult to defend against but offer a few more opportunities for lawyers to strut their stuff. TV stations cannot reject a candidate ad for being libelous, but if some other "independent" political committee supporting the candidate shows up—say, the Committee to Defend America from Bob Bauer—and runs an attack on poor Bauer, stations have the discretion to reject it. They don't have to give reasons. A candidate or candidate's party who wishes to stop that sort of advertising can hire a lawyer to complain to a station that the anti-Bauer ad is false or libelous or tasteless—the possibilities for lawyer drivel are limitless—and should not be run.

Stations don't often grant the campaign's request, in part because they don't want to arbitrate these clashes between campaigns. They also don't readily forego the handsome fees for airing the ad. I made these sorts of demands on behalf of my candidates for years with weak results. I do recall fondly the occasion when the demand successfully resulted in a committee's ads being pulled off the air during a Senate race in Nevada. The committee then sued my client for wrongfully interfering in the committee's contractual right to have its commercial run. I was called as a witness, having authored the legal memorandum distributed to the stations with the demand that the offending ads be taken down. For five days, I waited for my day in court. My client insisted that I be comfortable and booked me into a two-story hotel suite at Circus Circus with an offer of unlimited room service. That was a first, and it was also a last. Only in Vegas. We won the suit.

When lawyers screen ads for libelous content, they do pay close attention to the civilians who may be caught in the crossfire and who could stand a better chance than the candidate of prevailing in court. An ad might attack a candidate for keeping company with suspect allies, such as a donor or a former business associate, and those allies could take offense and sue if the attack is carelessly drawn. There have been occasions when ad makers have had to retreat before a threat of a libel suit from this quarter. The private plaintiff can more afford the time and money, and may have the incentive, to seek the vindication that may be years away.

What's missing in this inventory of the victims of false advertising? The voters, of course. They have a recognized interest, the overriding interest, in not being lied to. Their right to vote is at risk in the lies they are told. The damage to those interests can flow principally from the effect of a lie in inducing the electorate to cast an uninformed or misinformed vote. Or their confidence in democratic institutions can be dangerously shaken. When the Trump campaign embarked on a program of systematic lies that the Democrats cheated in 2020 to win the election, the primary casualty was public faith in the electoral system that is indispensable to the functioning of the democracy.

Political lawyers and other senior campaign aides have to guard against lies with this destructive potential. In campaigns that are euphemistically described as "hard fought" but are outright brawls, someone has to speak up when the rhetorical attacks heat up and boil over. Sometimes someone does; just as often, if not more frequently, no one does. And when a concern is expressed, it is often enough attentive not to the ethical question but to the potential political blowback. If the campaign could get away with it, it would.

The only control of significance on these kinds of lies is ethical responsibility. The law cannot do the job. Under pressure from reform groups, Congress has tried to legislate at the margins, with poor if not amusing results. It has required federal candidates to affix to their paid advertising, in their own voice, the now familiar "I am Susan Jones, and I approve this message." The purpose of this "stand by your ad" disclaimer was to encourage candidates to take responsibility for their advertising and, by doing so, to deter negative ads that are false or seriously misleading. The candidate might at least think twice before launching a viciously negative, misleading ad if they had to own up to it right then and there, in the body of the message, in their own voice.

The effect of this well-meaning reform? None. Whether the public takes notice of the disclaimer, it does not factor into either the candidate's choice of what to approve for broadcast or the public's response to the ad. Unethical candidates, prepared to attack and lie with impunity, have not been deterred by this requirement. They continue to practice their dark arts with enthusiasm. While some states have experimented with laws against campaign statements that are false, or made with reckless disregard of the truth, with the intention of supporting or defeating specific candidates, these enactments have encountered serious constitutional challenges in the courts.

The ethical standards of candidates and their lawyers and aides are the crucial, often the only, line of defense. And it should be obvious why these lies are especially damaging if the lawyers themselves are telling them, such as the one that has cost Donald Trump's personal and political lawyer, Rudy Giuliani, his license to practice law in New York. In the aftermath of the 2020 election, he told one lie after another about election fraud costing Trump his victory. He had every reason to believe that he could get some part of the hard-core Trump base to buy what he was selling. As lies go, this was hard-core stuff to undermine public confidence in the system for the elections, and he both supported the lying and personally engaged in it.

There are special cases, no less troubling, where the voters are told the truth, but the goal is not to sell them on a lie, but to use the truth to manipulate them. An example that made headlines during the 2022 midterm elections is the Democratic Party's decision to support Republican candidates for nomination, because those candidates, extreme in their views and plainly unqualified for the office they sought, were thought easiest to beat. The party spent significant sums to persuade the other party's voters that the extreme candidate is one they really wanted to put up for the general election. None of these appeals revealed the motive behind them: that the voters were being encouraged to vote for a loser. And in 2022, this strategy seemed to work: many of these candidates lost.

This kind of manipulation was pioneered by former Democratic senator Claire McCaskill, who claimed to have successfully engineered the Republican nomination of Todd Akin in the 2012 campaign for the

U.S. Senate in Missouri. Three years after the election, McCaskill wrote a memoir in which she provided details on how the effort was planned and how her campaign understood the costs and benefits. At a time when Akin was far behind in the primary and short on funds of his own, the Democrat McCaskill acted energetically to boost his lagging prospects. Her campaign spent money, as did the party, to persuade the most conservative Republican voters that Akin was the true, conservative choice. An ad was designed—one she later called a "dog whistle"—that would get their attention.[1]

And quite apart from her campaign's hope to improve Akin's standing with Republican voters, the strategy depended on what the senator termed "reverse psychology": Republicans would construe a McCaskill ad stressing Akin's conservatism as an attack by the Democrat—and a sure sign that he must be as conservative as alleged. The senator relates how Republican voters flooded her office with calls to declare triumphantly that if she disliked Akin's conservatism, then he was sure as hell the right conservative for them.

The senator has acknowledged in express terms this "manipulation" by which her campaign sought to "control the outcome" of the Republican primary. The voters were the immediate target for the trick. If these voters understood that McCaskill was asking them to pick the candidate she would likely defeat, and that this was her intention in touting his conservative bona fides, they might have chosen another conservative. They certainly would have been surprised about the extent of the McCaskill support of the Akin nomination.

I am unpersuaded that electoral success redeems this strategy. There are two reasons. One is that systematic, strategic manipulation of voters is bad, whatever the outcome. It is all too easy for a party to assert that it is resorting to this strategy in the exceptional case, a defense on the model of "desperate times call for desperate measures." Once done, and particularly if done successfully, it is ready to be done again. Satisfying the conditions for voter manipulation—judging the circumstances to be exceptional and desperate measures to be warranted—can only be easier the second time around, and every time thereafter. The party alone decides the state of emergency, and, in politics, nothing succeeds like success. The operatives who mastermind these moves display their tough-ness of mind and will to win, and who, if it might work, can complain?

These strategists also count on short memories to minimize account-ability. In 2016, many Democrats were rooting for a Trump nomination. We are still picking up the pieces left from that election. By 2020, it was the same gamble, better results. It appears that the primary objection to voter manipulation is that in some cases it doesn't get the job done, and the ostensibly persuasive answer is that the next time it might. Of course, if things take a really bad turn, dangerous candidates wholly unqualified for office may finish first. The election of a would-be autocrat may mean that the next time is a long way away.

In reflecting on this world of lies and manipulations, two episodes come most to mind as studies in how a campaign might define its responsibilities for truth and falsity on the campaign trail. In one case, the controversial claim was a slipup, as a campaign just got carried away. The question then was whether a lie or misleading remark should be left to stand, or the campaign should undertake to "clarify" or correct it. On the other occasion, the claim was a lie that the campaign refused to admit and even doubled down on, spreading it even farther and wider.

In 2012, in the Obama reelection campaign, I participated in a con-ference call with reporters about our opponent Governor Romney's ten-ure at a private investment firm, Bain Capital. We sought legitimately to call attention to his responsibilities for that company's business interests and practices. The extent of that responsibility depended in part on how long he had held his Bain management position. Our call was prompted by Securities Exchange Commission filings and related press reports that suggested he was claiming to have left the company three years earlier than he did. The Obama campaign pounced; I suggested that he had a credibility issue and that this was "serious business."[2] This was a political claim. Another campaign adviser on the call went further, suggesting that he may have committed a felony arising from false SEC filings. This was a more serious, legal claim.

The press ran with this more sensational piece of the story, as one might have expected. The Romney campaign demanded an apology for effectively charging him with a crime. The Obama campaign conceded that it had gone too far: the claim of criminal activity was not planned or even necessary to the credibility issue we wished to raise. Our candidate Senator Obama made clear he wanted the matter cleared up. It just was not the kind of campaign—his campaign—that he wanted it to be.

When I need the example of a lie told with shamelessness and a refusal to correct it, I think back to the 2000 presidential primary between former senator Bill Bradley, whose campaign I represented as general counsel, and then-vice president Al Gore. The Gore campaign made a major and damaging charge it knew to be false and reiterated without the slightest regard for this falsity. In a major debate on January 8, 2000, Gore told the audience that Bradley had opposed emergency flood relief aid for Iowa farmers and cited a no vote Bradley had cast on the bill. To make the point as poignant as possible, the Gore campaign had planted an Iowa farmer in the audience who had lost farmland to the floods, and Gore asked him to stand as a fresh-and-blood witness to Bradley's heartlessness. The farmer stood there, a prop, as Gore repeated three times that his "friend" was left without help or hope because Bradley would not vote for the relief:

Why did you vote against the disaster relief for [the farmer], when he and thousands of other farmers here in Iowa needed it after those '93 floods?

And there were many other droughts and disasters facing farmers where you were one of a handful who didn't help the farmers . . .

But, again, what was the theory on which you based your vote to vote against Chris Peterson getting some help when his farm was underwater?[23]

The Gore campaign well knew that Bradley had voted for $4 billion in flood relief, but not for the particular measure that Gore cited. This "pre-mortem" published in *Slate* lays out the cynicism in telling detail:

Bradley had, in fact, voted for $4 billion in flood relief. He had merely failed to support an additional $1 billion in aid that the Clinton-Gore White House also originally opposed. The next day, Bradley explained this back-ground, which rendered the charge absurd. But for the next two weeks, the

Gore campaign hammered Bradley in Iowa with 30-second TV and radio spots featuring Iowa Sen. Tom Harkin, who charged that Gore was "the only Democratic candidate for president who has been there for us in our times of need."[4]

Gore not only egregiously misrepresented Bradley's position, but he did so in citing a vote on a bill that his own administration had originally opposed. The press covering the contest saw this as a failure of the Bradley campaign. It was also impressed with the blood-toothed ruthlessness of the Gore operation. A winner, that Gore.

Perhaps in one respect it was a Bradley campaign failure. We had not prepared the candidate with the history of his own vote on the issue. The Gore campaign had telegraphed the attack in a press release on the eve of the debate. I recall clearly the particular moment. We were in debate prep in a hotel in downtown Des Moines, and my role was playing the part of Al Gore—Bradley's sparring partner in the prep. We recessed to consider the vote cited in the release, which struck the assembled staff as very odd. How likely was it that Bradley would oppose flood relief? We checked the vote; there it was. The key vote he did cast, for the $4 billion, somehow escaped attention, only to be discovered after the debate, when it was too late to correct the record with any meaningful political impact.

But the Gore campaign was lying to the voters. As is so often the case, this exchange was reported as just another no-holds-barred skirmish in the candidate wars, decisively won by Gore.

One supposes that Gore campaign defenders would reply that there was technical truth to the claim: Bradley had voted against some flood relief. But this defense won't do. The Gore campaign argument was not a complaint over amounts, for it could not have made much of a Bradley vote for $4 billion rather than $4.9 billion. They wanted the voters to see Bradley as a cold bastard who had left the flood-affected farmers all alone and penniless in their time of need.

Only later did the press reflect on the question of Gore's tactics, and then only as the campaign went on and other issues about his way with the truth found their way into press coverage. A lengthy piece in the *New York Times* over a month later pronounced the Gore claim as "false and unfair."[5] One commentator, Phil Gailey of the *Tampa Bay Times*, wrote a thoughtful piece on "the differences between a negative campaign and a dishonest one."[6] He dismissed the suggestion that Gore's tall tale about flood relief was just standard hardball politics. "Gore's attack on Bradley was not negative campaigning. It was a lie, and Gore got away with it."

Too late for us. We did not catch it, but the key missing check was in the Gore campaign itself. Did anyone in the Gore campaign, lawyers or others, speak up to suggest that maybe this charge was best not made at all? Or perhaps could be framed as Gore voting for more funding than Bradley did? I don't know. What is known is the result: the Gore campaign put even more money on the air to drive the falsehood home as forcefully as possible.

Analysts saw the lie as pivotal in the campaign's outcome. Kathleen Hall Jamieson, a leading scholar in the field of political communications, concluded that the lie had a crushing impact on Bradley's Iowa prospects. She pointed to "polls [that] show the Bradley collapse began the day after the . . . debate. You could argue that Gore built his Iowa victory on a significant deception."[7] I am less sure. There were other reasons for his win and Bradley's loss.

And yet even if the lie might not have explained Gore's massive win in the Iowa Caucus, its effectiveness should not count in judging the ethical choice he and his campaign made. It was a fraud on the voters, intended to have a devastating impact, and the open question of its success does not make it any less a fraud.

The false attack on Bradley occurred in one campaign context—a candidate debate—which is supposed to represent the best that campaigns have to offer the voting public. The competitors agree to put themselves forward, on the same stage, for probing evaluation as they answer the same questions from moderators and, in some debate formats, audience members. They can show their poise under pressure, the quality of their preparation, and their nimbleness in responding to the unexpected. They spend considerable time getting ready for the event, freeing up hours and days to map out their strategy and absorb facts and figures they can recite as needed to show their command of the issues.

This is a moment of the highest accountability to the voters: candidates are expected to agree to debates, and with few exceptions they agree except for those who have explaining to do—and usually a price to pay. It is one event on the campaign calendar when candidates cannot hide behind the nicely packaged advertisements or the interventions of spokespeople and surrogates speaking on their behalf. Whether it meets this expectation depends, in part, on what choices the candidates and their campaigns make, but there are other choices—the formats for the debate, and the role that the debate moderators, drawn from the news media, are supposed to play and how they play it.

I have been involved for years in debate preparation in presidential campaigns. Just as I played the part of Gore for Bradley, I was the "Bernie Sanders" who prepped with Joe Biden in the primaries and the "Donald Trump" in the mock sessions and rehearsals for the 2020 general election debates. And I cannot say that presidential debates serve the voters, or the process, as well as they might, and they are far from the sentimentalized version promoted by the press as it sets up countdown clock graphics to build audience anticipation and give excited previews of the combat to come.

The problem starts with a flaw at the heart of the premise of the debate: that the debates will offer unscripted moments because candidates will have to answer questions they might wish to avoid, in formats and under rules over which they have limited control. These conditions create risk for campaigns: a question they cannot answer, a fumbled response, the varying capacities that candidates have for working within time limits, especially on challenging questions. The response of the campaign is to prepare in every way to reduce the risk. One standard technique is to answer as you wish, with the response in the "can," a canned response that may not really answer the question asked. As one debate manager rightly said in my presence, "you can't choose the questions you are asked, but you can choose the answers you give."

Then it is up to the moderator to push the candidate to answer the question, which the moderator may or may not do. Even if the moderator decides to press for a responsive answer, the audience is then treated to a struggle between the moderator and the candidate, and it does not always accept that the moderator should be a Debate Cop. It is often unquestioned that the press is uniquely best prepared and credentialed to moderate debates. This is not an unreasonable view, and yet the press are also celebrities in their own right who know that their performance in the role will be evaluated and compared to others who in past debates have had the same chance to shine. They are rated on the quality of their questions, the extent of their follow-up when candidates are evasive, and their enforcement of the rules, such as those that impose limits on answers and seek to give each candidate roughly equivalent opportunity to participate in the debate. The moderators then become factors.

A working group of which I was a member, convened in 2015 by the University of Pennsylvania's Annenberg School of Communication, recommended a series of reforms in the debate formats championed for years by the Commission on Presidential Debates, a private tax-exempt organization that achieved for decades a monopoly on presidential debate sponsorship. The working group concluded that "debates are not giving voters an understanding of the candidates as they might." It correctly reported that "candidates and their party representatives use them as a hybrid of Sunday morning interviews and gladiatorial clashes, and express frustration with the constraints the joint press conference structure imposes on their ability to communicate their positions, priorities and core political messages, and to clarify distinctions between or among the candidates." The working group proposed the following reforms to the process:

- *Increase direct candidate exchanges and otherwise enhance the capacity of candidates to engage each other and communicate views and positions;*

- *Reduce candidate "gaming" of time-limited answers and create opportunities to clarify an exchange or respond to an attack;*

- *Enlarge the pool of potential moderators to include print journalists, university presidents, retired judges and other experts;*

- *Use alternate formats for some of the debates, including a chess clock model that gives each candidate an equal amount of time to draw upon;*

- *Expand the role of diverse media outlets and the public in submitting questions for the debates; . . .*

- *Embrace social media platforms, which are the primary source of political information for a growing number of Americans and facilitate creative use of debate content by social media platforms as well as by major networks such as Univision, Telemundo, and BET, by providing unimpeded access to an unedited feed from each of the cameras and a role in framing topics and questions.*[8]

Nothing much happened. The Commission on Presidential Debates sent one of its members to object to our usurpation of their role. It was not our place, apparently, to question their control of the presidential debate process.

For all its commendable efforts over the years, the commission's time may be running out. The Republican National Committee has announced that its nominee in 2024 will not participate in a commission-sponsored debate. I was not surprised. In 2012, when I represented the Obama campaign, Ben Ginsberg,[9] the Romney campaign counsel, suggested that we break away and just negotiate, candidate to candidate, our own debate schedule and rules. Let the candidates take control, he argued.

We did not agree then, but he had a point. Why should candidates not take responsibility for these debates—whether they take place, and if they do, how they are structured? It is worth a try, unless someone makes the case, which I find hard to credit, that the debates we have today are highly informative and functioning well when measured by their own declared objectives. At every stage, why not flush into the open the candidates and their commitment to informed engagement with the voters? If the debates don't happen, as they did not in 1972 when Nixon refused to debate Democratic nominee George McGovern, the voters can decide how much they care. Nixon won in a landslide.

Whatever happens, I will have the memories of the Biden-Trump debates in which I, as Donald Trump, played my part, lying and blustering and bullying my way through the mock sessions. To prepare, I watched hours of tapes of the 45th president, as a businessman, 2016 candidate, and then in office, and read transcripts of his extemporaneous remarks on every conceivable topic. I got into the role, as the mock debate performances require. In her memoir, Valerie Biden Owens, the president's sister, kindly says I had figured out "how to get under her brother's skin."[10] She also said it was more of a controlled performance than Trump could ever have given.

I do not recall that I was much controlled, but it is hard to judge your own performance. We set aside special sessions during which I was expected to be at my Trump-worst—as personally insulting and unhinged as Trump can be. Valerie may be right, though. It could well be that nobody can really be Trump as only Trump can be.

To get as close as I could to the genuine article while remaining useful rather than distracting with my theatrics, I did not attempt a full-scale impression of Trump. I did not bother with makeup or dress details, in the mode of *Saturday Night Live*. I did not bother with a red tie; our dress was casual. I did work hard at mimicry of a few of his standard gestures: the use of his hands, and the positioning and movement of his body as he launched what passed, for him, as an argument or point. I did a light imitation of his voice and inflection. And for all this to work, I needed to become comfortable with heaving insults at Joe Biden.

Just as important, I used as much of the language he did on the topics that would come up in a debate. The role-playing depended on getting this right, on answering a question with the catchphrases and slogans Trump had uttered time and again. Those who do debate prep appreciate that politicians are nothing if not repetitive. They may vary their wording in this way and that, but the demands on them to talk in a host of settings, on the same subjects and often in response to the same questions, lead them to fall back on the familiar and repeat past comments or riffs. It makes sense that they would do so; it is more efficient and reduces the potential for error or gaffe. Improvisation comes with high risks.

For the most part, I delivered a dependably Trump-like Trump, the same one who later showed up for the debates (two of them, as he dodged one). Once I badly missed the target. In replying to a question about *Roe v. Wade*, I had Trump going well beyond his right-to-life rhetoric and calling for the decision to be overruled. As of 2020, he never had. I knew he hadn't, and I still somehow had my Trump say that he supported the end of *Roe*. When we recessed the prep for discussion, Ron Klain, who along with senior adviser (and my wife) Anita Dunn played the role of moderator, asked why I thought Trump had gone that far on *Roe*. I immediately agreed that I had botched the reply. And I apologized. We redid the exchange a few more times over the course of the next two days. (Postscript: by 2022, Trump was taking credit for building the Supreme Court majority that did away with *Roe v. Wade*: my debate prep Trump had just gotten a little ahead of himself.)

In any event, "Trump" was met with some rough justice during one of these debate preps. During a break, I stepped outside, where there was a swimming pool with a tarpaulin cover laid over it for the winter. To relax, I picked up a tennis ball and tossed it out on the lawn in a game of go-fetch with Joe Biden's dog Major, who was a regular presence at these preps and always looking for a playmate. Major returned the ball to me, I heaved it yet again, and as I released it, I lost my footing and fell into the pool, up to my waist in water. I sloshed back into the prep area, a chastened Trump: all wet. I hoped to hide my soaked lower half from view, behind the lectern. As I left hurriedly after the session concluded, the president bade me farewell and told me to "get dry."

"How did you know?"

"Major told me."

CHAPTER 6

Money in Politics

After an early commitment to the cause of reducing the role of money in politics, which includes losing a campaign finance case before the Supreme Court, I become a skeptic. I come to question the politics and effects of campaign finance regulation and worry more about the ethics of fundraising. A regulator tells me I am a bad Democrat. One of the leading congressional supporters of reform, Senator John McCain, also dislikes me and urges my party to fire me.

In 1980, the Democrats were fighting a furious and eventually doomed effort to maintain control of the U.S. Senate. I fancied I had a unique role to play in saving them. I plotted out a lawsuit to significantly limit Republican Party spending for their own candidates and against ours. This legal strategy took me all the way to the Supreme Court of the United States. Where I lost, 9–0, and deservedly so.

The question in the case was whether the national Republican Party could effectively double its spending in Senate races. For each of its Senate nominees, the law allocates one spending limit to the national party and another to the state-level party unit. The Republicans arranged for the national party to "borrow" the limits provided to the states. This was a nifty move: the national party had a lot of money, and this was the most efficient way for the national and state units to match their overall spending authority and the available funds. There was also an argument to be made that this sensible ordering of its affairs violated the law.

I made this case through the Federal Election Commission, a U.S. District Court proceeding, and then the Court of Appeals, where I won, garnering the vote of then judge, later Supreme Court justice, Ruth Bader Ginsburg. The Republicans appealed on an emergency basis to the U.S. Supreme Court, which—dashing my hopes of heroism—"stayed" the appeals court ruling, which meant that nothing would change for the pending election, and the national Republicans could proceed to spend within the vastly expanded limit through the election. The Supreme Court would only hear and decide the case the following year.

A month later, I gamely tried to defend my position before nine skeptical justices, who ruled unanimously against me. What in effect was I arguing? This was the core of my claim: that the federal government could micromanage the spending strategies of each political party, directing so much spending by this party unit and then so much spending by another. It made no sense to the justices, and so caught up was I in this legal adventure that I didn't truly appreciate that this technical legal case—and I did have a technical legal case—was justifiably tossed out.

It was only gradually, throughout my career, that I became skeptical about the regulation of political money. When I started out, representing the wing of the national party committed to winning Senate races, I was exceedingly conservative in my approach and fairly or unfairly wound up with the nickname "Dr. No." Lawyers do have to say no and put up with client exasperation. I was doing my job, though not happy to carry the reputation of being a legal killjoy. I felt more like a scold than a lawyer.

Over time, I came to appreciate that some of the applications of the rules, and in some cases their very design, made little sense and just got in the way of perfectly reasonable campaign activities and programs. Clients had good reason to grind their teeth over my legal lectures. It also seemed likely that the tensions between the strictest application of the law and the realities of campaigning would eventually doom the entire reform enterprise.

This realization did not lead me to become reckless in my advice, but I did not mind at all, indeed relished, exploring the gray areas within which my clients could raise and spend creatively and aggressively to come out on top on Election Day. Dr. No was replaced by a more venturesome Dr. Very Possible, who might reply, "Let me take a look and get back to you—there may be a way."

Soon I was out of step with the expressed policy views of my party. It was no secret. One news account in 2005 reported specifically on what it suggested made "Bauer stand out" as a party lawyer: "[He possesses] a point of view on campaign finance regulation that—at least until lately—has been close to heresy in the Democratic Party."[1] Reform groups were offended in the extreme. So were their allies among the regulators, one of whom—a senior lawyer at the Federal Election Commission—told me that he could not understand how a Democrat could take the positions I did on campaign finance regulation.

It was fine to appeal to the party's principles, but not to be overlooked was a fact of political life: for decades, Democrats worried endlessly about money in politics, because they were reasonably sure that they would always be outspent by the other side. Now it is true that some wings of the party were then, and still remain, dedicated in principle to limiting the role of money in politics. They have believed that cash could only corrupt the way politicians behave, the commitments they keep, and the quality of public debate. Those who had money, spending it for their own self-interested purposes, would have leverage to pressure politicians into doing their bidding. It was not that politicians would pocket the money and pay their household and recreational expenses with it. The graver danger was that politicians would take the money and then run a government to reward the financiers who helped them into office.

Then, when Democrats became far more competitive, and in some key national races might have appreciably more resources at their disposal than their Republican opposition, the fear of corruption—the horror of money in politics—dissipated. The delights of having a lot of money were unbounded.

The Obama 2008 presidential campaign I represented was awash in cash. Barack Obama could raise money from large donors who were excited about his candidacy, but also from newly available sources of small donor giving via the internet. The campaign raised more money than it could possibly spend and wound up with a surplus. It had to stop raising money a few weeks before the election because it had no real need of more funds and no rational way to spend it. If Obama's general election competitor John McCain put up an additional amount in some state, the campaign could easily answer with double that amount. It was exhilarating.

The Obama electorate, excited beyond measure about his candidacy, had no qualms about how much money he raised, and they didn't imagine for a moment that the large sums wealthy donors might contribute would somehow corrupt him. The more money the better if this was how the victory could be achieved.

The national press, so much of which was enchanted with Obama, was less taken with this whatever-it-takes view of how he could win. They were particularly alarmed that Obama opted out of a broken system of public financing that allowed participating candidates to obtain public money in return for an agreement to limit their private fundraising. For a long time, liberal Democrats (later to be denominated progressives) cared deeply about replacing private with public money. The idea is simple enough, and in the main, compelling: treat campaigns as a public function better paid with public funds than with the cash supplied by special interests. The risk of corruption would be lessened, and candidates without immediate access to wealth would have a chance with public support to get a hearing.

The problem, of course, is that voters are not enthusiastic about providing money for politicians and their campaigns. They fall for the charge that public funding systems are "just for politicians." The presidential public financing system was designed to work around these concerns by inviting taxpayers to simply check the box on their tax returns and gift a few dollars of what they already owed to the government. In other words, they paid no additional money to the federal government for campaigns; they simply and voluntarily allocated a portion of their tax liability for this purpose. The government would give up its claim to the checked-off dollars and manage the delivery to the candidates, but it was not providing new money generated through new taxes.

The welfare-for-politicians charge still haunted this and other public financing programs and proposals. At any rate, the public never participated in the system at very high levels. The high watermark of taxpayer contributions was roughly 28 percent, and then it rapidly slid down. Reformers made endless excuses for the lack of public interest. They suggested, among other claims, that tax preparers were not adequately advising their clients of the tax check-off option. The true explanation for the lack of public interest was simply lack of public interest. Perhaps taxpayers did not see any reason to help fund the campaigns of those they would never vote for. Under this program, taxpayers did not check off funds for specific candidates, but instead it was a system in which all qualified candidates would receive a share.

To make matters more complicated, the money available through public financing didn't come close to what, as campaign costs consistently increased, a reasonably competitive presidential campaign would eventually need to meet its vast expenses. Candidates who could raise far more money on their own came to question the utility of taking public money and limiting in turn their access to private sources. George W. Bush participated in the general election grant system, but not in the primary system. Barack Obama participated in neither. John McCain, Obama's opponent in the general election and celebrated for his support of campaign finance reform, objected that he and Senator Obama should honor the very principle of public financing, foregoing all considerations of competitive advantage. Our supporters laughed that off.

When the Obama campaign made the only sensible choice, which was to opt out of the system and rely entirely on private funding, Robert Gibbs, the campaign and later White House press secretary, accompanied me to a breakfast with reporters to announce the decision. The response was hostile. Many of the reporters and columnists present subscribed to the proposition that campaign cash soils politics—that it requires endless vigilance and energetic regulation. Now, from their perspective, the Obama campaign was getting dirtied up. They were bitterly disappointed, and their questions were pointed, but those in the room who knew me from my representation of the national party and its candidates were not surprised. They saw me as always looking in every possible way to loosen campaign finance restrictions to enable Democrats to spend sufficiently to be competitive. The sour faces turned in my direction said it all: there's Bauer, up to his old tricks.

I don't repent. Nothing over the many decades I've been involved in politics has suggested to me that this money has nearly the corruptive effect that reformers claim. The drive for money does affect how the politician behaves toward donors. Candidates "dial for dollars" in airless cubbies, and the donors who succumb to these appeals have to be celebrated and kept warm for the next request. Candidates cannot afford to ignore their friends, and any campaign that does so will suffer the consequences. The contributors' calls have to be returned; appreciation has to be expressed. The good politicians know how to manage all of this without selling out their office. Politicians who fail in this task are not so much corrupt as they are inept—or just unethical. I represented politicians who raised vast amounts of money and never experienced, or deserved, a single serious charge of corruption related to their fundraising. They were nonetheless able to pat their donors on the back, express their gratitude, and lock them into another cycle of successful fundraising.

Sometimes politicians with the most honorable of intentions did not know quite how to manage this task—and in comic moments, they might be so nervous about the appearance of corruption they would alienate their supporters to the point of insulting them. I represented the late Senator Robert Byrd of West Virginia who rarely faced a serious challenge to his reelection, but in 1982, he did, and his campaign had to raise meaningful sums of money. The senator was briefed at length on all the fundraising rules and the suspicions confronting politicians as they built up their campaign treasuries. I advised him of the law prohibiting fundraising on federal property: the campaign had to be kept out of official space. One day the senator met with constituents from his state to hear their thoughts on pending legislation, which involved no mention of the campaign or contributions. One of the visitors closed out the meeting by saying that he had long admired the senator and wanted him to know that he and his colleagues stood squarely behind his reelection. Byrd flushed a bright red, slammed his hand down on the table, and shouted that he wanted to hear no such thing in his office. The poor soul berated in this fashion slid back into his chair, entirely in the dark about the reasons for this rebuke.

Decades of social scientific research do not support the conclusion that politicians are motivated primarily by campaign contributions or the hope of raising them. Instead, they are moved by a range of factors, which include ideology, staying in sync with their constituency on major issues, the imperative of following congressional leadership on major votes so they can ascend the career ladder, and so on. By and large the press, especially the investigative press, resists this view of the world. One reporter very schooled in these matters once told me that if you were to understand any major policy decision you should simply "follow the money."

This is false, no truer than a claim that reporters will disregard any professional or ethical standard to sensationalize a story and get it on the front page. It is on major decisions that campaign money in national politics generally plays the least impactful role. Far easier to satisfy donors by giving them access on less visible and significant issues, when the officeholder is not in danger of helping out the wealthy supporter at great political cost. This access, fairly described as "special access," is not to be dismissed as of no concern in a democracy. While it is entirely legal, how it is managed is an ethical issue. Officeholders have to be mindful of the legitimate demands of fundamental fairness in how they carry out their responsibilities.

It is also true that wealthy donors are frequently motivated by ideology and politics, or just the joys of being in the game, and they have funded antiestablishment political activity when resources for those purposes were badly needed. Wealthy people funded Eugene McCarthy's opposition to President Johnson's Vietnam War policies by underwriting his decisive challenge to the president's reelection candidacy. They were behind the Democratic Party's efforts to defeat George W. Bush and bring an end to the war in Iraq in 2004. To this day, with few exceptions, wealthy donors I have represented, or I have had occasion to deal with on behalf of the client, have cared far more about policy or political direction, or just the gratification of political engagement, than serving their own personal financial self-interest.

In truth, wealthy people don't really need politicians all that much, most of the time, and many of them don't care to keep their company. Contributions they make for "business" reasons are largely downside.

Their involvement in politics may annoy their customers, and if they run public companies, it is not helpful in their relations with their shareholders. They do not rationally see this activity as essential to running their business, just one of the costs. Still, they feel they have no choice but to provide some campaign funds to answer the incessant appeals from cash-hungry politicians. When they spend money, and a lot of it, to move government policy, they prefer to spend it on lobbying activities. More money is spent, less accountably, on lobbying, than on campaigns. Lobbyists may think that the political contribution here and there makes their job easier by buttering up their lobbying targets. And in some cases, that may be true. However, skillful and well-paid lobbying does not depend on it.

The ugly stuff in campaign finance happens in unsophisticated circles where crude views of the American political process can be found, and those who hold them flatter themselves that they are savvy players. Now and then, the corrupt businessperson or entrepreneur finds a match in a corrupt or stupid politician. Their clumsiness will also land them in trouble. It is not the way of this world, but it does happen. It simply does not define the political process or the source of its ills.

Another cost of campaign finance regulation is that some kinds of political activity are favored and others disfavored. We have restrictions, for example, on what nonprofit tax-exempt organizations can spend on politics. Those who enjoy the most tax benefits, including deductions on the contributions their donors make, cannot, by law, have any role in electoral politics at all. This includes churches. A pastor who delivers a political sermon to the congregation is putting the church's tax exemption at risk. The IRS is given the task of deciding what constitutes a political sermon, not just an expression of moral views but an illegal "intervention" in a campaign.

This spawns the usual hypocrisies. Democrats want to protect their political activity in the pulpit when it rouses the congregation to action on progressive issues, whereas Republicans are suspicious of liberal churches but anxious to protect the interests of evangelical congregations that are conservative in their politics. It is not surprising that the backstory of this restriction is then-Senator Lyndon Johnson's act of revenge against nonprofits that sprang up to spend against him in one of his campaigns. This sort of regulation is rarely born of the purest of motives.

The regulatory system doesn't just penalize religious institutions. It can haunt other associations little equipped to manage the maze of rules and the risk of liability. Years ago, I received an appeal over the internet from a biking club in California, whose members wished to use one of their weekend outings to leaflet against a Republican congressional candidate. The question was whether this relatively innocuous activity posed any legal questions. It did, and while I normally never gave out legal advice over the internet, I took pity and offered in general terms a picture of what they had to avoid, and what they could do with relatively little risk. I took one look at the email I drafted, which ran to several paragraphs, and wanted to throw up. Why should bike club members have to hire a lawyer, or troll for one on the internet, to run a political biking expedition with club funds?

When Congress attempted to shore up the failing law and add new layers of rules by enacting, on what was basically a party-line vote, the McCain-Feingold legislation, I warned my party that this would end badly. The law was designed primarily to close loopholes by which the parties could get around legal restrictions on the sources and amounts of money they could spend. The filthy lucre in this instance, the product of weak spots in the law, was known as "soft money": monies from large donors, corporations, and unions. It seemed obvious to me that the law would fail in its goal of closing loopholes, but in so doing, would damage political parties and empower "outside" business and ideological groups that were not so restricted. I was right.

Senator John McCain did not think I was right. As he did with other issues important to him, he advocated for and defended the law bearing his name with a fierce righteousness. At a Senate Rules Committee hearing at which he and I both testified, he assailed me for being an "ardent opponent of the law" and suggested that I "invented" criticisms of it. When Senator Diane Feinstein replied that "he advised us and we take that advice," McCain replied that Democrats should look elsewhere for legal counsel. He also suggested that my position on these issues was "well rewarded"—that I was paid for opposing his law.[2] It wasn't a pretty performance, but I did not mind in the least. The senator was just drawing attention to my position. He also was highlighting the influence I might be having on the Senate Democratic Caucus.

It was never the case that I questioned whether federal law should limit individual contributions to candidates or require candidates and parties to disclose their finances. I never did, and federal law does. It is all a matter of degree, and any ambitious program of restricting money in politics, like McCain-Feingold, was both sure to disappoint its supporters' expectations and undermine the conduct of perfectly legitimate, necessary political activity. Cycles of aggressive reform debate and activity itself were dangerous, as each major party plotted out rules that would give it an edge over the other. George W. Bush signed the McCain-Feingold bill into law, a curious choice by a Republican, and it was apparently a consequence of hearing from advisers that Democrats would be the party with the most to lose from the enactment of this reform.

I have supposed, too, that my resistance to this role of government in politics is in some measure rooted in my family history and my parents' experience of governments seizing control of politics. The role of governments in politics—in the regulation of the terms and conditions of political participation—is unavoidable. There must be rules to structure a fair political process accessible to the electorate on broadly equal terms. Public confidence in the democracy rests on the perception of that fairness and equality; citizens must experience it at their various points of contact with the system. There then comes more quickly than many reformers imagine or acknowledge a tipping point when an expansive role conceived for regulation draws government into a very different role. It becomes a tool the contesting parties seize and manipulate to pick winners and losers. We see this in the fight over voting rights, where politicians use voting laws, some of them enacted for blatantly discriminatory purposes, to give their side the upper hand. Campaign finance regulation poses similar, if not always such dramatically evident, risks.

As in any consideration of a complicated issue that gets people very worked up, one qualification to all this is in order. My experience is with congressional and presidential campaigns, and with the effects of and arguments over reform at that level. I don't doubt that in a school board or state legislative race, money could make a significant difference. Lower visibility elections in which fewer voters participate may well be swung one way or the other by massive disparities in the funding of the competing campaigns. States and localities might experiment usefully with public financing and other reforms to address that problem. They will not escape all the traps in regulation, such as unintended consequences and the gap between their goals and the actual outcome. They can do their best, and it might still work better in some jurisdictions, some of the time, than it has in the unhappy case of elections to the presidency.

To see extensive federal campaign finance regulation as dubious in concept and hopeless in implementation is not to dismiss concerns with the quality of our national politics. I am troubled not so much by how *much* money is spent, or by the sources of the cash or interests behind it, as by the various *ways* it is spent. Politicians, parties, and other political organizations pour cash into ever more innovative, technologically sophisticated techniques for winning over and turning out voters and depressing the turnout among the opposition.

The microtargeting of voters allows strategists to better manipulate the emotions and manage the motivations of citizens whose personal data can be collected and put to this use. Lies can be told with greater effect and with less chance of detection and rebuttal. The sums devoted to polling and focus groups encourage the recruitment of candidates who lack meaningful convictions of their own and who can be equipped with campaign techniques and programs evaluated mostly on the basis of their vote-getting potential.

I also favor in principle public funding for as many campaign functions as possible, but I recognize that it's not popular and will certainly not happen in my lifetime. It is better, for sure, for candidates to be spared having to spend huge amounts of time raising money. It just takes up too much of everybody's time. We would also want candidates without immediate access to resources to have an opportunity to bid for public attention, and perhaps succeed, which would be impossible for many without some kind of seed money available through a public financing program.

What most matters in containing the ill effects of money in politics is the exercise of ethical responsibility. It does not fall principally to the law to answer the question of how politicians should manage with integrity the raising and spending of campaign money. In my years of counseling candidates and the parties on the uses of money in politics, the advice of greatest importance, of most value to the client, was about the ethics of raising and spending money. It is not hard to explain a clear legal prohibition, and it was exceedingly unusual in my experience that advice in this category was disregarded. Then other questions would come up in a very different category of "gray areas" and "appearances." A happy constituent commends the lawmaker for taking her position on a pending vote—a position already announced, or a vote already cast—and hands her a campaign contribution. Does the officeholder, quite clearly not taking a bribe, accept the check—or advise the contributor that the discussion of the vote or policy position should not occur at the same time as a contribution? How does the officeholder explain the position without giving offense to a supporter who did not intend to act corruptly or compromise the candidate? At what point would the candidate be free to return to any such satisfied constituent and ask for financial support?

These are relatively common issues on which a lawyer (or other campaign aides) might counsel. Among the others is the vetting or screening of contributors who could lawfully make, but from whom for appearances' sake a candidate might not accept, a contribution. Presidential and congressional campaigns screen or vet major contributors for background or other issues that suggest a reason to decline their support. Some of these contributors play expanded, visible roles in campaigns, hosting events and helping the campaigns to identify and contact other potential donors. A campaign must know if a prospective financial supporter or volunteer fundraiser has paid a heavy fine in a regulatory proceeding, or appeared in a story about associates who were indicted for a business-related criminal offense, or gone through an angry divorce involving charges of infidelity or domestic abuse. These histories could be recent or long ago. The candidate or party has to decide whether to take the money or the offered assistance with fundraising.

In large part the campaign vetting standards are a protection against bad political stories and demands from the opposition that they disgorge money from questionable sources they should not have accepted in the first place. There are other, ethical considerations, having to do with how these choices reflect on a candidate's character. The conversation within a campaign about a vetting issue is both political and ethical in nature.

The law struggles with many of the issues in this category. It is far better designed when it deals with the grossest abuses of power and deficits in integrity. It cannot be wielded with any precision, and it can be the source of real harm, in managing the day-in and day-out choices that politicians make in balancing political self-interest and public responsibility.

CHAPTER 7

The Press

Politicians and their legal advisers who don't understand the press are doomed to frustration and failure. Sometimes they are at fault for this unhappy state of affairs; sometimes the fault lies with the press, and the responsibility can also be shared. But what can go wrong is part of the story of failed ethics in public life. I learn the limits of defending a client who faces a career-ending story based on anonymous sources. I make the mistake of alienating a major political reporter early in my career. I become a member of the widening circle of lawyers commentating in print and on the air and learn that it is perilous work. I write a blog post that leads to calls for Barack Obama to fire me from his presidential campaign. I decide it is best to stay off Twitter.

In my lifetime, the press has never been modest about its position in the democratic firmament. Nor is the immodesty altogether misplaced. When Thomas Jefferson famously wrote in 1787 that "were it left to me to decide whether we should have a government without newspapers, or newspapers without government, I should not hesitate a moment to prefer the latter," he may have oversimplified the choice, but he made a point that has resonated for over two centuries.[1] Another question altogether is how well newspapers have stood up to the task. Just twenty years after that pronouncement, Jefferson confessed to a bleak view of how well these publications were performing: "Nothing can now be believed which is seen in a newspaper."[2]

The press and the politicians are locked in a state of perpetual mistrust, and much of the quality of democratic debate rises with the successful—or falls with the failed—management of this conflict. Those who advise politicians cannot, of course, successfully discharge their representational duties unless they understand the press and have some skill in working with it. Their clients care deeply, rightly, and are often obsessively concerned with their press coverage.

When in trouble, and with lawyers by their side, the politician or public official (frequently the same person) has added reason for concern with how the bad story plays out, and for how long. Lawyers worth the name have to advise on how to constructively manage the press—what to say or not, and on which conditions of engagement: off the record, on deep or other background, in writing, or just on the phone.

This is not just another facet of a political or public communications program. A candidate can lose an election, or an elected official his job, if a critical story or series of stories are seen as serious enough and not, as the hope is often expressed, "contained." Scandal is more than a legal and political drama: it may affect who will acquire, or hold onto, political power.

Lawyers in this line of work also know that badly handled press can complicate the client's strictly legal troubles. Prosecutors and regulators follow the stories and will notice when, in a misbegotten press play, the politician who is ham-handed or panicked lies or dissembles in his own defense. The politician indignantly insisting he has nothing to hide has then, for all to read or see, given the opposite impression. Prosecutors can say all they want that what counts in the end are the facts and the law, that disdain of the accused has no part in the final reckoning, but the way they size up the politician they are investigating is not without impact on the outcome. The politician may need the benefit of the doubt; the one who has exhibited bad character may not get it. Years ago, representing an officeholder under intensive investigation for public corruption, I listened to two prosecutors explain to me that my client was a "bad person," and that I would one day understand that. Not just guilty but bad. That client who is deemed a bad person is not going to get the benefit of the doubt.

The politician may also mistakenly give in to the impulse to rush out an exculpatory account of his action. He just wants to tell his side of the story. He launches a defense in the press. His account is incomplete, as it can only be his side. It may seem that he has done himself some good on the day, in the one story, when he reels out this made-for-the-press defense, but it also supplies investigators with new avenues to explore. The press and investigators will turn their attention to testing it, picking it apart, combing through the details for follow-up. This "tell all" defense is not typically the best legal defense, which often requires time, patience, and care. This means putting up with damaging press—that is, politically damaging coverage—in the interests of effectively working through the legal process.

This is hard for politicians to accept. They are accustomed to tracking their press and expect that their communications specialists will talk reporters out of a critical line of questioning, or when this fails, fight off the worst turn the story can take or battle to a draw. Not "engaging" is by and large political malpractice, while from the political lawyer's standpoint, engaging the wrong way, or even at all in some cases, is legal malpractice.

In this case, as in so many others, the press core routinely calls for "transparency," for getting it all out. This demand for transparency works well for the media. Self-interest and a fervent commitment to openness in government and politics blend well in claims like the one that emblazons the masthead of the *Washington Post*: "Democracy Dies in the Darkness." The detail they search for and demand is good copy and, they claim, a healthy outcome for all concerned. Reporters argue that it is self-defeating for the politician to try to hide. The story will just proceed in fits and starts—drip, drip, drip—as reporters hunt down material from witnesses and other, often anonymous, sources. Far better to have it all out on the record, once and for all: the only way to stop the bleeding. In one case, a reporter of some distinction from a leading news outlet patiently explained to me that disclosure to her would serve both our missions, as it was as "good" for my client as it was for her reporting. How fortunate for both of us! I declined.

The problem: this is simply untrue as a general proposition (just as it was false in the particular instance in which she was making that appeal). Democracy does not invariably go to die in the darkness. Sometimes, it needs a little more shade, a little less light. The legal system is constructed around protections against exposure where it could only do harm, prejudicing core interests. Grand juries meet in secret; the leaking of grand jury information is a crime. Clients can invoke the attorney-client privilege to prevent their lawyers from revealing confidences, and, as criminal defendants, they can exercise their Fifth Amendment rights to withhold their testimony. Presidents can assert various privileges to shield from disclosure the advice received from their senior aides. The Supreme Court deliberates in the darkness, stepping out only for oral argument (from which cameras are excluded) and in the publication of opinions, and the leak of the draft opinion overruling *Roe v. Wade* was widely seen as a catastrophic breach of institutional norms. And on and on.

Nor is transparency indisputably, in all other contexts, what a democracy requires to stay alive and kicking. Politics does not thrive in a continuous glare of exposure and publicity. One obvious and basic example is the right to vote, which is exercised in secret. No citizen is ever called on to say for whom they cast their ballot or to give their reasons for their choice. Many nonprofit organizations active in public policy battles zealously protect their donors' anonymity in order to shield them from harassment or adverse effects in their nonpolitical business or social circles. Members of Congress are not subject to any legal requirement to make their schedules public or disclose the names of those seeking assistance with legislation or constituent casework. Negotiations toward political compromise are often impossible to conduct successfully unless the parties are not looking over their shoulders at a public audience monitoring every tentative offer. And members of the press resist, as they should, transparency about critical details of their reporting, energetically concealing sources.

At any rate, the political lawyer has to balance the transparency favored by the press against other requirements for the appropriate and successful management of the defense. In 2023, representing President Biden in a special counsel investigation into the handling of classified documents, the press's complaints about a lack of transparency prompted me to issue a press statement in my name to clarify when the president's legal team would provide timely information about the inquiry.

We had not engaged in any sporadic, selective disclosures in the first instance—the notorious "drip, drip, drip" of information into the media. The first on the record statement to the press came in response to a leak about the original discovery of documents in private office space the president had periodically used, after his vice presidency. We confirmed that much and said no more, for which the president and his team were roundly criticized. We then clarified our position on transparency issues in a statement that stressed that "the President's personal attorneys have attempted to balance the importance of public transparency where appropriate with the established norms and limitations necessary to protect the investigation's integrity."

The statement noted that "the public release of detail relevant to the investigation while it is ongoing," such as the identification of witnesses or the narration of specific events, "may complicate the ability of authorities conducting the review to obtain information readily, and in an uncompromised form." To put out the detail we knew was, by definition, putting out only the detail we knew. It could only be part of the story, not all of it, which "pose[d] the risk that, as further information develops, answers provided on this periodic basis may be incomplete."[3]

These considerations might guide lawyers in any sensitive, public representation. Prosecutors cannot prevent lawyers from saying what they will, but that does not mean they have to like it, and in many cases, tensions over what a defense is doing to complicate an investigation is not in either the government's or the client's interest. This consideration is of particular importance to lawyers representing a president of the United States, the chief law enforcement officer in the constitutional system. Public officials, certainly the president but others as well, might also choose to limit litigating the case in the press with necessarily one-sided accounts of the facts if they are concerned at all with avoiding the accusation later, when all the facts are known, that they were misleading the public.

As far as I could tell, this statement made little impression on the press. It was worth a try, and it served the purpose of a foundational statement of our position to which we could refer as necessary later.

All in all, political lawyers find that their politicians are in an impossible position, having to pick their poison—lousy press or a compromised legal defense. *Because* they are politicians, they cannot be faulted for worrying about the very real problem posed by bad press that could haunt them in the next election and end their chosen career path. The best intentioned may also be anxious about what their troubles mean for what they can accomplish in office. Budding scandal or the full-bloomed variety drives into the background everything else they might say or do. They proclaim a new policy initiative, and by the second sentence or paragraph, the reader or viewer is reminded that this dutiful announcement comes amid "mounting questions" about the unrelated allegations of misconduct, or if an investigation into those questions has been previously reported, this is prominently noted.

It is also not uncommon for reporters to throw in an observation or quote someone to the effect that the besieged politico may have taken a stand or been vocal on a topic only in a desperate bid to divert attention from their troubles. The politician's attempted return to normalcy backfires: it has invited still more press attention to the trouble they are hoping, even for a small slice of the news cycle, to escape. They are left to fume, and the ones so disposed yell at the lawyers and staff they judge too incompetent to impose more control over the rampaging reportorial hordes.

It was in 1989 that I received my first education in the fraught world of managing the press in a major investigation for the party and its political leadership. The client was Tony Coelho, the Democratic House majority whip, whom I had represented since his days as chair of the Democratic Congressional Campaign Committee, the arm of the party charged with seeking or regaining majority control of the House. Tony's DCCC days had earned him considerable renown for his organizational and fundraising skills. They were formidable. He was a man in perpetual motion. The Republicans were on the march in the Reagan and George W. H. Bush years, counting among their victories Ronald Reagan's forty-nine out of fifty states reelection triumph; and yet the Democrats kept their control of the House through the 1980s, an accomplishment for which Coelho rightly shared the credit. He was a Democratic Party superstar, and it was not difficult to see him on a path to the Speakership of the House.

He did stumble here and there, and a notable misstep, which cost him in the moment and then again later when scandal struck, was one decision he made in managing his otherwise favorable press. Brooks Jackson, an investigative reporter with the *Wall Street Journal* who specialized in money-in-politics issues, approached Tony with the proposal that he cooperate on a book Jackson would write about his successful leadership of the DCCC. Jackson would be allowed to report at close hand on how Coelho ran the committee; he would have access to internal DCCC meetings and materials and a chance to speak regularly with the congressman. Tony was intrigued, the staff less so. He saw it as a chance to show how he turned the DCCC, only years before a small, low-budget outfit, into a juggernaut. The staff was unnerved by the prospect of having an investigative reporter turned loose in their office and present at least at some of their meetings. Tony green-lighted the proposal. He had had plenty of usually favorable press about his hard-charging ways, and he did not imagine that Jackson's narrative would do more than give more detail and context to an already established and accurate chronicle of political success.

He miscalculated. The book eventually published, titled *Honest Graft*, might have reinforced the impression of Tony as a master political crafts-man, but it took a sharp turn in a more critical direction. As its title suggested, it recast the plot and etched a less flattering picture of purportedly sleazy fundraising practices. In Jackson's account, the stench included a whiff of actual sale of office. The *Los Angeles Times* review suggested that Jackson's "implicit" message was that "America has strayed from its mission as a 'government by and for the people.'"[4] Others concurred in the substance of that message but thought it not quite explicit enough. In the *Atlantic*, Jackson's book was cited among others as support for the proposition that American politics "stinks."[5]

Coelho got past this slip, which did not precipitate a full fall. It would leave its mark, however. It provided background to the troubles he later could not get past. These involved problematic financial dealings critics would view as updating and bolstering the Jackson narrative.

In the spring of 1989, only months after *Honest Graft* came out, Chuck Babcock of the *Washington Post* published an investigative piece about Coelho's purchase of a junk bond issued through the investment banking firm of Drexel Burnham. Babcock was a careful reporter who worked closely with primary source materials. If the phone rang with Babcock on the line, one would have every reason to fear that he was not just fishing for information but that he had a sound, well-reported basis for his questions. He would have been developing a line of questioning rooted in investigative leads he had already pursued and evaluated. In my experience, Babcock was also eminently fair. It never seemed that he would cling to a story that did not merit follow-up. Now, in the Coelho case, he was sure of the merit of inquiring into the circumstances and details of Tony's purchase of the bond, and he published first one story and soon thereafter a second.

The basic details as Babcock reported them revealed that Thomas Spiegel, chair of a savings and loan and an active Democrat who knew Tony, recommended the bond purchase. As Tony had to borrow funds to buy it, Spiegel reserved the bond out of the limited number available until those financial arrangements could be made. Spiegel did more. He arranged for his S&L to loan Tony $50,000 of the $100,000 purchase price. Tony bought the bond, but the reporting of the purchase, on financial disclosure forms members of Congress must annually file, omitted the $50,000 loan. It also turned out that when Tony bought the bond, he did so at the original purchase price when offered to him, not the amount he would have paid at the later date when he had the borrowed funds in hand. His IRS returns also erred in the tax treatment claimed for the purchase.

At Coelho's direction, I prepared a full account of the facts for the House Ethics Committee, which was released to the public. Coelho, who resisted at the outset answering all questions, adopted, along with the release of the report to the Ethics Committee, a communications strategy of "getting it all out." This was complete transparency—which in this instance ended badly.

The reporting problem originated in accountant oversight, but the deal in its essential and politically problematic details were Tony's to explain and answer for. The bond offering was not available to the public: it was of the "friends and family" variety, and Tony had access to the investment through the offer from the chair of an S&L who both held the bond until Tony had the means to buy it and loaned him part of the purchase price. Babcock did not suggest that Spiegel was looking for a return on his favor to Tony, nor that Tony ever acted to reward him. He was writing a story of those with power, in the business and political communities, playing an inside game of mutually rewarding relationships. Tony got a deal that other members of the public could not get, and Spiegel could bank, so to speak, a favor from a national politician on the rise. He might not ask for anything in return, but who knew what the future would bring? This was a time of sharpened attention to mismanagement and corruption in the S&L industry and the protections that executives might have hoped to buy with federal officeholders by making contributions and bestowing other favors.

All of this was ample cause to imagine that the story would take off and seriously damage Tony's standing and career prospects. The other problems—a reporting violation and the erroneously claimed favorable tax treatment—could only darken the picture.

It was a fair and serious story, and we knew it. Babcock reported it with scrupulous accuracy and sensitivity to fairness. It was the next phase in the coverage that highlights the challenges when the press, mobilized by the first taste of scandal, marches on like a small army to move the story forward.

I cannot recall whether Jack Nelson of the *Los Angeles Times* first called me or the Coelho communications office, but he advised us that he would report that the Department of Justice had opened a criminal investigation into the bond purchase. The department does not announce that it is proceeding on the basis of press reports or other evidence to initiate a criminal inquiry. Nelson was basing his reporting on a "source" within the DOJ. I am confident that he had one or believed in good faith that he did. He was a well-respected reporter who would not have lied to me. The anonymity of his source meant, however, that I could not evaluate for my client the reliability of the claim. Nor could the *LA Times*'s readers.

It was certain that, however reliable, the story of a criminal investigation would hit Coelho hard, likely a blow from which he would not recover. Managing a House ethics inquiry would be difficult enough, but his colleagues might be willing to see how that turned out. However, a criminal investigation was not obviously survivable as a political matter for a House leader. The chance that in due course the bond purchase could be seen to reflect bad judgment and accounting sloppiness, but no more than that, was shrinking, close to the vanishing point. A House ethics committee inquiry could take time to conclude, but critics and even neutral observers would appreciate the longer period of time a criminal investigation could consume. A question about Tony's compliance with the congressional ethics code could not, of course, rival in seriousness one about potential violation of U.S. criminal laws.

I argued strenuously with Nelson about the fairness of reporting on a story with consequences this severe from an anonymous source. Tony could not defend himself against this purported development. Not knowing the source, he could not deny it. Also unfair was the impression left with readers that the department's opening of an inquiry represented even a preliminary judgment that Tony's actions had violated the law. I was aware from other representations and from conversations with former federal prosecutors that the department might "open a file" based on press reports, which could remain open but inactive for lengthy periods of time—and quickly close it after a brief investigation. And it stung, as it always does, that the story would emerge from a breach of professionalism and confidentiality by a department employee who may not have been closely involved with the inquiry, but whose willingness to share what he knew or imagined he did with a member of the press was unethical and a violation of department policy. The department answers publicly to this misconduct only by refusing to comment on the story, which does the victim of the anonymous source no good at all.

Nelson was unmoved by my arguments, and the *Times* published the story. Not much time passed between the publication and Tony's decision to resign. He was a skilled politician. He could try to keep going and try to catch a break, but his perseverance would come at a high cost—to his party and to his colleagues who had elected him to a leadership position and now would be in a politically awkward position. And to his family.

My role as political lawyer was to represent him in any criminal inquiry, since his resignation from the House ended any House Ethics Committee inquiry. When the department looked into the matter, the investigation was short-lived—so brief I can recall little about it—and Tony, now out of Congress, was informed that the DOJ was closing the file.

To the degree that it is a story about political lawyering and the press, the Coelho saga offers contrasting examples of press engagement with scandal. Babcock's stories were built on fine-grained reporting. None of them depended on anonymous sourcing. I could not be frustrated with him, and I do not remember that Tony or any member of his team groused about Babcock's commitment to reporting and writing this story. I felt quite differently about the *LA Times*'s part.

It did not surprise me. This is often the course that these stories travel, as editors demand that their reporters catch up and then scoop their competition. The reporting becomes looser, the sourcing more disguised, including the "sources familiar with" and "sources close to" labels attached to those who speak behind the veil. It cannot be passed off entirely as a routine reporting choice made in the public interest in a story like the one about the Coelho bond purchase. The *LA Times* story resounded as it did because it put Coelho's actions in the worst possible light, overstating for the public the stakes, which were now converted to the stakes in a criminal investigation. It diminished any possibility that his defense of his actions on the merits—whatever critics may have thought about it—could be heard. The words "criminal investigation" have that effect, driving everything else out of view. The lawyers and communications team can always appeal to editors and plead the imperative of fairness, at least playing for time. Most often—and if the story is hot and competitive enough, with the rarest of exceptions—those appeals are known to press and political lawyer alike to be largely pointless.

Shortly after leaving office, Coelho met with reporters, conceded his mistakes in the bond purchase, and registered his frustration with the press coverage. The story would have been impossible without the financial disclosures that he and other members were required by law to make, and these transparency laws reflect a shift toward a Congress more open and accountable than ever before. Yet, as Coelho saw it, "members of the press . . . take the very thing that is helping correct the system . . . and then say the system is more corrupt."[6] They lacked perspective or succumbed to cynicism.

It was understandable that Tony saw things this way. And he was right that the Congress of the 1980s and beyond was an institution in far better ethical order, more regulated and governed by accepted norms of right conduct in office, than its predecessors. The cynicism he detected in the working press was apparent to me as well. In my experience, many reporters see politicians as compromised by the very requirements of succeeding in their work. They make promises to win elections they might not be able to keep; their political rhetoric, a form of salesmanship, can cross quickly over into blarney, more serious misrepresentations, or outright lies. They raise money on the strength of their achievement of influence and power, and the risk or just the perception of the quid pro quo hovers over all they do to assemble the campaign war chest. The world of transparency is not their natural habitat.

In the gap between speech and intention, and in developing political strategies and making deals, the political arts thrive in the shadows. Reporters might admire the politicians who pull it all off, but they are watchful, suspicious. When their ready distrust is triggered, as it was in the Coelho matter, they are primed to strike hard with a frenetic coverage that can be fatally short on balance and without strict adherence to sourcing and other journalistic standards.

The task of the politician is to foresee the possibility that they will face these questions, whether fairly or not, and build buffers. When the bond purchase came into question, Tony already stood associated with "honest graft" in building a powerful party committee. He had conditioned the press to think of him as something of a latter-day machine politician, leveraging power for the large sums of money he then fed into the Democrats' electoral operations. The major donors he recruited, including some in the scandal-ridden S&L industry, would associate him with wealthy people who ran into their own troubles, which would, however unfairly, rub off on him. By the time that Babcock published the first of the bond purchase stories, and before the *LA Times* landed the final blow with the report of a criminal inquiry, Coelho was highly vulnerable to political death by press. It is like a run on a bank. The momentum toward collapse is, at a certain point, unstoppable, and there is nowhere to turn for a bailout.

The helplessness of the politician and his advisory team before this flood tide of bad coverage can turn into a lot of teeth-grinding about the press. These aggravations need to be kept under control. The client will be angry enough for two, and the lawyer has to keep his head about him, recognizing that railing about the barrage of damning stories does not make a whit of difference, and it certainly does not aid the cause of managing the next round of the conflict more effectively than the last. Also, each profession battles the same ethical demons, having to balance professionalism against commercial or competitive pressures. Reporters in red-hot pursuit of a story have to work through these conflicts the best they can, just as lawyers have to acknowledge that there are reasons for the storied distrust of their political clients' stumbles or excesses in the pursuit of money and glory.

And lawyers in the political world have an investment in good relations with the press. The reporter who is hounding the lawyer and their client in one case will show up in the next, and it will not help matters if the dealings between the two in their last encounter ended on a bitter and recriminatory note.

The point of no return will have been reached if the reporter concludes that the lawyer lied to or misled them. I made one such mistake early in my career, and I regret it to this day. It was not a lie, but a hyping of material my client wanted to sell to the press as worthy of coverage. The Republicans were outspending Democrats in the Reagan years, and one effective outlet for this money advantage was their use of "independent" committees that, unlike parties at the time, were not restricted in what they could spend to support or defeat a candidate. Democrats made a fuss about this, alleging that these committees were not truly independent: they were a fraud on the campaign finance laws. I prepared a "study" of this issue, which pulled together what was known about the formation and operation of the most prominent of these committees. I provided it to one of the finest political reporters of his generation, David Broder of the *Post*, who took an interest in it. He asked me if the report broke new ground in the controversy.

Well, it did and it didn't. The report did not bring to light new facts but collected the available information in one place and refreshed the argument about the problem to which we were hoping to draw attention. I oversold its originality and he published, only to decide that he had been snookered into writing a story that did not merit the space given to it, much less his byline. The report was not false, just not anything really new. Broder was miffed and he let me know it. This was an avoidable error, which occurred when my client was trying to get coverage of a legitimate issue.

The worst of all dangers in the press relationship is when a politician asks a lawyer or other campaign representative to front for on- or off-the-record denials of facts known to be true, usually in the hope of quashing a story in the making. It is not necessary, of course, for the lawyer to confirm bad facts or produce a client for a public confession, but lying, on or off the record: never.

It is always open to the lawyer to downplay the significance of the story in early development, explaining that it is truly not the material for a Pulitzer Prize–winning saga of corruption in high places. It is mostly these arguments over the scandal-worthiness of what the reporter is pursuing that have required me to keep my cool. The reporter wants a big story and believes that she has one in the making, and however sincere this belief, it is in her interest that it hit the front page or be prominent in the online edition, and then reverberate throughout the media universe and across social media platforms. The political lawyer presses for the opposite outcome.

In these conversations, reporters can exhibit an exasperating over-commitment to their story. A sure sign of this is a certain moralistic preachiness about the public right to know of bad things happening. For example, in working a story about a legal "loophole" a political party discovered or has begun to exploit, the reporter might begin to frame it as the End of Days. This detection and reporting of loopholes is standard stuff, legitimate enough for the press to take an interest in, but it can be dramatized for effect, and for front page treatment, by the layering in of the reporter's moral disapproval. *Ah, these dishonest politicians are at it again: shocking!* And the lawyer is then stuck with arguing that this is not quite the crime scene it is being made out to be, often to the extent of minimizing the conduct he is attempting to defend—which further enrages the reporter who does not wish her hard reporting work dismissed in this fashion.

All of these were recurring issues in the political lawyer–press relationship over many years. Another, more recent, involves the press and lawyer not as antagonists but allies in the presentation and explanation of stories with legal content.

This is the rise of the legal commentator. I have tried my hand at this, in writing op-eds and appearing on cable to comment on legal cases in the domain of political law, or on political controversies with a legal dimension. This world of legal commentary emerged with a bang during the controversies of the Clinton presidency, culminating in the impeachment process in 1998–1999. I did a few cable appearances and joined other Democratic lawyers in defending Clinton.

At that time, some concerns surfaced about the responsibilities that legal commentators had to the public: duties to competently describe the legal process and to be attentive to conflicts of interest that would raise a question of whether they were expert neutral observers or representing the views of a party or specific interest. Years before social media revolutionized political news and communications, lawyers' cable performances troubled some observers as "lead[ing] to oversimplification and polarization and to certain disparagement for the process."[7]

These ethical concerns largely faded away over the years as legal commentary became embedded in the coverage of politically controversial scandals, investigations, and courtroom dramas. There has been more of this kind of news, as heightened political conflict in the United States is so often expressed in legal charges and countercharges that set law enforcement machinery into motion. The more conflict, the more call there is for lawyers to explain, analyze, and opine on panels, or in one-on-one interviews, arranged throughout the day and into the evening hours. Neutrality is not commonly a virtue in this programming. The audiences on MSNBC, Fox, and social media, among other news sources, are not hungering for objectivity.

Lawyers have signed up to deliver the product. The best outcome of all for the lawyer is a chain reaction of a published op-ed, which produces an invitation to discuss the piece on air, and all the while social media platforms are talking up the piece before the show airs and circulating interview segments afterward. It is a complete ecosystem of self-focused newsmaking, and it is intoxicating.

During the investigation by Special Counsel Robert Mueller into Russian interference in the 2016 election, the legal commentary overflowed. It was a troubling time for all concerned, and lawyers, like others, were caught up in the fever pitch of feeling and opinion. But much of this commentariat, of which I was a member, lost their bearings and wound up giving a lot of opinion mistakenly taken for "expert analysis," which was all too often what they wanted to believe or what their audience wanted to hear.

The problem, of course, was that lawyers on the outside of an investigation can't really judge what is happening on the inside. They know what everyone else knows from the daily media, and they have to work off media reports and leaks of varying degrees of accuracy—or in some instances, none.

When the Mueller Report concluded with disturbing findings but no recommendations that charges be brought on "collusion" between the Trump campaign and the Russian government, or on obstruction of justice, the audience for the anti-Trump commentary was gobsmacked. After the shock wore off, the disappointment turned in Mueller's direction. Criticism of his investigation and final report was fair game, but it is hard not to think that the degree of anger and disbelief was partly a consequence of the legal commentary on the air, in print, and on social media. It was supposedly clear from this avalanche of comment and analysis that Trump had violated the law. When the Mueller Report came out, those earnestly awaiting the merciless judgment, taken to be a foregone conclusion, could not understand what had gone wrong.

I have enjoyed commentating from time to time, and especially writing opinion pieces that afforded me the chance to develop a point and control more closely its presentation than is possible in an interview. I appreciate its rewards. Lawyers, like others on the network and cable circuit, can find out quickly if their comments found an audience. They get congratulatory emails or texts; and if the online op-ed generates enough clicks and comments, it might go into print for a second run. They have established themselves in the debate.

I also have recognized the perils. The sharpest comments, shorn of qualification or nuance, get the best reception.

Here is a little thing, maybe very little, but it has stuck with me, and it is chargeable to my account. In 1986, Democrats were vying for control of the Senate in the midterms and money was being spent left and right. The *New York Times* published a story with the thesis that both sides were cheating on the campaign finance laws. It opened this way: "Political strategists have found so many ways to evade Federal statutes that the laws on campaign financing have been seriously undermined in the election cycle that ends next Tuesday, according to experts in the field." The *Times* came to me, counsel to congressional Democratic Party committees, and asked for comment. This is what the reporter, quite correctly, reported, with a quote from me: "Robert F. Bauer, a lawyer specializing in election law, says the parties 'have got their legal departments working overtime' searching for ways to get around the restrictions governing Federal elections."[8]

At least I was suggesting that lawyers were looking for loopholes: we were not absolutely flouting the law, just getting around it. But I was chagrined that I had lent my name and support to a story about "whatever it takes" politics and implicated my own clients in it. I called a member of the House leadership to admit my error and apologized. He had not seen the story. "Where did it appear?," he asked. "On the front page," I responded. "Above or below the fold," he asked further. "Above, right at the top." "Oh, good," he chuckled. "It will get your name out there and no one will really remember much else." He was comfortable with the "whatever it takes" politics, and happy for me that, in championing it, I had my day in the sun.

I was relieved at the time, as I had escaped censure. I knew then, as I know now, that I had made the comment to show we—Democrats and their lawyers scheming behind them—were prepared to compete with legal limits as barriers easily enough overcome if we worked overtime. It was self-aggrandizing and irresponsible. It was also surely the product of vanity. The *Times* came to me, and I could not resist putting my name in print, "above the fold."

Again: a minor episode, but had I stopped and considered what obligations were attached to my public comment, I would not have given in to the temptation to inflate my role and prove my legal know-how and mettle. The comment did reflect a state of mind, and this is my point about the little things: an attitude exhibited in a comment like that does not keep to the small things. It can begin to infect the bigger ones.

Everyone who accepts this sort of invitation to engage with the media understands that the commentator on the air is also at the mercy of the show host who might run a short piece to frame the issues before the interview, and who decides on the questions and tone that will define what kind of show, emphasizing what kind of storyline, it will be. An introductory video recounting the background of the issue might open the segment with a strong point of view. It will tell the audience that something dreadful has occurred or been said, and the host then may follow with something on the order of "yes, just awful, and here is [Bob Bauer or someone else] to discuss it." In the Trump years, I was among those who believed—in my view, rightfully so—that something dreadful was happening or being said, and I was very ready to discuss it.

It also became clear to me over time that I could easily get cornered into losing control of what I wanted to say, either because I did not have the time or skill in a short interview to give a thoughtful, well-supported view, or because the structure of the interview made it even less possible for me to do so. Panels of interviews—when two or more commentators share the time—are especially treacherous ground for someone worried about stumbling. The other commenters might send the discussion off into a direction you are not comfortable with. The interviewer asks a question, and after one of the copanelists responds, you might be asked the same question or encouraged to respond to your fellow panelist. There is also less opportunity to contribute clearly and intelligently when the questions are spread among the various interviewees in a segment of no more than a total of three to five minutes.

Soon I steered clear of certain shows, preferred others, and made one choice—I would stay off Twitter (now "X"). The 240-character social media comment was not for me. I would not excel at it and could easily imagine shooting off a comment I frantically regretted only minutes later but could not retrieve.

It was this policy toward social media that reflected experience with my own mistakes in the business of legal commentary, both of which caused me trouble with my client Barack Obama.

When blogging was fresh and popular, I set up my own blog, *More Soft Money Hard Law*, and wrote a piece on political law every day of the work week, rising early in the morning to do so. I set a deadline more or less strictly followed of 10 a.m. daily publication and wrote at other times as well. Some of my pieces were analyses of legal developments in my field. Others were more pointed opinion pieces. The blog's readers were members of the practicing political law community, press who reported on these issues, regulators, and Capitol Hill staff who also worked on and followed the topics I wrote about. I was the sole author and the only one responsible for what I wrote. While I kept an eye on writing anything that could cause problems for clients, I had some freedom, I thought, to write as an expert and let things fall as they would.

After the Obama campaign in 2008, I wrote a piece critical of a statement made by Senator John McCain, with whom I had longstanding differences over campaign finance policy and regulation. The McCain office complained to the Obama White House, which in turn contacted the senior staff traveling with the president in Europe. Jim Messina, the deputy White House chief of staff, called me from Germany and cautioned me to take better note of possibly annoying a senator who, while a former presidential campaign opponent, was still a senator the administration would have to deal with.

This mild rebuke did not compare to the problem I caused, if briefly and with blessedly limited effect, for the 2008 campaign itself. The *Huffington Post*, which had followed my blogging, asked whether I would write pieces for them, and the second of my contributions was on the subject of the famous Valerie Plame case. The investigation concerned a leak to the press of Plame's identity as a CIA agent after her husband, Joe Wilson, a former diplomat, had written a widely discussed *New York Times* piece challenging the Bush administration's claim of good faith in believing—and arguing as justification for an invasion—Saddam Hussein's development and stockpiling of weapons of mass destruction. There was a reasonable and serious question of whether the leak was administration retribution for Wilson's published conclusion that intelligence on Iraq's weapons had been distorted to justify the war. An investigation of the source of the leak yielded an indictment and conviction of the vice president's chief of staff, Scooter Libby, for false statements to a grand jury and obstruction of justice.

Amid speculation that President Bush would pardon Libby, whom Cheney and others believed to have been unjustly prosecuted, I wrote a piece arguing that perhaps clemency would be justified, as it would force Bush to take responsibility for the leak, rather than allowing a little-known White House official to take the fall. The piece was critical of the leak and meant to locate the ultimate responsibility where, I thought, it belonged—with the president.

I misread the situation. Word leaked out from the *Huffington Post* that Obama's lawyer was publishing a piece that exculpated Libby. Bill Burton, the Obama campaign press secretary, called to ask me if this was true, and I said that it was not: what he had heard did not accurately resemble the content of what I had written. He was satisfied. For a while.

Then came the piece, with this headline: "Pardon Scooter Libby," with my author identification informing readers that I was general counsel to the Obama presidential campaign. Progressives saw the Libby case as more evidence of an administration covering up lies told to sell the public on the Iraq War, and punishing those, like Plame's husband, who had dared tell the truth. Now I was seen by them to be calling for Libby to be excused, his conviction wiped off the books. The *Drudge Report,* a conservative outlet friendly to Bush and not Obama, published this with glee. Obama supporters called the headquarters to demand that I be fired.

I wasn't fired. Obama was not happy, nor was his campaign team. I received an email from David Plouffe, the campaign manager, who noted lightheartedly, *"You made Drudge!"* and, then more soberly advised me that I needed to be "very careful" from that point on.

I tried. The Libby and McCain cases exposed for me how public comment by political lawyers can misfire. In the Libby case, I failed to carefully consider the reasons for refraining from any public comment on the war in Iraq. It was a major issue in the middle of a presidential campaign in which I represented a leading candidate for the Democratic nomination. And I knew well that readers often stop at the headline or read some but not all of the story that follows, and that a misstatement of my argument I would be powerless to clarify would instantly make the social media rounds. The McCain case mistake was somewhat similar. I could have made my policy point without critiquing McCain directly and causing discomfort for an administration that did not need this irritating point of conflict with an influential senator.

At least by the time Twitter came along I had begun to learn my lessons.

I recognize that politicians and their advisers complain about the press all the time, and that their critiques of press coverage are surely influenced by self-interest and the advisers' very professional responsibility to defend their clients and protect them from harm. Reporters and editors who fight with campaigns and politicians about the fairness and accuracy in their coverage may not aways feel that, of all people, lawyers in particular have much of value to contribute to questions of journalistic ethics.

I cannot see it this way. Both lawyers and the press in their fated interactions in politics have choices to make, and how they resolve them have repercussions in the particular case and cumulatively over time. The reporter who wants to hammer away at the storyline that in order to understand politics all the public needs to do is "follow the money" is doing a disservice—and not only to the poor wretch of a politician who is cited as an example of this corruption. It has an effect on the poor wretch but also on public confidence in the democratic process. It feeds into the populist insistence that the system is rigged, rotten all the way through. And it can determine who keeps their office or appears or stays on the ballot. At a time of extreme financial and competitive pressure on news organizations, their choices of the stories to pursue—and how to pursue them—may be more difficult, but also more important, than ever.

The lawyers defending the politicians have their own set of obligations to consider: not lying to the press, which is a lie to the public, but also not giving in to demands for "getting it all out," which may undermine the fair workings of the legal process. Taking a beating in the press may be the price clients pay for lawyers doing their jobs. The press has to decide whether to administer the beating, and if the beating is administered, is it because the public has a right to know or because the story is too good to be abandoned—*and aren't all politicians sketchy anyway?*

CHAPTER 8

Impeachment

Impeachments have become more common, one more "hardball" maneuver by which a party may seek to challenge the legitimacy of a president's election and cut their term short. Representing the Senate Democrats in the trial of Bill Clinton, I observe at close quarters how failed norms result from bad individual and institutional choices. The worst of the mistakes was one made by a lawyer. I make my own modest contribution to the mess by completely flunking a test of political lawyering as I try to help House Democrats fight off an impeachment vote. I worry that the failure to reform the impeachment process has weakened it as a vital constitutional protection against abuse of power.

My experience with presidential impeachments has been intensive in one case—the Clinton impeachment and trial of 1998–1999—and in another, one of monitoring closely the House impeachment and Senate acquittal of Donald Trump for pressuring the government of Ukraine to concoct an investigation of his likely 2020 opponent, my client and then former vice president Joe Biden. In the Clinton impeachment, I was counsel to the Senate Democratic caucus during the trial; in the House, I assisted my client, Democratic leader Dick Gephardt, in assembling the legal team to defend the president.

The impeachment process by which presidents can be ejected from office may seem a partisan charade that routinely ends with no change in the occupancy of the Oval Office. The "constitutional crisis" comes, and then it goes. No impeached president has so far been convicted. In the nineteenth century, Andrew Johnson was saved by one vote. In the twentieth and twenty-first centuries, the script has played out the same way, with acquittals. The party out of power has moved toward impeachment, acknowledging somberly the seriousness of the step and expressing sorrow to go with its anger that it must initiate this constitutional process for removing the president from office. The president's party quickly questions both the basis and the motive for impeachment, usually laying the blame on partisans' refusal to accept the result of the last election and conspiring, in the name of "high Crimes and Misdemeanors," to cancel the voters' choice.

This is not how it will always end. That the parties have failed up to this point in ousting a president is wrongly taken to mean that they likely will not succeed in the future. We are passing through a period when partisans accept with reluctance, or not at all, that they have lost an election. The aftermath of the 2020 election showed the lengths to which partisans would go—the lengths to which the president who lost would go—to contest the outcome. Impeachment is one more chance, available throughout a presidency, when partisans can plot to end a term in office they could not prevent but can now try to cut short. In the past, they may not have had the votes. One day, they will.

Impeachments in the twentieth and twenty-first centuries have been closely tied to elections. Nixon was impeached for illegal acts and abuse of power committed in the service of his 1972 reelection campaign. Both the Trump impeachments arose out of campaign-related acts: one to use his power to weaken his likely opponent's prospects, and the other to remain in power after he lost. Of course, in the last case, the impeachment, if it had been successful, would only have removed him from office within days of the end of his term. But a key objective of the process was to follow a vote to convict with another, provided for under the Constitution, to prevent him from running for another term in the future.

The Clinton impeachment might seem to have been different, less connected to an election outcome partisans continued to contest, as it arose out of charges of lying in legal proceedings about personal matters. Yet the mismatch between a lie about a personal matter and the removal of the president from office had only so much to do with beliefs about morality and fitness for office. The sorry episode was rooted in a broader rejection of Clinton's presidency: "[A] sizable group of detractors—conservative Republicans, in particular—viewed Clinton as an illegitimate and unworthy president from the moment he moved into the executive mansion."[1] The impeachment process followed an organized Republican Party attack on the president's 1996 reelection victory, organized around allegations that it was tainted by cheating and foreign government interference. In 1997–1998, congressional Republicans conducted with great fanfare an investigation into these claims, but the evidence fell well short of the hype.

When this line of attack on the legitimacy of the Clinton presidency failed, another opened up a year later, made possible by the revelation of the president's relationship with a White House intern and his ultimately unsuccessful efforts to conceal it. In an extraordinary collaboration of an independent counsel and organized political opposition to Clinton, a trap was laid for him to deny the affair under oath. The legal jeopardy in which he found himself was sure to prompt calls for his impeachment, as it did. The Republican enemies of Clinton could not prevent him from winning reelection. They could, however, end his presidency through impeachment and conviction.

Congress can run an impeachment as it pleases and convict on any grounds it asserts. It fashions the "constitutional test" for impeachment and conviction. For all the time devoted to arguments about what constitutes "high Crimes and Misdemeanors" justifying removal from office, there remains no clearly defined agreement. Perhaps former President Gerald Ford's blithe assertion, that an impeachable offense is whatever a Congress at any given moment in history says it is, may have captured a basic political reality but it was far from an impressive contribution to a serious constitutional debate. It seemed to endorse a power play by any party with the votes to bring it off. No doubt he was only right to some extent: it cannot be the case that *any* charge or collection of charges against a president, alleging misconduct of the widest variety, is enough to support a successful impeachment. Politicians are sensitive to public opinion, which sets some limits to unrestrained partisanship. But these limits are variable, and in a highly polarized politics, when politicians cater to the narrowest base opinion and ignore the rest, the limits may be set very low.

Every presidential impeachment and trial is restructured largely as if none came before it, even if there is lip service to past practice. The rules and standards are made and argued on the fly, as political circumstances dictate. The process the House (if the House impeaches) and Senate will follow is largely designed for the particular case. The extent of the fact-finding each institution will conduct before it votes ranges from the more or less extensive to virtually none at all.

Even the committees with jurisdiction may vary. In the first Trump trial, Speaker Pelosi decided that multiple committees would proceed with an official impeachment inquiry: an investigation by six committees in all, under an overall impeachment umbrella. The House adopted a similar approach in 2023 in voting for an impeachment inquiry directed at President Biden. The Senate does have standing rules of impeachment, but they don't lock the Senate into procedures of most consequence. It may and does historically proceed by resolution to make up more procedures as needed to deal with the circumstances—the political circumstances—before it.

It is not even clear that if the House impeaches a president, the Senate is obligated to hold a trial. If the two Houses are controlled by different parties, they are not obligated under the Constitution to cooperate. The Senate might decide to entertain a "motion to dismiss" which, if successful, would speed the proceedings to a conclusion with no serious consideration given to the record that the House built in support of its vote to impeach. Or the Senate could delay holding a trial indefinitely, perhaps seeing a political advantage in slowing things down and cooling off public opinion while it mounts an attack on the House process. This procedural flexibility can work the other way as well. In the first Trump impeachment, Speaker Pelosi directed that the House delay the transmission of its Articles of Impeachment to the Senate as she struggled with the Republican Senate leader over the question of when (and if) witnesses would be called in the trial.

It is no doubt in part to preserve their political flexibility that the two Houses have left the impeachment process to case-by-case political choice. Impeachment is becoming more common at the same time as it remains ungoverned in critical respects by an ethics grounded in constitutional and institutional considerations. The metastasis of irresponsibly threatened impeachment is a serious consequence of this state of affairs. This is a problem not only where the impeachment process is pure politics—either a sideshow engineered by an opposition determined to disrupt a presidency, or a more serious attempt to defy voter choice and accelerate a president's departure from office, or both. A crudely politicized impeachment process, unconstrained by settled procedures and clear standards, will also be drained of credibility when it is needed—when there is a strong case for removing the president from office. It will afford presidents like Trump that much more of an opportunity to cry witch hunt and make Congress the target.

The Clinton impeachment was a warning sign that this process was no longer a once-in-a-century event but a political plaything in which partisans would see themselves as free to act to suit their political interests. Those who had the votes and a favored constituency cheering them on would be rewarded for seeking to terminate a presidency.

I did not come to this conclusion as a die-hard Clinton political associate. I wasn't a Clinton associate at all. I had represented Democrats competing against him, as well as his wife and future Democratic nominee Hillary Clinton. In 1992, I represented Gephardt when he was considering bidding for a nomination that Bill Clinton sought and eventually won. In 2000, I was general counsel to the Bradley campaign challenging the presidential candidacy of his vice president, Al Gore. In 2008, I was the Obama campaign general counsel in a primary contest with Hillary Clinton. On only one occasion do I recall meeting Bill Clinton, as he was ushered into the Gephardt House office when I was leaving. When in the White House, I only had occasional contact with Secretary Clinton.

I never minimized Bill Clinton's personal failings and errors of judgment in the Lewinsky matter. But from the beginning, I could not see this conduct, including his misrepresentations and prevarications, as conceivably rising to the level of an offense for which Congress should impeach and remove him. This was not only because it struck me as plainly outside any reasonably articulated standard for impeaching and convicting a president. The partisan Republican cabal preparing for impeachment, and the members of Congress who then went about implementing the plan, degraded the impeachment process, exposing it as vulnerable to the crassest manipulation.

The most serious of the problems, from which the proceedings never recovered, was the role of a lawyer—Independent Counsel Kenneth Starr. Congress had mistakenly included in the law an obligation for the independent counsel to report to Congress the potential commission of any impeachable offenses. This was bad enough. Congress should not have outsourced even a preliminary judgment of that nature to an official outside its membership. What in the way of expertise or accountability did an independent counsel bring to the already highly contestable question of what constituted an impeachable offense? Lawyers think like lawyers, and prosecutors who were investigating a potential crime might decide that an apparent criminal offense would have to be sufficient to call into question a president's suitability for office. Once they reach that conclusion and, as in the case of Starr, send it officially off to Congress, they have prejudiced the proceeding and spared members some measure of their work required to examine the constitutional relevance of the charges through to impeachment and conviction. Republicans were all too eager to rely on Starr.

Starr was the first of those with public responsibility to make a choice he could have avoided. The mandate to report to Congress "substantial and credible evidence received" in the course of an investigation was unclear in the precise obligation it imposed on the independent counsel. Starr might have chosen to read the requirement narrowly. An example: provide a short report of the essential findings having to do with alleged perjury and obstruction of justice but decline to affirm that the evidence is "substantial and credible" for impeachment purposes. He could have provided Congress with information if and when the relevant committees demanded it, subject to limitations such as those designed to protect grand jury secrecy. Especially in a case with this subject matter of alleged sexual misconduct and strenuous attempts to conceal it, Starr could have declined to offer any conclusion about the commission of an impeachable offense.

Instead, he produced a thick book, emphasizing the seriousness of his findings and soon to appear in bookstores throughout the nation. It became the authoritative guide to the case that only Congress may constitutionally make: that Clinton had committed offenses so serious as a constitutional matter that his presidential term should be cut short. It is remarkable that in a memoir written some years later, Starr recounts how he and his aides pored over the authorities on impeachment and then concluded that it was at its heart a political judgment only Congress could make. He went ahead anyway and supplied Congress with just that judgment. The Starr Report to Congress was a brief for impeachment.

Starr made two additional moves to put himself, and his support for impeachment, front and center in the process. He included extensive detail about the sexual contact between the president and Ms. Lewinsky. Its apparent purpose was to hit as hard as possible on the conflict between Clinton's denials of a sexual relationship and the graphic details of that contact. It was the device an advocate would adopt to swing the audience his way. Now Starr had not only presented a conclusion about the substantial and credible evidence of impeachment, all the while noting that it was really Congress's to make. He was also moving from providing the evidence to making the case. He was a lawyer for the prosecution in the House impeachment process.

And also the chief witness. Rather than keep some distance from the proceeding, he agreed to become the House's chief witness. It was his evidence and his case, and now his testimony, about the investigative record he had compiled, which became the record for the House to vote on. Starr states in his memoirs that he was taken by surprise by the House majority decision to make him the key witness and to excuse themselves from building an independent record to support impeachment. He discovered, he writes, that he would be "flying solo" in the majority's witness list.[2] But he did not resist or argue for a limited role; he threw himself into the task.

At every turn, Starr acted not only irresponsibly but without any ethical appreciation of the part he was playing in the House's distortion of the impeachment process. He knew, as he and his team concluded, that the process was inescapably political, one for legislators to manage as responsibly as possible. He rode right into the midst of the politics.

Starr's ethical blindness to his proper role may have been less a surprise than it should have been. His appointment and investigation had taken on a dangerously political coloration. A conservative panel of the Court of Appeals, Special Division, which was responsible for independent counsel appointments, had inexplicably refused to extend the appointment of his predecessor, Robert Fiske, installing Starr in his place and necessarily raising the question of the motive for this move. Why did Fiske have to go, and Starr get the job?

A natural concern among Democrats was that Fiske lost his position because he did not have conservative or partisan credentials as sturdy and reliable as Starr's. Years later, it became known that one member of the three-judge panel who appointed Starr had resisted this choice internally for just the reason that Starr was too political a choice or would appear to be. Whether this was the reason for the appointment, these concerns, voiced by Democrats immediately after the appointment, should have led Starr to do whatever he could to proceed judiciously to build up his bipartisan credibility.

He did not, and it gradually appeared, particularly as his investigation into Bill Clinton's financial dealings expanded into an inquiry into his sex life, that Starr was a man on a zealous mission. Starr learned, for example, that Clinton was unaware that evidence of his relationship with Lewinsky had surfaced and that he likely would fall into a trap laid for him to lie about the relationship in a civil deposition in a sexual harassment case brought by Paula Jones. Starr chose to wait out the moment, then pounce along with the conservative legal network that had made a crusade out of distorting the Clinton presidency. As one commentator, Robert W. Gordon, wrote in an exceptionally insightful assessment of Starr's performance, "[a] prosecutor is supposed to prevent crimes [of alleged perjury and obstruction of justice], not to facilitate their commission. Instead, Starr and his team took every step they could to ensure that

Clinton would fall into the trap the Jones lawyers set for him."[3] Gordon effectively brings the political ethical dimension into clear focus:

> At the time Starr learned of Clinton's affair with Lewinsky and his impending testimony about it, he was not an interested party but an Independent Counsel with no mandate to do anything about these matters. . . . Starr was a citizen and a highly placed government official. What he learned was that the President was about to blunder into a course of action that would cause serious trouble to himself and his office. A friend to the country and to the Presidency, a citizen interested in preventing what damage he could prevent at little or no cost and trouble, an official with the republic's interest at heart, should have acted to prevent it.[4]

There is no better statement of Starr's ethical failings—a failing of political ethics in a public role.

This was not all, as Starr then pushed actively and successfully to have this jurisdiction expanded to include the Lewinsky matter, when a reasonable alternative would have been for another special counsel to be appointed to handle it. He proceeded to conduct this inquiry into a covert extramarital relationship as if it were the pursuit of a drug cartel. Among other instances of overkill, he cornered Lewinsky in a mall and removed her to a hotel room where his colleagues actively discouraged her from exercising her right to speak with a lawyer.

This was the long background to Starr's decision to play the leading role in the House impeachment process. The House of Representatives wrote its own chapter. By its parasitic reliance on the Starr case, Congress was evading accountability for building its own. House Republicans might add a rhetorical touch or two, summarizing the Starr evidentiary record. It would remain Starr's record, bolstered by Starr's testimony. The House decided to impeach on the basis of an ongoing criminal, not constitutional, case.

I became involved when House Democratic Leader Gephardt asked that I make a recommendation of a legal team to represent the Democratic side of the aisle. It was not clear at the time that the House Republicans would dispense with their own fact-finding. The team, eventually to be led by Abbe Lowell, seemed to require a mix of skills and experience, and I sought out an expert on sexual harassment and other issues in the legal regime governing sexual relations. I foresaw a House investigation in which Lewinsky, Paula Jones, and perhaps other women would be called as witnesses for depositions and possibly public testimony.

One name that quickly came up was Deborah Rhode, a professor at Stanford Law, who agreed to join the team, but in a case without any independent House development of the facts, it turned out that there was little for her, within her field of expertise, to do. The Senate eventually deposed Lewinsky, but the House did not. The House impeachment inquiry turned into a set piece, each side arguing its conclusions about the material contained in the Starr Report. To my mind, it was an embarrassment, and the vote on party lines—to impeach—was a foregone and entirely political conclusion.

Before the impeachment process progressed past the point of no return, Gephardt instructed me to explore one alternative: a House censure of the president, essentially a vote to condemn his actions, with no impeachment to follow. A censure would be for the constitutional record, expressing as appropriate its disapproval of the president's behavior— both the relationship with Ms. Lewinsky and his maneuvers to escape acknowledging it. The president would stay in office, serving out the term to which he had been comfortably reelected two years before.

This was a project of political lawyering. Of course, it was not the text of a proposed censure, the fine touch of the lawyer, which would entirely decide the success of the option. Politics overrides all else. Either there was room for censure, or there was not. Early on, we had word that while leaving open the possibility of accepting censure as the escape from full-fledged impeachment proceedings, Clinton was at best ambivalent about it. He was not keen to give in to his adversaries in this bitterly personal conflict. Without White House support, there was no chance that Democrats would rally to censure and bring enough Republicans with them.

I was nonetheless asked to meet quietly with a White House intermediary, prominent Washington lawyer Lloyd Cutler. He suggested that the White House might be open to censure: it all depended. He invited me to send him some language. Had there been an opportunity for a good faith, bipartisan consideration of censure, it would have helped to have a draft text to encourage and guide the negotiation.

I went to work, trying to conceive of an approach to censure that seemed serious enough to answer the concerns about the president's behavior but did not adopt the Republican narrative that absurdly treated this lapse in private morals, and his understandable wish to conceal it, as an all-out assault on the foundations of the American Republic. I wound up building what Peter Baker, the reporter for the *New York Times*, later described as "an elaborate mechanism intended not only to sanction Clinton but to clean up the damage he had done to the institution of the presidency."[5] It was ambitious in design, focused on teasing out the important institutional issues.

And it was utterly misconceived.

In writing about it now, I am following the Baker account in the book he published a year after the impeachment process concluded, *The Breach*. He seems to me to have gotten it right, and I say "seems" only because in key respects it is consistent with my recollection and he also cites sources, including a copy of the censure draft he obtained through his reporting, which I no longer have. I have always found Baker to be a careful reporter: I may disagree with the overall shape of a particular story, or the moral of the tale he is telling, but I have never had reason to doubt the particulars of what his reporting unearthed.

The draft I produced had the sort of general censorious language one might expect. The president had engaged in "misconduct unbecoming the stature and high responsibility of the office that the President holds." It referred to the harm done by this behavior as breaching the "bond of trust with the American people essential to the discharge of the President's duties" and compromising the "ability of the country to conduct other business." His evasiveness had prolonged the investigation and added to its cost.

Built into this critique was a penalty and series of processes for curtailing the impeachment process that would never sell. The proposed penalty was the loss of his presidential pension for a period of five years, and for this piece of the solution to pass constitutional muster, Clinton would have to agree to it. There was no reason at all to think he would accept this punishment—and not because he needed the money. The president's acquiescence in the penalty would elevate the impression that he committed a very serious wrong, and this was not a concession he was at all ready to make. It gave away too much to the other side. Strong words of disapproval, yes; stripped of five years of his pension, no way.

Then there were provisions for good government reforms intended to sort out controversies that had beset the investigation. One was the role of the White House counsel in hewing appropriately to the job of representing the institution of the presidency, not the person of the president, and the resolution would call on the Office of Government Ethics to help clarify the line between the two. Another would address the conflicts over privilege which the president asserted to deny information to the independent counsel, and here, the resolution was friendly to the president's side in the dispute over the breadth and aggressiveness of the Starr investigation.

At one point, the president had asserted a "protective function" privilege to keep the independent counsel from obtaining testimony from his Secret Service detail. The courts had rejected it—unwisely, as it seemed dangerous in the extreme to establish the principle that the Secret Service should be called on to testify to the president's personal habits and activities. The Service's mission is guarding the president with his or her full cooperation. Turning them into witnesses in an investigation or prosecution struck at the core mission. This was one casualty of the investigative war. In addition, the courts rejected other claims of attorney-client privilege the administration asserted to protect communications between government attorneys and the personal Clinton legal team. The draft censure resolution would establish a study of executive privilege, through a Joint Committee of the Study of Privileges. One of its aims would be to reconsider and perhaps rehabilitate the role of the protective function privilege.

There was more. This magnum opus then called for a series of steps by which Congress would try to bring the impeachment process to a quick end. I don't quite understand from the Baker account or my memory how this was supposed to work. It called for President Clinton and Starr to negotiate a resolution by the time of the president's 1999 State of the Union address, and failing that, Congress would vote on whether to end funding for the Starr investigation. Baker quotes from a memo he reports that I wrote to Gephardt in which I described the goal as a "congressionally mandated plea-bargaining arrangement designed to put pressure on Starr but also to allow for a vote on his investigation."

The entire censure proposal I developed could be defended as a miscarriage of good intentions. Clinton would be held accountable, but so too, Starr. Some of the debris from their clash, such as bad and confused law on executive privilege, would be put on a path to more careful consideration. But it was wholly unrealistic as a political matter. Too many moving pieces. Too harsh for Clinton, nothing to really offer impeachment-hungry Republicans. And in no survey of public views was there anything to indicate much interest in the state of executive privilege and the role of government lawyers in the personal defense of the president in a criminal investigation.

Maybe there was never any hope for censure as a way out of the Clinton impeachment. Certainly, what I put together would not make it any more likely.

In any event, Republicans moved quickly to kill off censure's already distant chance of serious consideration. Tom DeLay was at it again, pushing his House Republican colleagues to rule it out. It was not constitutional, he argued. This was not true. A joint resolution of disapproval without a penalty was entirely within Congress's power to consider and pass, and if a penalty was included, the constitutional issues would be overcome by a president's consent. Nonetheless, DeLay told the conference that "any talk of censure or 'censure-plus' should be stopped."[6]

The impeachment of Bill Clinton sped ahead. The House Republicans lined up behind the Starr Report and voted to impeach. I watched the vote on C-SPAN in the Gephardt leadership office. By that morning, it was clear that the verdict would turn out as it did. Yet the aides watching with me seemed a bit taken aback. One asked whether I thought there was anything they could have done differently in battling the pro-impeachment forces. I did not and said so.

I was surprised by their surprise. The Republicans had locked themselves into the indefensible position that a president could be removed from office for personal failings that did not bear in any way on his fitness for office. Their scramble to make it appear a matter of perjury and obstruction of justice put a thin veneer of pompous rhetoric on what was a political sting operation. Enormous partisan energy was devoted to catching him lying about sexual misconduct.

The stage was set for the Senate trial, in which I assumed the more formal role of counsel to the Senate Democratic Caucus. First came the November midterm elections, which visited a surprise on Republicans who lost five seats when the party out of power normally gains a few, not infrequently a lot. The voters, it was widely thought, were expressing their view of how the Republican Party was spending its time and resources.

Republicans took note, and by the time the Senate got ready for a trial, it could not have been clearer that at least the Republican Senate leadership had had enough. They wanted out. Even the hardest-core opponent of Clinton knew that the public had no patience for impeachment. Democrats were uniformly opposed and, if they remained united, could block it.

It is not quite right to suggest that the Senate just went through the motions. The House managers appointed to prosecute the case for the House showed up with suitably long faces and did what they could to dress it up. The result was rhetoric puffed up to an almost comic level. Henry Hyde, who had chaired the Judiciary Committee hearings, may have outdone them all. In his closing statement, at the conclusion of the managers' presentation, he spoke of the decision before the Senate as one that would redeem or diminish the great sacrifices Americans had made over the span of history for their liberty. Suddenly he was citing the "50th anniversary of the American landing at Normandy," when he visited the cemetery there and, among the crosses, found one without a name but inscribed with "Here lies in honored glory a comrade in arms known but to God."[7]

And then Hyde asked: "How do we keep faith with that comrade in arms?" Apparently by throwing out of office a president who had an inappropriate relationship he sought to conceal from the prying eyes of his political opponents. The future of the republic depended on it.

The rest of the trial was farcical. The House Republicans and their Senate allies who had rested their case on the Starr Report now wanted to call witnesses. It was at this point that the Senate heard from its most prominent institutionalist and constitutional expert, Senator Robert Byrd of West Virginia, who argued for cutting short the proceedings and, to that end, filed a motion to dismiss the House case.

Byrd had no use for Clinton's conduct and made that very clear. But as an institutionalist to the core and a former majority leader, he rightly saw that the Clinton impeachment process was more harmful to the institutions and the public trust than the conduct it had been instituted to investigate and would only "foster more of the same hallway press conferences and battle of press releases that are contributing to the division of our parties and our nation." He called for "reconciling the differences caused by these events and address together the issues, challenges, and opportunities facing our nation."[8]

The vote was held but the motion failed for want of Republican support. The trial ground on. In the end, only three witnesses, including Monica Lewinsky, were deposed, but they were not called to the Senate floor to testify. Only videoclips of her and the other witnesses' deposition testimony were used during the trial on the Senate floor.

Over the course of the trial, Democrats caucused daily to assess the latest developments and prepare for the day ahead. Senator Daschle would ask me to open with observations and my best counsel. Discussions and questions followed. Some senators were caught up in the investigative details, deeply interested in how the Clinton defense might poke holes in the House managers' (and Starr's) claims. It was a trial, after all, and some members were taken with the idea of acting as defense counsel and aiding the president's lawyers by checking for inconsistencies and weaknesses in the prosecution's case.

Most members appreciated from day one that none of that mattered. The polls showed a strong majority against removing Clinton from office. The Lewinsky story may have been sensational and lurid, but it was not fit material for the invocation of an extreme constitutional remedy to address presidential abuse of power. Some argued in the caucus that the obvious answer to what Clinton had done resided solely with him and his personal sense of responsibility for his actions and misrepresentations to the public, his aides, and his cabinet—by resigning from office. If he decided he would not resign, and he remained in office with broad public backing, that should be the end of it.

The absurdity of the impeachment process triggered by Ken Starr and advanced by House Republicans to a Senate trial played out in various embarrassing ways. One moment stands out: the deposition of Monica Lewinsky, which took place at the Mayflower Hotel in Washington, D.C. I attended as the counsel to the senator assigned to represent the Democrats at the deposition, newly elected John Edwards of North Carolina. The caucus respected Edwards's reputation as a trial lawyer, and I found him easy and enjoyable to work with as we prepared for the deposition. Within five years, he was the party's vice presidential nominee; four years later, he was a candidate for the Democratic presidential nomination; and when another three years passed, his political career ended—in another sex scandal that became, foolishly, a criminal prosecution that did not move the jury.

Nothing that occurred in the Lewinsky deposition had an effect on the outcome. But it was an event—the hottest ticket in the trial: not all staff or senators could attend, but if Ticketmaster had been open and operating for this purpose, the site would have crashed. The hotel conference room was crowded. When Lewinsky arrived, the assembled staff and senators did their best, which was not all that good, to hide their gawking. She was poised and highly likable. Her Republican interrogator was polite, even considerate. But what in the world, I thought, are we doing here?

In writing this book and reviewing materials on the public record from this period, I came across a memorandum from then-Senator Joe Biden to his colleagues, circulated in January of 1999. He argued that the Senate could choose to hold a trial, or not: it need not call witnesses. The choices it confronted were necessarily political, but in a noble sense. It had to consider the wider public interest and the significance of the decision it made for the institution.

This seems entirely correct. The Clinton impeachment was not about obstruction of justice. It was about abuse of the constitutional impeachment process. Senator Byrd was right, and so was Joe Biden. The Senate should have dismissed the case and ensured that it became precedent for defending the constitutional process from this form of subversion.

Twenty years later, the House initiated, and the Senate tried, two more impeachments, and these two ended in acquittals. The unfortunate Clinton experience is not to blame for somehow breaking open, somehow routinizing, resort to the impeachment process in unconstrained political conflict. The Trump years are a story all their own. Elsewhere in the legal process, in the New York case involving payment of hush money to conceal an affair with an adult entertainment actress, his personal life certainly figured into his political and legal troubles. In Congress, the charges against Trump directly concerned abuse of office for political ends: the manipulation of national security policy to advance his reelection prospects, and his role in encouraging a violent attack on the Capitol to stop the constitutional process for the final tally of electoral votes. The Trump impeachments were like Nixon's, not Clinton's.

A large and continuing problem with impeachments is that Congress continues to make up the process as it goes along. In the first Trump impeachment, where he faced the charge of withholding military aid to Ukraine to force it to contrive an investigation of his likely reelection opponent, the House Democratic leadership adopted makeshift changes in process. In addition to dividing the responsibility for developing the case among multiple committees, the House skipped the step of voting as a body to authorize the investigation, as it had done in the past. The impeachment process opened when the Speaker determined that it should. The House Intelligence Committee then replaced the House Judiciary Committee in its traditional role of leading the process and conducting public hearings. The Democrats also decided on the role that would be afforded to Trump in his self-defense.

As constitutional scholars pointed out, the House does have all this flexibility, and the Speaker committed no constitutional offense in proceeding as she did. The House might have voted in the past to authorize an impeachment inquiry, but it was not required to do so. It could accelerate the process as the majority chose and establish as it saw fit Trump and his lawyers' access to the prosecution's evidence or forum for self-defense. There may be constitutional "due process" rights for a president subject to impeachment, but there is ample room for disagreement between the two branches about how far those rights extend.

The price of this flexibility is inevitably presidents' complaints about fairness. And this is where Trump and lawyers happily went. Process issues are always fodder for defense counsel, as it was for the Trump legal team who not only argued that the House was denying him due process, but that this made it necessary for their client to refuse his cooperation. The Trump position was over-argued and intemperate. It also served the purpose of many such attacks on process. He could portray himself as a victim while directing attention away from the charges he faced to the way they were being brought. The basic move is to suggest that if Congress is trashing due process, it must mean that its case is weak. Trump's White House counsel, a government lawyer, went further and excoriated the House for proceeding against Trump for no reason other than to attempt to reverse the outcome of the 2016 election.

Congress could build on this experience by reforming more extensively its standing rules, rather than continuing to adjust the process in the immediate and always hothouse political circumstances of a particular case. The extraordinary remedy of forcing from office a democratically elected president would benefit from a process established in most material respects in advance.

There may be an upper limit to what can be done, and Congress may have to improvise where it has no principled choice. The second impeachment is an example: a president on his way out of office seeking to upend the electoral process and retain power. Congress did not have much time to respond to this attack on the constitutional order, and among the issues it had to confront and resolve was the constitutionality of an impeachment that would only conclude after the president had left office and became a private citizen. Congress had every reason to move quickly and keep going after Joe Biden took the oath of office—to ensure that the running of the clock did not defeat a clear statement on the record that the president had committed an impeachable offense and that, upon conviction, and just as important, Congress could take the separate vote to prevent him from ever again running for the office.

But any revision of the basic process, unless absolutely unavoidable, should occur within rules cleared and fixed in their details far more than is presently the case. By updating its rules and not refashioning them on the fly, Congress could take a small step toward restoring the credibility of the process. Considering rules outside the particulars of a specific impeachment, which implicates the fate of a particular president, holds out some hope that the issues will be thought through on a bipartisan basis. The range of questions that this sort of constitutional reform would take up include the standards for impeachments and conviction—a sober reconsideration of the meaning of "high Crimes and Misdemeanors"— and the requirements of a trial in the Senate. Whether the Senate is even obligated to try a House case is an issue that will come up again and is better not left to debate and resolution in the passions of the moment. The availability of other alternatives, such as censure, can be entered in the rule book, to end all doubt.

These reformed rules would help channel the choices that members might make in proceeding with impeachment. It would engender a climate for responsible action and encourage the consideration of alternatives such as motions to discuss and censure. It would impose limits on brazen political self-interest and partisan motivation in the construction of standards and procedures. Of course, a majority could move to change the rules to suit their political purposes, but the reformed rules would force them to *explain* the departure from the bipartisan institutional foundation the rules were meant to establish.

Given that the process remains unavoidably open to some revision on the run, it is all the more critical that the political actors face up to the individual choices that each make. In what way are those choices ethical? Robert Byrd suggested the reasons. The members of Congress who convert the constitutional impeachment into a "soap opera event," following the script for two-party duels but playing with real weapons, have failed in an essential personal responsibility. Byrd, like Biden, feared that this politics-as-usual in the most unusual of circumstances would inflict severe damage on the institution, and it is to the institution and its role in safeguarding the democratic process that their responsibility was owed in the first instance.

That impeachments have occurred more regularly in recent decades in American history cannot be easily dismissed as happenstance. There are, of course, substantial differences between the cases: in my view, Trump clearly committed impeachable offenses and Clinton did not. What links them all, however, is the rise over many decades of zero-sum politics, in which the victory of one party is unthinkable and unacceptable to the other, with the result that the very legitimacy of elections is contested. Impeachment is one route to challenging an election outcome.

There is another link: the connection between the institution of criminal prosecutions and calls for impeachment. Throughout their presidencies, Clinton and Trump faced criminal investigations. It is now standard practice for partisans to pursue their opponents in the legal process. Congress regularly looks for the reasons or excuses to call for the investigation of presidents and their administrations, and yet under executive branch law, presidents cannot be indicted while in office. One answer frustrated partisans have at their disposal is impeachment. The convicted president is out of office and now at last beyond the legal protection that holding office provides.

Among the "profiles in courage" John F. Kennedy wrote in his book by that name was Senator Edmond Ross, who joined six other Republicans to cast the deciding votes to acquit impeached President Andrew Johnson. Kennedy may have oversimplified his tale of political bravery. Apart from the quality of the history in that particular case, Kennedy was making the larger point that individual decisions—even one decision—guided by a respect for democratic institutions can be highly consequential. Starr did not get that point. Robert Byrd and Joe Biden did. Future members of the House and Senate will be tested as well, and not only in a future impeachment, when a presidency is on the line. Whether to leave the process unattended and unreformed is also a choice, which will determine whether this constitutional process is a degraded political weapon or can escape this fate and serve its critical purpose of removing presidents who are a danger to the democracy and therefore unfit for the office.

CHAPTER 9

Representing Presidents

As personal and political counsel to two presidents, and White House counsel to one, I advise two national leaders who are also lawyers. I have the challenge of sorting out in practice the identity of my "client"—the person who is president, or the office he occupies—and not confusing legal with political advice. I am heavily criticized for taking an expansive legal position on presidential war powers. I don't spot the problems with a regulatory proposal that is denounced as inappropriately political. Republicans who should know better accuse me of obstruction of justice. I know when I leave that I will never have a better job.

In early 2005, when the newly elected Barack Obama was setting up his Senate office, I was summoned to provide him with legal support. He had chosen as chief of staff Pete Rouse, who had served in that role for former Democratic leader Tom Daschle and was widely respected on the Hill for his management skills, judgment, and work ethic. As Daschle's political counsel, I had worked closely with Pete. He was also a treasured friend. Daschle lost his seat in the same year that Obama won, and the new senator from Illinois had pushed hard for Pete to organize and run his new office. Pete called me: would I meet with the senator to go over a few housekeeping matters?

I was to brief him on the various laws and institutional rules that defined how his personal and political lives should intersect with his official position. Senators may not, for example, use the same office communications equipment and resources for campaign or political work. This is what I recall of the kind of issues I addressed on the first encounter.

The three of us sat together in a room in a drab transitional office the senator was provided before his new suite was ready. Obama was friendly but had before him some papers, not on the same subject, which he was reviewing as he listened to me. And yet—a skill I do not have— he would look up from what he was reading to ask me questions, having managed to closely attend to what I was saying while going over other unrelated material. He was multitasking. This was my first introduction to the senator as a client who was also a lawyer, and a very good one, with remarkable skill at picking up facts and anticipating the legal issues embedded in them.

On this occasion, I was probably also boring the new senator who, in three years, would be elected president. The material I was covering was routine and basic. It was a standard review of the rulebook, which I had delivered to many freshly elected members of Congress over the years. Far more complicated issues in my representation of his political and official interests lay ahead.

I was struck by a comment he did not make. He said nothing about my originally having signed up with one of his opponents in the campaign for his Senate seat. I had represented a wealthy businessman named Blair Hull. Hull had taken his outsider status and his heavy spending to an early lead in a crowded field. My wife, Anita, as a senior adviser to the Hull campaign, had astutely read the polling data to suggest that if Hull faltered, State Senator Obama stood to move quickly ahead of the pack. Hull's candidacy faded after an initial surge, Obama began moving up, and I had nothing more to do with the Illinois Senate race. I have known politicians who would have made a good-humored or needling comment about this history. I have known some who would have questioned having as a legal or other close adviser someone who had previously aided a political opponent. Obama could not have cared less.

Both my wife and I became quickly and deeply involved with his Senate career and his presidential campaigns, and both of us served on his White House senior staff. This relationship with Barack Obama also led to my representation of the man he picked as his vice president. I had met Joe Biden and knew even better his chief of staff, Ted Kaufman, who would attend legal briefings I would give from time to time to Senate Democratic senior staffs, but I had never represented the Delaware senator. In 2008, after Obama named Biden to the ticket, I began advising him in my role as general counsel to the Obama-Biden campaign, and the connection continued into my White House years as counsel to President Obama, and then beyond.

I have represented these presidents in three dimensions: personal, political, and official. As White House counsel to President Obama, I had to keep my advice to the purely official. A government lawyer does not advise the president on personal or political issues. It is often said—simplistically—that the White House counsel does not represent the president, only the presidency. The role is supposedly institutional, not personal.

This is overstated, not true to the complexity of the role of legal adviser to the president. The White House counsel is not the president's personal lawyer and should not be involved in balancing his checkbook, preparing his tax filings, or helping family members with traffic tickets. At the same time, the presidency is, for better or worse, an office defined by an intense interest in the person who occupies the Oval Office at any given time. And not just an interest: a belief that there is a crucial connection between who he is and how he performs in office. The president's political position rests, of course, in great measure on personal credibility and authority. In his excellent book *The Cult of the Presidency*, Gene Healy lays this out unsparingly and critically: "He's our guardian angel, our shield against harm. He's America's shrink and social worker and our national talk-show host. He's a guide for the perplexed, a friend to the downtrodden—and he's also the Supreme Warlord of the Earth."[1]

And many years before Healy wrote, Lyndon Johnson's former press secretary George E. Reedy directly questioned the "personal" versus "official" distinction: "the president cannot have problems which are personal to him alone. His troubles are the troubles of the nation and if they become disastrous, the nation is in peril."[2]

As a broad statement, the distinction between the particular president and the office holds up well enough—such that for me to resume my
political representation of the president in his reelection campaign, I had
to leave the White House—but the lines between the personal, official,
and political do not all the time separate neatly.

The so-called birther episode is a case in point. The claim that Barack
Obama was born outside the United States, and hence was ineligible
under the Constitution to be president, made the right-wing circuit in
2008, and then flamed back to life after his election. It was a complete
fabrication, of course, and by 2007 the Obama campaign had already
posted his official birth certificate from the State of Hawai'i. It was a
campaign "issue" at the time, but once he won the presidency, the continued attack on his eligibility was official, too. The press unaccountably
continued to cover these charges from time to time, and once Donald
Trump took up the attack, the coverage became more intense. Trump
never failed to attract a press crowd, and he joined others in this smear
in questioning why the president did not answer all doubts by producing
his "long-form" birth certificate.

The long-form is not the official certificate, which had been made
available years before, but it is an original document that resides in a vault
in Honolulu. It did not trouble the birther mob that this demand was a
contrivance, or that, along with the official birth certificate made publicly
available years before, there was other contemporaneous documentation
of the president's Hawai'i birth: a birth notice in the Honolulu paper
when Barack Obama came into this world.

In April of 2011, the president decided to put an end to the nonsense
by requesting that Hawai'i retrieve and provide the nattering press with
a copy of the long-form. Someone had to fly to Honolulu to get it, but it
was personal documentation, and I was a government lawyer. I arranged
for my good friend and former law firm colleague Judy Corley, who
remained in private practice when I left for the government, to make
the trip.

When Judy returned with the document in hand, I took it with
press secretary Robert Gibbs to the White House briefing room for
distribution. The birther nonsense straddled all the lines. It started with

the campaign, became a "communications" issue for the administration, and required personal counsel to be involved as well. I suppose one could argue that it was also a constitutional issue—did Barack Obama rightfully hold his office?—which justified the commitment of official time and resources. It was nothing of the sort, of course: it was a fraud, a scam, a purely political distraction.

The birther episode illustrated another aspect of political lawyering—the political aspect, which is unavoidable in the course of the official representation. The president possessed a copy of the certificate that the hospital in which he was born would give to families as a keepsake. It bore the imprint of the newborn's hand, along with the date of birth and name of the parents. Would this spare us the need for the trip to Hawai'i—one more piece of evidence, mooting the need for the president's personal lawyer to travel thousands of miles to fetch the long-form? It seemed to me that this would be a mistake. The conspiracists and fraud merchants would also question this document's authenticity and the reasons why this was being produced in lieu of the long-form. They would reel off challenges the press would find irresistible. Why had the president never produced this before? Where did he keep it all this time? And it was, in fact, only a keepsake: it had no official standing as documentation of the president's birthplace.

Is an analysis of this kind political or legal? Does it go to the president's personal, official, or political interests? All of these.

The lawyer representing the president cannot be unaware of this full range of interests. But the contribution he makes must remain a lawyer's contribution. The president is fully staffed with communications and political expertise; no one is looking for the White House counsel to venture well beyond his training and get in the way of the political pros. In my time in the job, I guarded against mission creep in my office, especially concerned that younger lawyers stick to lawyering and resist playing political or policy or communications consultant. It was not only a matter of having lawyers keep in mind that they were there to provide legal advice. A manifest enthusiasm for playing politics could strain the office's credibility. Those we were advising, from the president on down, could begin to wonder if they were getting straight talk about legal issues or receiving their law heavily seasoned with political and communications judgments no one had hired these lawyers to provide.

Even worse would be the suspicion, if it were to take hold, that this scrambled mess of legal, political, and personal advice reflected the lawyer's judgment of the right outcome of policy disputes. This doubt about whether the White House counsel's office was "staying within its lane"—sticking to legal advice—had dogged my predecessor Greg Craig's tenure in the job. Craig was a fine, highly experienced lawyer, well-liked by the president, and he brought to the job both legal and more general government experience. He had been head of the State Department's Office of Policy and Planning in the Clinton administration. Fairly or not, senior staff members groused that he had not kept under control his intense engagement with foreign policy issues and that his office had a policy agenda, particularly in advising on the reform of counterterrorism legal policies. The president had campaigned on this reform, challenging the Bush administration legal positions on issues such as the lawful detention in Guantanamo Bay or elsewhere of enemy combatants captured during the "war on terror." His White House counsel was rightly in the middle of this complex process—in a supporting, legal advisory, role. Lawyers in the White House, the State Department, the Department of Justice, the Department of Homeland Security, and the intelligence agencies were all involved in delineating or clarifying the legal options. Critics complained, fairly or unfairly, that, in the guise of giving legal advice, the White House counsel was pushing the policy in his preferred direction.

In trying to keep my office out of this kind of conflict from our place in the West Wing constellation, I could go to extremes. In 2010, after Republicans had staggered the Democrats with a sixty-seat win in the midterms, the president convened discussions of the right policy and political response to the new Congress. I would attend among other members of the senior staff, ready to give legal counsel where it might be needed. On one occasion, the president asked me point-blank a question without any legal component whatever about some aspect of managing the relationship with Congress in the now-divided government. I paused, then declined to answer. I tried a graceful way out, correctly admitting that I had not come prepared to address an issue of that nature, but offering to gladly reflect on the question and arrange to speak to him later. I never did, and he did not ask further. It was not that I had no opinion on the subject. I had opinions galore. But I thought it necessary to signal to the rest of the West Wing that I was not looking to be a player in the wider policy and communications battles ahead. I was the counsel.

It was for this reason that when the president considered who he might pick to succeed Rahm Emanuel as chief of staff, and for whatever reason my name cropped up in press speculation, I asked that the White House affirmatively advise reporters that I had asked to be taken off the list of possibilities. I raised the issue at one of the senior staff meetings convened by Rahm every morning at 7:30: I brought it up at the end, saying I wanted to raise a "point of personal privilege." I had no interest in being considered for chief of staff, I assured the room, and any suggestion I was in the running was harmful to the credibility of my office. Our advice on key issues would come under scrutiny as possibly influenced by my wish to curry favor with the president or to build support among other advisers for a promotion. I was happy with my job; I wanted no other. Rahm then agreed to have me work with Dan Pfeiffer, the communications director, to put the word out that I had taken myself out of consideration for the job.

The hard part of holding to this position on my role was that I did, as in the birther case and others, have to advise on the press implications of managing attacks on the president. I would be useless if I was oblivious to the press and political dimensions. The key, and no easy trick to pull off, was holding these considerations in balance with my overriding obligation to provide legal counsel. Because the birther matter was a challenge to the president's honesty and integrity on a requirement of holding his office, namely, his birthplace, it was entirely within the remit of the counsel to advise on. It was further consistent with that obligation to advise on how best, most persuasively, to put the craziness to rest once and for all. It was something like a lawyer's choice of the best line of argument to present to particular judges, taking into account their judging history and style, or advising witnesses on how to present their testimony to the jury. Our jury was the press and wider public, and the legal answer to the smears and lies needed to be as telling and definitive as we could make it. In that way, the question of using any documentation or evidence other than the long-form certificate was indispensable to the quality of any legal counsel in that situation.

Keeping to this discipline about the role could only enhance the trust of the president and senior staff. The political lawyers who try hard to be honest brokers, keeping in check their political enthusiasms and vanities, will find their counsel all the more valued—or at least respected, even if the advice they ladle out is disappointing or unwelcome. And when they do have to give advice with some attention to the political and press background and potential consequences, they will have more of an audience. They will have earned a hearing on these issues because it will be clear that they are not just indulging their passion for political sport. They are being the best lawyers they can be. And, it seems fair to note, they always appreciate when the non-lawyers on the staff reciprocate and refrain from giving legal advice, which has been known to happen from time to time.

I had every advantage in trying to win President Obama's trust because as a lawyer, he well understood what legal counsel should be expected to bring, and what I hoped to bring, to the operation of the White House. The standard of good lawyering in a public role goes beyond the obvious one that lawyers must give sound legal advice—that she read a statute, understand what proposition a judicial decision stands for, and then with the aid of standard tools of logic and interpretation, correctly advise on legal risks and pathways. On the most difficult questions, this is the beginning and not the end of the analysis.

The lawyer has to understand how the law fits in and affects all the other considerations a president weighs in mapping out courses of action. Whether a legal position is sound depends in the first instance, of course, on what the law is. But whether the administration goes with one legal position or another varies with the issues on which it is taken and the circumstances in which it has to be argued.

Some issues just matter more than others, and this can cut both ways in sorting out the legal options for navigating them. When a president acts on a sensitive policy question, the legal authority under which he proceeds becomes one line of attack on the policy choice he has made. Critics will dispute the policy choice, but also readily question whether what he proposes to do is even legal. This may require the administration to set aside the most aggressive legal position and drop back to one that is less open to objection, but the less preferred legal position may also require adjustments to the proposed policy. Virtually by definition, the more expansive the view of the president's legal authority, the more expansive the action available to the president; the less expansive the claimed authority, the more limited the scope for presidential action.

It is also possible that the sensitivity of the issue requires the administration to take risks with a legal position because it has no alternative. The only way to achieve its goal is to craft a novel or creative interpretation of the law to support what the president concludes must be done. Strong lawyering in this context means taking into account the need for a president to effectively advocate for and advance a policy and endeavoring to provide a skillfully lawyered rationale for the proposed executive action. That is the best support a lawyer can provide, and what President Obama valued in his lawyers.

It is hard to get these calls right. You can only expect to do so some of the time.

An example of botched performance on this measure of sound lawyering was a proposed executive order in 2011 to require federal contractors to disclose their political spending as part of the process of bidding for government work. The notion was simple. Those who seek profitable government contracts might hope that making a contribution to the president's campaign or party would make their pitch easier. Why not have the president by Executive Order (EO) address the risk that government contractors would "pay to play," hoping that they could buy goodwill and build their business? In bidding for a government contract, the aspiring vendor of goods or services would have to disclose their political spending, and if this spending appeared suspiciously robust and timed for maximum effect on the contracting process, it might be disqualifying. A disclosure requirement like this might dissuade contractors from trying to use political money to better their prospects for taxpayer-funded business.

The White House senior staff had asked us to examine various potential proposals for political reform, and this showed up on a list prepared for my review. It seemed on a first look to make good sense, and I shipped an early draft of the possible EO to the agencies for review and comment.

This was early in the development of the draft: the proposal was not public. The White House staff had yet to recommend it to the president. The draft leaked. Republicans promptly denounced it, as did no small number of Democrats.[3] The technical details were not really the problem. What we had not considered was that the technical feasibility of the proposal was easily overwhelmed by the political argument against it. Rather than a measure to keep political money out of the contracting process, the proposed order could be seen as the government *inviting* it in. Contractors with Republican sympathies would fear discrimination against them in a Democratic administration, and potential contractors who supported Democrats would seem to have the advantage. So, too, the reverse.

To this same point, and yet even worse, the order was under consideration in a presidential election cycle in which the incumbent president was a candidate for reelection. Critics could reasonably argue that this was a bad look, certain to trigger suspicions that Obama was planning to use unilateral presidential power to reward political friends and punish adversaries as he sought a second term. Less reasonable critics could convince themselves and try to persuade others that this was the plan, not just a matter of appearances.

The president had no such plan. His staff and his counsel had less a plan than a notion, and it was a bad one. It was lousy political lawyering. The issue itself was not one of central significance to the president's program. It did not warrant risk-taking, either in the conception or the design of the program, especially in a reelection year. Eventually, the administration retreated, and the plans were shelved.

Perhaps I could have taken comfort in the tentative nature of this policy initiative. The plan was in draft form only, and when it leaked, it had been circulated for comment and discussion, with no final decision made about proceeding with it. This rationalization doesn't wash. It was my job to anticipate the problem with the proposal and to recognize that once it had left the West Wing, it was leak bait.

One of the pleasures of representing Barack Obama was that, unlike some politicians I have represented over the years, he did not habitually look to assign blame for mistakes and to suggest that, with a tad more competence and forethought, any staff mistake could have been avoided. He might wince or scowl at a mishap, but he did not fly into an accusatory rage. He tended to see the world as a novelist might: a site of human error and folly and bad luck. He appreciated a straightforward account, with no excuses, of a blunder or misjudgment, and it well served whomever had to bring the bad news to have ready a plan for the cleanup.

Even better from my perspective, President Obama had a knack for seeing that what might seem like the beginnings of a major political storm would fade away and appear, maybe only a day later, less cataclysmic. The White House is always on edge. Everywhere mounted television sets are turned to cable, and laptop and desktop screens are flashing instant word of activity on social media and the web. Reporters, supporters, and friends on the Hill are calling in alarms. *This* is happening now, and then *that*, and decisions have to be made on commenting, not commenting, or adopting one strategically prudent response or the other. Staff who haven't slept enough and who probably enjoy politics in part out of an addiction to perpetual excitement are rushing to and fro with apparent purpose and in keen states of anticipation or despair.

Throughout all of this, I found that the president kept his cool, almost eerily so. It is true, as reported, that he was a "no drama Obama." It reflected his distaste for staff intrigue and conflicts. He expected those he relied on to come to their senses and work things out when tempers got out of hand and emotion overcame clear thinking, muddling the presentation of issues. This "no drama" moniker circles around but does not quite land on what was distinctive about Barack Obama's response to pressure. Most important, he often had a better sense than staff of what would outlast the news cycle and justify attention as a serious, ongoing problem. This is no small gift, as not many in D.C. possess it, and he did, in abundance. In the crazed environment of the West Wing, he had a special capacity for judging the moment, for leading the conversation away from noisy distractions that can bewitch the Washington community, with the press corps leading the pack.

In a case like the wayward federal contractor rule, and on other occasions when the building would be seized with some new excitement, he would hear what had gone wrong and how we proposed to fix the problem or contain the damage; he would ask a question or two, and then he would indicate by tone, gesture, or comment that the time had come to move on. There was plenty on a given day to worry about, and his approach limited the waste of time and energy invested in finger-pointing and twenty-twenty hindsight on issues that would prove, in relatively short order, entirely forgettable.

Lawyers and other advisers perform best for powerful clients who, like Barack Obama, don't lose their heads over the inevitable frustrations of daily press coverage, or the misfiring of a strategy because it was either poorly conceived or bungled in execution. This is because the advisers can claim a little time and space to think through the response and then be heard—maybe even listened to—before positions taken in a panic have hardened and patience is limited for further deliberation and discussion. If the Boss becomes immoderately agitated—face drawn, teeth clenched, voice raised—then the staff is under pressure to fall in line with a similarly gloomy view of the challenge ahead. The leader who remains composed is helping everyone do their jobs—and better serve her.

And the president who is also a lawyer makes successful political lawyering possible in still another way. The relationship of client to lawyer is not especially productive if the lawyer counts on doing the talking and then hopes for the president to nod appreciatively, if not break out into applause. Lawyers should want the client to probe and test, to put them through their paces. An engaged rather than passive client is one who is fully listening to and evaluating the advice. This is the kind of client who takes seriously the legal piece of the problem under consideration. It is also the kind for whom the lawyer, aware that she will face questions, will prepare that much more thoughtfully. And the president who is also a lawyer will, on many issues, have a surer, more informed instinct for the best questions to ask. The lawyer and the client both benefit from conversation.

Not all lawyers are the same, and Obama and Biden have approached the conversations with me from different angles. I tend to see it this way: Obama would have excelled in the judiciary, and Biden would flourish before a jury. Obama took an interest in discussions of fine points of constitutional doctrine, and he would pick up on them in reading a briefing or decisional memos involving legal issues. Biden was well familiar with doctrine, having also taught constitutional law, but he would anticipate how the issue would play out in the public. One could see the one president as analyst, developing a novel perception of weakness or possibility in the law, whereas the other would make the sale for a client before a jury.

In meetings, these varying strengths would be on display when I briefed on a legal issue or made a recommendation about a course of action. I recall one instance when, as White House counsel to Obama, I explained a case of significance pending before the Supreme Court and referred to the "standard of review" the Court would employ in judging the constitutionality of a statute. A standard of review ostensibly determines how closely a court examines the legislature's action in the light of constitutional limits, such as free speech protections. A member of the senior staff asked for more explanation. Before I could respond, the president, reprising his role as law professor, took up the point and elaborated on it. He knew the stuff. On another occasion, after the election of Joe Biden and in the middle of legal struggles over Trump's denialism and the obstacles thrown up to a smooth transition, the president-elect presided over a call on a legal issue. I pressed for consideration of an option. The president-elect balked. He appreciated the theoretical strength of my position but doubted its timing or persuasiveness with the press or public. We did not go in the direction I favored and, looking back, I can see that he read the situation more correctly than I did. I was right on the law, but that was not good enough.

Presidents don't *need* to be lawyers, of course, for their administration to show respect for the rule of law while exploring every possible avenue for the assertion of presidential authority to advance their core policy programs. They should have at least an elemental understanding of the lawyer's role, however. Trump did not. He preferred his lawyers to be enablers, to get him what he wanted, and his model is Roy Cohen, the infamous lawyer who worked hand in glove with vicious demagogue Joe McCarthy during the Communist witch hunts of the 1950s.

Trump was unique among presidents in publicly attacking administration lawyers who did not deliver as demanded or expected. Trump was not exceptional, only extreme, in his failure to see why presidents have to have good lawyers. Republicans have told me that George W. Bush never quite grasped the qualities of counsel. The lawyers he personally liked and trusted were good enough for him. Franklin Roosevelt before him was happy if lawyers aided him in doing what he wanted to do, and not so happy when they did not. When Dean Acheson, later President Truman's secretary of state, served in the Roosevelt administration as a senior lawyer in the Treasury Department, he annoyed his president with the eminently sound legal opinion that the chief executive did not have the legal authority to fix the price of gold. Roosevelt did not forget and arranged for him to be fired. Robert Jackson, his attorney general and later justice of the Supreme Court, recalled years later that Roosevelt just did not value lawyers or have much tolerance for legal impediments to his governing plans and programs. FDR was, Jackson wrote, "a strong skeptic of legal reasoning" who "found difficulty in thinking that there could be legal limitations on his judgments."[4] I fortunately have served two presidents who respected the role of lawyers and didn't distrust legal reasoning.

The job of White House counsel was the best job I had or ever will have, but the risks of the office, which has ballooned in size and influence over time, have given me pause. It should be trimmed down, and a large share of the lawyers now hired into the office should work instead as Department of Justice lawyers working out of the department offices, not in the West Wing or the adjacent Executive Office Building. The president should have lawyers close at hand, able to walk down to the Oval Office when needed and without delay, but a counsel and perhaps two deputies on location should be sufficient.

To have a small- to medium-sized law firm in the White House, rarely smaller than twenty to twenty-five lawyers and in the past topping forty in total, dangerously confuses the role of counsel and other staff.

The White House counsel is a member of the senior staff, and right there, in that status, is both the allure of the role and the threat it poses to the lawyer maintaining the necessary distance and independence to properly advise as a government lawyer. All senior staff should naturally be expected to give their best advice, always mindful of the duty to facilitate whenever possible the president's goals but undaunted by having to deliver bad news. It is especially important that lawyers be insulated from the pressures of "team" membership that could lead them to bend in considering what legal advice and judgment to offer.

Of course, nothing would prevent a president with less of a law firm housed in the White House from staffing the Department of Justice, top to bottom, with sycophants and enablers who happen to have law degrees. Bad faith can travel down the street. We know that by the end of his administration, Trump had tired of taking on lawyers who only disappointed him—two attorneys general (Jeff Sessions and Bill Barr), and one White House counsel (Don McGahn). He was comfortable with lawyers of the caliber of Rudy Giuliani, Sydney Powell, and Jeffrey Clark, and in the last two cases, he tried to install them in senior government lawyering positions: Powell as special counsel to look into Trump's fantasies about a stolen election, and Clark as attorney general, who Trump admired for inventing legal strategies to keep him in power after he lost at the polls. Had he won a second term in 2020, he surely intended to install cronies everywhere it mattered to him—first of all in the Department of Justice. The Senate's advise and consent role can have some effect on these dangerous decisions, but even where it responsibly discharges this duty (less of a chance of that when the president and the Senate are controlled by the same party), those controls do not apply to nonconfirmed positions. There are plenty of those in the White House and elsewhere around the government.

But even if Trump turns out to be the outlier, the history shows that presidents gravitate to the expansion of their powers and lawyers represent a key check on abuse. A more limited White House counsel's office does not solve the problem of lawyers acting as reliable team members, but it might help in keeping it within bounds. Institutional culture matters. The Department of Justice is by no means a complete sanctuary, free of institutional flaws and challenges of its own. It is a superior choice of home for the lawyers who advise the president. They would go to work each day with other lawyers who are Department of Justice lawyers, not members of the president's staff.

Picture this: the walls of the department are adorned with murals and statutes that depict the American historical experience and allegorical representations of Justice and the Rule of Law. The West Wing walls are covered with beautiful photos of the incumbent president and vice president, regularly rotated to capture them in impressive moments at work and on both domestic and international travel. To say it again: institutional culture matters.

Would these questions of location and culture have affected my own performance as counsel to President Obama? It is impossible to say. Even on my plan for moving the better part of the office to the Department of Justice, the White House counsel (and a couple of deputies) would remain on-site, passing those photos daily in the movement up and down the stairs to the Oval Office. Their role would feel very staff-like, as full membership in the inner circle. Unknowable, then, is how much of a difference a bit of professional distance would have made in my tenure in the job. I can at least ask the question of whether I succumbed to the pressures of team membership—enabling rather than wisely advising— by examining two instances when my advice drew fire for seemingly sacrificing sound advice to the president's political and policy needs.

One such episode has long receded into the archives and the memories of only a handful of practiced Washington junkies. It was a dustup rather than a full-blown scandal. It remains worth recounting since I was charged by critics with throwing myself between the White House and a criminal investigation and, in so doing, committing obstruction of justice.

It all started with the political team's concern with the potential that Democrats would have an unwanted primary contest for the 2010 Senate election in Pennsylvania. The incumbent Republican, Arlen Specter, had switched parties, and the Democrats warmly embraced him as their own. A House Democrat, Joe Sestak, considered challenging Specter, which he eventually and successfully did.

The White House chief of staff Rahm Emanuel set out to dissuade Sestak from this course. He thought Democratic prospects were better with Specter. He asked former president Bill Clinton to intercede with Sestak and talk him into staying in the House and out of the Senate primary. Sestak was offered a modest sweetener: he could hold the House seat but also an uncompensated executive branch advisory position.

Washington got ready for a new scandal, this time about an allegedly shady deal to lure Sestak out of the race with a government job. Republicans had been chafing at their failed attempts to tar Barack Obama with an ethics charge. They eyed Rahm Emanuel's selection as chief of staff, a former party operative and congressman, as one way to describe Obama as something other than how he presented himself. His choice of Emanuel to run the White House staff gave him away, proved that he was a politician like any other, and like any politician, he could soil his hands in the political muck. Now came the Sestak matter: seemingly misusing government positions to accomplish political objectives, not making an appointment on the pure merits.

My office reviewed the matter and briefed the president, and I released a short report on our findings: nothing there, sorry. The report made no attempt to deny the basic move Emanuel had made. Yes, the goal was to "avoid a divisive Senate primary." The offer of an uncompensated advisory role on a presidential commission or board would enable Sestak to take on "additional responsibilities of considerable potential interest to him," and he could assume them while remaining in the House. The interests served by this proposed arrangement were entirely legitimate and lawful and consistent with "numerous reported instances" in the past when prior administrations of both parties had "discussed alternative paths to service for qualified individuals also considering campaigns for public office."[5]

Critics were unimpressed, though along the way Rich Lowry of the *New York Post* delivered the backhanded compliment that I had produced an "exquisitely crafted exculpatory document."[6] He meant that it was evasive and unconvincing. The *Wall Street Journal* called for a criminal and congressional investigation of the affair.

Others' criticisms were even sharper, more personal, and could not be taken, even backhandedly, as a compliment. Two Republican establishment lawyers, William Burck and David Rivkin, published an opinion piece to accuse me of improper conduct—indeed, obstruction of justice. They characterized my investigation as "unprecedented," and "misguided," charging that "at worst . . . [it] impeded any legitimate Department investigation, harmed the cause of justice and reinforced public disgust with Washington."[7] By this account, it was not only Rahm Emanuel and others who had engaged in potential criminal activity. So had I.

I was more than slightly put out by these claims. Friends in private practice, experienced former government lawyers and white-collar defense lawyers, volunteered to write a rebuttal and submit it to the *Post*. They did and the *Post* declined to publish it. It would only print a rebuttal from me. Why in the world would I do that, unless my intention was to draw even more attention to these charges? So I didn't, and left their accusations hanging, unanswered.

Now my annoyance flared in two directions: Republican second-guessers from the bar and the fourth estate. The Burck and Rivkin argument was meritless, notable mainly as two Republican lawyers taking a shot at a White House counsel who was a Democrat. Would they have published this critique if Republican notables had adopted the course of action I did? Of course not. In fact, at least one prior counsel, in a Republican administration, had conducted years before just this kind of review of charges against a member of the White House staff. Burck and Rivkin either did not know this, because they did not bother to check, or they passed over this history for some other reason.

A White House counsel alerted to the potential of improper conduct by a senior staff member—in this case, the chief of staff—owes the president a reading of the seriousness of the problem. There's a government to be run. Had I concluded on a preliminary review that Emanuel's stab at keeping Sestak out of the Pennsylvania primary posed serious criminal or ethical problems, I would have so advised the president and the next steps would have been different: the need for Rahm to step down, or perhaps a referral to the DOJ. The chief of staff of the president cannot carry on in the job under the cloud of scandal, the pressures of a criminal inquiry, or both.

But I quickly found that there was no basis for concern on the facts as I was able to ascertain them. I so advised the president, and given the public interest in the matter, the White House concluded that I should issue a brief report for public release. This was the responsible course of action.

It was mostly in the manner of execution that I could fault this plan of action. The report was a bit short, and Lowry could fairly note that it was a "classic in the use of the passive voice: Options were raised, and efforts were made." There was a reason for writing it this way: the more detail provided, the bigger deal we would appear to be making of it. It was just not a big deal. Also, our Republican critics were not going to be persuaded by any presentation, but the more we had to say about how we conducted the internal review, the more we would offer ourselves up for bad faith follow-up questions. *Oh, you said you did X, but when did you do it, and with whom, and who was with you at the time?* The choice we made was to keep it to the point, generally stating the relevant facts—keeping Sestak in the House, avoiding the primary fight, offering other opportunities for additional but uncompensated service—and then concluding, correctly, that none of this involved the violation of any law or ethical rule.

It all came to seven paragraphs, and it bordered on the cursory. We might have ventured additional discussion in defense of our position, such as a little additional background on why the president directed an internal review, the history and basis for those kinds of reviews, an extended discussion of the law. I can see that now; I did not then.

It might have made no difference at all. Except that choices like this become a part of the history of the counsel's office, a precedent of sorts that other counsels in the future have to consult if faced with similar situations. The counsel's obligation is to both solve the immediate problem but keep in mind long-range institutional interests. This is an example of the tension between defense of the individual president and the representation of the presidency. The limited document we released served, well enough, the president then in office. It was not a model of how to balance that against the institutional record for future presidencies we were always building. My statement read too much like a press release.

L'Affaire Sestak was over quickly. The making, then duration, of "scandal" is often mysterious. Occasionally it looms as a real possibility, and the city tenses in anticipation of all the familiar stages: the first revelations, then the press's hot pursuit day by day of reportable developments, then the opinion pieces examining its meaning and significance for the future, and then some event or series of events that mark the gradual easing of excitement as the scandal seems to have run its course.

Lawyers and their colleagues in the press and communications staffs like to imagine that they had the skilled hand in blocking early press interest or a bad story from lifting off to scandal. Or, if they cannot do that, they might shrewdly maneuver to keep its trajectory short and its consequences for the client limited. Luck plays more of a part than the lawyer would like to admit. Some candidates for scandal are just not made of the right stuff. The Sestak story did not have it. In the end, who really cared all that much if Democrats wanted to avoid a Senate primary battle and tossed an unpaid advisory position into the arguments and incentives to talk Sestak back into his House seat and out of making the race?

I did not care for the allegation in the Sestak matter that I had engaged in obstructive conduct inconsistent with my duties as counsel. But this was a mildly irritating slap at my competence and integrity, and the source and motivation could be dismissed as transparently partisan. It was in advising the president on a national security matter that I ran into far weightier criticism. I gave advice roundly denounced among legal commentators and among members of Congress from both parties, some of whom filed a lawsuit with no prospects for success but to underscore their unhappiness.

The question on which I had opined concerned presidential war powers and the precise issue was whether the War Powers Resolution limited the Obama administration's flexibility in providing continuing military support for NATO air strikes in Libya against the forces of the Qaddafi regime. The administration and its allies took action out of concern that Qaddafi, seeking to quell an armed rebellion in the eastern part of the country, appeared ready to massacre civilians in the defense of his beleaguered government. NATO and the United States launched strikes to disable Libyan air capabilities and establish a no-fly zone over the threatened area.

My part in the controversy came after an already much-criticized opinion was issued from the Office of Legal Counsel that the president did not require congressional authorization for U.S. air strikes at the outset of the military engagement because the conflict was not a "war" that, under the Constitution, only Congress could declare. Some commentators agreed; others did not.

The unhappiness with the administration's legal position became more widespread when the U.S. support for the mission extended beyond the sixty- to ninety-day limit set by the resolution for the continuation of "hostilities" without explicit congressional authorization. The administration took the position that, by the two-month point in the bombing campaign, the United States was playing a supporting role only, supplying refueling, targeting, and other services for NATO air forces. It was not taking fire, its planes and troops were not at risk, its mission was limited: there was no path toward escalation of the U.S. role. Hence, no "hostilities" within the meaning of the War Powers Resolution.

The *New York Times* correctly reported that administration lawyers had disagreed among themselves about this legal position. The Office of Legal Counsel would not render a supportive opinion on this theory of "hostilities," and lawyers for the Departments of Defense and Homeland Security were similarly unwilling to endorse this position. On the other side were the legal adviser to the State Department, Harold Koh, and me. The president eventually took and acted on Koh's and my advice. The bombing campaign continued beyond the sixty-day limit without a request for congressional authorization.

I came under attack, explicitly or implicitly, for being just the sort of White House counsel critics of the office feared: a presidential enabler. I had disregarded the weight properly given to the Office of Legal Counsel. Koh and I had formed a rump group. The prominent constitutional scholar Jack Goldsmith of Harvard Law School wrote in clear terms what others who took issue with my opinion were thinking: "I discount the legal input of the White House counsel; Bob Bauer is a smart man but neither he nor his office is expert in war powers or situated to offer thorough legal advice on the issue."[8]

I did not think that the criticism was either surprising or, for that matter, entirely unfair. I was not a national security or war powers expert. The dissent within the administration ranks was unfortunate, not helpful to the president who would have benefited from unqualified support from his senior legal advisory circle. He did not, however, have it, and I still had a job to do, which was to clarify for him the basis for the disagreement and enable him to exercise his unquestioned authority to resolve the disagreement. He had the final word within the Executive Branch, not the Office of Legal Counsel or the State Department Legal Adviser or me. On many national security issues, a president's decision cannot be challenged in the courts. Congress has the power to challenge him in various ways, most dramatically by instituting impeachment articles alleging that he had abused the powers of his office.

To prepare myself for informing the decision Obama would ultimately make, I read all the available precedent on the core legal question and was surprised to find, as Harold Koh later testified to Congress, that there was ample support for the proposition that the U.S. role in Libya did not involve "hostilities"—as a legal matter. Congress had deliberately avoided defining the term "hostilities" in the statute. One of the lead sponsors of the resolution explained that it was subject to "different interpretations," that it was a "fuzzy area," but the "decision would be for the president to make." The Office of Legal Counsel had long conceded that what did or did not constitute hostilities depended on the facts of the particular military engagement, such as whether U.S. forces were engaged in active exchanges of fire, the mission was limited, and the risk of escalation was low.[9]

Naturally I was comforted that Koh agreed with me. There is no way of knowing for sure, but I very much doubt that the president would have proceeded on my advice alone. Moreover, I gave every opportunity for the lawyers on the other side of the argument, OLC included, to air their views and I made sure to relay them in detail to the president. I certainly understood this opposing point of view and appreciated as well that our legal position was open to attack. How could a sustained bombing campaign not be "hostilities"? There was an answer, well supported by precedent going back many years. Later, when I was out of government, critics of our position who discussed this controversy with me admitted that it had a basis in law. They just were not comfortable with it. That's fine, but that's a different argument, isn't it?

From my perspective, the critics' complaint about the Obama administration's interpretation of its obligations under the War Powers Resolution was more appropriately directed against the law and its development over time. Congress had never successfully addressed by amendment the ambiguities and evident weaknesses of the War Powers Resolution. It consistently lacked motivation to push back against what it might publicly denounce as overly expansive executive branch interpretations. Regardless of whether Democrats or Republicans controlled the Congress, or the federal government was under one-party control, Congress has chosen to leave things where they are.

The law on which the president relied in maintaining U.S. support for the Libya operation was not an invention—or even as one critic claimed, "legal acrobatics."[10] The president was as sophisticated in constitutional and legal matters as any who has held the office, and he could make, on the advice received, an informed decision.

This was one of those cases where choice of legal position depended on the urgency or priority of the policy objective. When only so much is at stake, the executive does not need to provoke a conflict over claims of executive authority. A conservative legal position may suffice to achieve the objective, or if it doesn't, then the objective may be modified or even abandoned. It is not worth the fight. A president wisely declines to insist on broad powers and institutional prerogatives when their exercise is not essential to achieving a goal of true consequence. President Obama judged Libya to be a different case and the strong assertion of legal authority to be well justified.

A president, like President Obama, who came to office with a commitment to restore "rule of law" credibility to counterterrorism legal policy took care with the positions his administration crafted on national security legal policy. Unlike the Bush administration, heavily influenced in these decisions by Vice President Dick Cheney, Barack Obama was not looking to make a point of expansive claims of executive authority to deploy forces overseas as a president might see fit and Congress be damned. Cheney was a man on a mission in these matters; Obama certainly was not.

In Libya, there was a legitimate choice of legal position to be made, and the choice would determine whether a mission to protect against the slaughter of civilians in eastern Libya would succeed or fail. Qaddafi's threat to go house to house and kill people was taken very seriously, and from what I observed in the meetings I attended, support for an urgent international humanitarian mission to save countless lives is what drove U.S. policy. By the time the sixty- to ninety-day clock under the War Powers Resolution approached, it was clear that were the United States to abandon logistical support for the NATO-led military engagement, it would have serious consequences for any hope of eventual success. It was under this pressure that the Obama administration analyzed the legal basis for U.S. support of that mission and chose the position advocated by Harold Koh and me.

Critics later pointed to suggestions that what may have started out as a humanitarian mission turned into a policy of regime change. And they later added to their complaints the way things turned out: that Libya after Qaddafi became an ungovernable mess and a haven for terrorists. I have no clear recollections of the twists and turns in the course of policymaking, only of the specific question arising under the War Powers Resolution we were asked to address. I cannot hide a basic skepticism of arguments that draw with boundless hindsight on history "as it turned out" to question the wisdom of decisions when policymakers were working in the moment, with the best information available, and in good faith seeking to stop indiscriminate bloodshed.

In the meantime, Congress did what it generally does from time to time on sensitive issues, namely, refraining from taking a clear stand while reserving and often actively seizing on the right to second-guess the executive. It could not muster the votes for an action formally expressing one view or the other. This irresolution did not extend only to policy, but to the very definition and defense of its own constitutional authority over U.S. military deployments.

Some—but not all—members complained about the president's infringement on their constitutional war-making powers, and yet a number called the White House to assure the president that he should do what he thought best. *We have to criticize you,* we were told, *but don't worry too much about it.*

To this day, colleagues in the legal academy give me a good-humored hard time about my role in the Libya matter. I in turn have reflected on the experience and written in defense of the White House counsel's responsibilities to the president in national security crises. In a curious but delightful turn of events, Jack Goldsmith, staunch critic of my war powers legal position in the Libya episode, wound up coauthoring with me a book on presidential powers, and he and I have become good friends. In that book, we argue for a downsized, less powerful Office of White House Counsel. It can all get very complicated, really.

I left the White House in July 2011 to reprise my role as general counsel to an Obama presidential campaign, this time for reelection. My representation of a president would continue, but no longer within government. I know that the job of White House counsel is the best I will ever have. Now, back out in the real world, I would be responsible only for advice to presidents on personal and political matters, which has been more than honor enough and not really easier.

CHAPTER 10

Joe Biden's 2020 Campaign

Faced with exceptional threats to a fragile voting system, Joe Biden's presidential campaign devotes massive resources to anticipating and fending off challenges to the results. I take a leave from law school teaching and join his team of lawyers, who unite around the view that winning the election means ensuring that one actually takes place. Election officials rise to the occasion; social media platforms do not. Not too long after Joe Biden wins, it becomes clear that the threats to the democracy have become worse, and I start worrying about 2024 and the urgency of bipartisan defenses of the democracy.

I did not anticipate any direct involvement in the 2020 presidential campaign. Once I left my law firm and joined the New York University School of Law faculty on a full-time basis, I did not envision a return to political lawyering. I was happy teaching and writing; I no longer needed to worry about the reaction of clients when expressing views on the legal, policy, and political issues I cared most about. As it happened, I did carry with me into this new phase of my career a handful of legacy clients—those to whom I had made what I thought was a personal commitment to continue as a legal adviser. One of them was Joe Biden, and it was not a foregone conclusion that two years later he would run for president and be the party's nominee—then win. My retirement from practice turned out to be more limited than I had foreseen.

In the period before he launched his campaign, I advised on his charitable activities and on the support he provided to other candidates on the road, appearing on their behalf, or through contributions made by a political committee he had established. Then came the discussions of a possible presidential run, and I was back and forth to his home in suburban Virginia to help work through the details of building a campaign.

Biden decided to go for it, and as soon as my spring semester ended, I took a leave from NYU Law for the fall and joined the campaign as a senior adviser, charged among other responsibilities with overseeing the Biden program to protect voting rights.

We, along with so many others, were in an all-out fight more important than any in my career—to get Trump out of office. His notion of a well-run campaign lacked any semblance of ethical limits. Nothing was out of bounds. The Trump we faced had waged a 2016 campaign, and then conducted a presidency, in a manner we knew foreshadowed a 2020 reelection bid unlike any other since Nixon's criminal endeavors to retain his office. Biden would describe the fight as one for the "soul of America."

Yes, it was, and for the preservation of core democratic processes and norms. In the 2016 campaign, Trump had unapologetically welcomed the help the Russian government happily offered to provide him. The question of "collusion" quickly got mired in a fight over law. Those defending Trump could find no legal prohibition against collusion, no basis for the appointment of a special counsel to conduct a criminal investigation. On the other side were battalions of lawyers and other commentators insisting that violations of campaign finance laws and other legal problems arose from the political alliance with a foreign power that Trump and his campaign were actively exploring, and hoping to benefit from. I was among the legal commentators who, in writing about these issues in *Lawfare*, the *New York Times*, and elsewhere, made the case that, on some aspects of the alleged collusion, there were legal grounds for investigation and prosecution.

Then Robert Mueller issued his report, and he did not find a legally actionable basis for prosecuting collusion. It was known, and Mueller's investigation confirmed, that the Trump campaign welcomed campaign support from Russia and, among other notable decisions, chose to meet with a Moscow delegation traveling on a mission to volunteer the Putin regime's support. The entire senior campaign management team assembled to discuss what campaign gifts the Russians came bearing. Whatever else the Russians did on their own, in seeding social media with lies and misinformation, they apparently did not bring goods satisfactory, on that occasion, to the Trump campaign. The campaign could deny that anything useful came out of the meeting, but the fact remained that its leadership agreed to the visit and to the offer of assistance, and it communicated clearly an openness to an extraordinary alliance with a foreign power.

Trump and his campaign declared victory. Mueller had not found that this evident collusion constituted a crime. Right or wrong, the conclusion was a legal one, but the whole episode was yet more evidence that Trump and his campaign aides would do whatever it took to win, any consideration of his larger ethical obligations carrying no weight with him whatsoever.

The public record of the meeting on June 9, 2016, with the delegation from Russia does not include any suggestion that the campaign sought or received advice from Trump's lawyers. It is difficult for me to believe that if they did solicit advice, it was from their campaign general counsel Don McGahn, later the White House counsel, who stood up to Trump on other occasions when he sought the lawyer's help in disregarding legal and ethical standards. McGahn refused to carry out orders to fire Mueller, and he declined to falsify White House counsel records at Trump's request for the purpose of suggesting that the president had never issued the order in the first place.

Federal law bars foreign governments from contributing to campaigns, or spending on their behalf, and Congress has repeatedly amended it to make it tighter. Upholding this broad prohibition, the District Court for the District of Columbia, in an opinion affirmed by the U.S. Supreme Court, found that "it is fundamental to the definition of our national political community that foreign citizens do not have a constitutional right to participate in, and thus may be excluded from, activities of democratic self-government." This was a "foundational question about the definition of the American political community" and the basis on which foreign citizens were barred from participation in the U.S. electoral process.[1]

Would a sound political lawyer have concluded that the meetings and communications between the campaign and Russia were a neat loophole, getting around this "foundational question" about the requirements of democratic self-government? I doubt it, at least in McGahn's case. The test of what Trump and his campaign hoped to get from Russia is not strictly, perhaps not even predominantly, a legal one. Mueller might have decided that the campaign had illegally solicited a "contribution" from Russian, in violation of the finance laws, which would have met the demand in some quarters for Trump and his campaign to suffer the legal consequences of their engagement with Russia. In a strange way, this narrow legal resolution, even if better than no legal accountability at all, would have operated to diminish the ethical significance of what Trump actively sought from Russia—all the help he could get. It would have become the story of a campaign finance violation, consisting of an unlawful contribution at that particular time, in that particular form. It would have somewhat obscured the ethics of "colluding" with a foreign power to win an election, which cannot be defined by what the law permits but by our expectations of the limits that candidates and their operatives should honor in seeking victory.

Trump's lack of compunction about the methods he would employ to win infected every dimension of his campaign in 2016, and we knew it would again in 2020. He was not the first presidential candidate to lie to the public about his own record and that of his opponents, but he did not have any scruples about the unbridgeable distance he put between the facts and his claims. And as president, he had made clear that he failed to understand that the power of his office was not just an asset he could use as he liked. He imagined that the federal government was the successor to the Trump Organization. He trumpeted the advantages of political uses of his pardon power; he stormed against the resistance he faced in his wish to harness law enforcement to his personal political benefit.

Trump had also made clear for a long time that losing the election was, for him, out of the question. He was not a loser; and so a loss could only be a fraud against him and his supporters. He had been banging the "voter fraud" drum for a long time. After all, having lost the Iowa caucus in 2016 to Ted Cruz, he insisted that he was the victim of fraud in that unlikely situation as well. The Trump campaign was constructed around his maniacal refusal to accept rejection. We knew what was coming in the event that he lost his reelection bid.

While we were confident that he would fail to hold onto the White House in the face of defeat at the polls, his failure in no way precluded the possibility of lasting harm to democratic institutions. Facing defeat and an embittered postpresidential residence at Mar-a-Lago, Trump had the materials at hand to do real damage.

It is rarely appreciated that in the best of times, the electoral system is fragile, more so than anyone would like to believe or should have any reason to accept. Election officials spread across more than ten thousand voting jurisdictions have to work with limited resources. When elections go well, they receive little credit; when they come apart, the officials have to face an outraged community of voters and a skeptical press. Lawyers for each party continually press for changes in the rules to their candidates' advantage. If they don't succeed, they often sue and charge officials with intentional misconduct or incompetence.

Add to these standard, never-ending stresses on the system others that have soared in volume and impact in recent years: social media disinformation, including healthy helpings of lies propagated on the web by foreign governments, and partisan activities to restrict voting access for politically targeted communities of voters. All of these were vulnerabilities in the system that Trump could readily exploit and worsen, and he certainly gave it his best try.

When the public health crisis overtook the country in the spring of 2020, the system began to crumble. In the battleground state of Wisconsin, Milwaukee lacked virtually any capacity for safe in-person voting: five polling places were open on the day of the primary elections. Georgia experienced a similar breakdown. Turnout was disastrously low. The question we confronted at the Biden campaign was whether these were the conditions, the collapse, we would confront in the fall. What was required to hold any election at all, much less one conducted under rules fair to the voters?

Under the direction of then-candidate Biden, our priority was defense of the system. We largely stood back from the courtroom wars over voting rules. Only after the election did the campaign hire lawyers to fend off the lunacies that the Trump team visited on the courts.

In the years I represented presidential campaigns, I was cautious about litigation, and this influenced my approach, at least my priorities, in 2020. Lawsuits are expensive, unpredictable, and time-consuming; campaigns are concerned, often obsessed, with the careful use of resources, yearn for more rather than less predictability, and labor under a merciless calendar from announcement to Election Day. Campaigns do whatever is possible to limit bad press, and a lawsuit ending in failure is bad press. I also recognized that lawsuits can tie up election administrators who are trying to run an election. Constant contention over voting rules can confuse voters who may be unsure what rules apply to their participation.

But sometimes legal action may be unavoidable, and I did not always counsel its avoidance in presidential campaigns. In Ohio, during President Obama's 2012 reelection bid, the state decided to close the polls to most voters for early voting the weekend before the election. An exception was made for military voters and their families. The campaign did not object to the accommodation of military voting, which federal law facilitates in any number of ways. The offensive feature of the Ohio law was its unprecedented choice, unique among states, to keep polling places open but only for one defined group of voters. Under our view, if a polling place was open, then it should be open to all. And further propelling us into the courts was that this poll-closing for all but military voters was especially disruptive to the Black church-going community long accustomed to "souls to the polls" voting on the Sunday before Election Day.

We sued and we won. Ohio was thought critical to our prospects. A win on principle was also a strategic win. It was the only lawsuit the Obama campaign brought in 2012, and we estimated that it would mean 200,000 of our Ohio voters could cast ballots before Election Day. When news of the victory came my way from the court, I read the notice twice to be sure I read it correctly, and then emailed the campaign. "Holy shit," was the pleased response from a very satisfied customer at campaign headquarters.

Eight years later, the Biden campaign did not sue before Election Day, holding fire until the certain conflicts afterward. In 2019–2020, Democratic groups and a robust voting rights community litigated around the country. The dedicated Republican drive to add new restrictions to the vote, followed by the stresses of the pandemic, called for a response in the courts, and experienced and sophisticated voting rights lawyers provided it. The Democratic and progressive groups fought hard for more access to the polls, especially during a public health emergency. The Republicans argued for less, far less. By Election Day, the courts decided some cases in the Democrats' and progressive community's favor, but more in the Republicans'. Many victories in the lower courts were reversed on appeal. Roughly one in seven legal actions to facilitate access to the polls ultimately succeeded—some of them successful at the trial court level, only to be reversed on appeal.

The Biden campaign put its emphasis on political and field operations that would enable us to work within the legal system of rules in place after all the courtroom clashes had concluded. We assigned staff designated as voter protection coordinators to support election officials on the ground. We heard them out on what they needed and did what we could to provide it. We requested that supporters do what they could in their communities, through financial donations and other ways, to prepare for a functional election—one in which the polls would be open, properly staffed, and equipped. The urgent need was in some instances nothing more dramatic than plexiglass sneeze guards, an adequate supply of paper for ballots, and cash to recruit and pay the poll workers who would replace the many older veterans of Election Day who had to step aside in the interests of their health in the time of COVID. Nothing dramatic, and yet vital.

Lawyers still had plenty to do in looking ahead to the Trump attack on the outcome. Heading up the strategic planning was our "SG 3" team—three former U.S. solicitors general—the late Walter Dellinger, Don Verrilli, and Seth Waxman. They participated in strategic planning calls with me, our general counsel Dana Remus, and key members of our legal team, Pat Moore and Danielle Friedman. It was always the threat of protecting against Trump's attempted subversion of an election he lost that most commanded our attention. The first step was ensuring that there would be a viable election, the second was defending the outcome.

We mobilized major law firms and some six hundred lawyers to produce thousands of pages of legal analysis. Here are a few of the topics explored, drawn from our master index, the work having begun in the summer and done at a fast clip:

- Discussion of whether the federal Due Process Clause bars post-election changes to vote counting procedures.

- Discussion of governors' legal authority to respond to voter intimidation by private citizens or Trump administration officials.

- Whether state legislatures may change the manner in which presidential electors are selected postelection, and whether they can do so independent of any state constitutional limitations.

- Whether the president may exercise statutory or inherent emergency powers to interfere with an election.

- A review of federal statutory remedies for voter intimidation.

- An analysis of potential legal challenges to any Trump administration deployment of Department of Homeland Security officers in an effort to interfere with in-person voting.

- Potential legal challenges to the deployment of Department of Justice officials to interfere with voting in specific precincts.

- An assessment of whether the U.S. Supreme Court was likely to reverse the Pennsylvania Supreme Court's alteration of the deadline for receiving ballots.

It might seem that we were positively clairvoyant in anticipating what is now known about what Trump did or hoped to do to negate a loss. We don't deserve plaudits. Anyone thinking through Trump's track record, both what he did in 2016 and how he behaved thereafter, would have to have planned for the same contingencies.

With the research in hand, we assembled notebooks of sample pleadings to enable us to convert this research within an hour or so into lawsuits, and we identified the lawyers who would represent the Biden campaign in each state where this conflict might occur.

This was all activity in the campaign's interest, without a doubt. More important, it was also a defense of the system. This meant, too, that we had to reassure voters and election officials that all would be OK and then refrain from adding to their anxieties or to the difficulties that election officials faced. We had to dismiss Trump's threats to the system rather than appear to give them credence. In a handful of press statements before the election, I stressed that we had laws to protect against crazy stuff that Trump might plan—"a whole host of constraints," as I put it in an interview with John Heilemann on HBO's *The Circus*. Trump could "rage" and shout out orders "to have federal marshals go to polling places and have them impound ballots," but, I insisted, "it won't happen."[2]

From time to time, this strategy put us at odds in setting priorities and coordinating public messaging with allies and supporters. We had kept a close watch over the Trump campaign's preposterous attacks on mail voting and, in every way we could, we sent a message to voters that it was safe and reliable. This meant that we also followed closely the concerns that developed over the policies and operations of the U.S. Postal Service under the direction of Postmaster General Louis DeJoy, a Trump appointee. When Twitter erupted with claims that the postal service was hauling mailboxes off the streets to hamper mail-in voting, we checked out these allegations, consulting closely with the postal unions, and found that there was no basis to these charges. Worse, they could only scare away our voters, just as Trump was foolishly driving his own supporters away from using the mail-in voting option. We thought that vigilance over the post office was warranted, but not panic. We did not want to play Trump's game. It was a game played at the expense of the voters.

The danger to voters most troubling to us was Trump's and his allies' use of social media to spread lies about the election. It is fair to say that we were always disappointed in the behavior of Donald Trump and his allies. We had no reason to expect better, only that he would continue to plumb the depths of irresponsible, and as he believed it necessary, borderline or actual lawlessness. We were not just exasperated with Facebook, now Meta. It enraged us.

First quietly, then more publicly, we pressed hard for serious checks on the dissemination of false information and its amplification. We would hear that the company was working to refine its responses to the threats. Then more time would pass without the response we had been promised. Meanwhile, the President of the United States was posting claims that "Mail Drop Boxes . . . are a voter security disaster" and were not "Covid sanitized."[3] He made up facts about the voting process, as he did when declaring that "in New Jersey they want you to certify that you asked for the Universal Mail-Ballot." His son Don Jr. advised Facebook readers that the Biden campaign had a "plan to add millions of fraudulent ballots that can cancel your vote and overturn the election."[4] Facebook had a policy that these lies clearly violated—a prohibition on misrepresentations of precisely this kind. It just did not enforce it.

This was a problem with unpaid, "organic" content that Trump and his allies would generate to mislead and lie to voters. They could also pay for advertising on the platform to supplement this program of attacks on the electoral process. We pushed for a period of two weeks before Election Day when Facebook would fact-check these ads before agreeing to run them. Lies spread on the eve of an election are the ones hardest to chase down and expose because the clock has run out, and Election Day is at hand. Facebook eventually agreed to some limitation—but with a catch. It would not run any new ads in the two weeks before the election, but this meant that any old lie run before this period could be rerun, for a fee, right up to the day of voting.

Perhaps most infuriating was the company's view that elected leaders have vastly more room for lies than, say, some group of citizens who join together in a systematic campaign of falsehoods. Their position was that people should be able to hear from their politicians, which did not allow for a fact-checking of this category of speech. In this view of the world, the president of the United States would have special dispensation to lie as much, and on any topic, he chose. This high standing would perversely come with diminished responsibility, even when the president was acting in his own and purely political interest as a candidate for office. Lies about voting or encouragement for violent behavior would remain open to him in free postings or in ads placed for a fee.

Our fight with Meta fit in with the overall strategy of defending the process, and key to the defense was attacking the sources of lies and misinformation. The company did not rise to the occasion. Others did. Scores of individuals—primarily those who run elections and including Democrats and Republicans—were committed to the defense and success of the voting systems.

Once Trump lost, his legal team, such as it was, brought lawsuits all over the place, but we were not, for a minute, worried that he would succeed. The cases he brought were destined to fail. He had no facts and no law on his side. Our only job was to show up with our lawyers wherever his did, and we spent $13 million to cover all this ground. The outcome was never in doubt.

Trump seemed to believe that he had the Supreme Court he needed to salvage a win in a pinch. After all, some argued, he had rushed Amy Coney Barrett onto the Supreme Court in thirty days, shortly before Congress recessed for the election. She then joined two other conservative justices who owed their appointments to him, and they would make for a Court majority ready and willing to upset the election results and return Trump to power. This worry, often rising to a prediction, always struck me as silly. Barrett did not become a Supreme Court justice, with years on the bench ahead of her, so that she could define her tenure with one lawless payback to Donald Trump.

It turned out that the threat would not come from a corrupted legal system but from an armed attack on the final tally of votes in January. Of all the contingencies we planned for, this was not one of them.

We were ready for any choice Vice President Pence might make to satisfy Trump's expectation, which later became a public demand, that he disrupt the count and give his boss a chance to mount an attack on the election results in the state legislatures and courts. In our calls, we reviewed these concerns with Hill staff who were in turn engaged in preparations for January 6 with their Republican colleagues and the Senate and House parliamentarians. I remember only one call when the issue of security arose, and the discussion passed quickly with a report that the Capitol Hill police had matters in hand.

We were confident the day of the vote that all would proceed as the Constitution and law required. The Senate Republican Leader declared that Biden had won the election the day after the Electoral College met. The discussions among Democratic and Republican members of Congress were sober-minded and productive. To be sure, we knew that we would face a protracted session because of pointless and baseless objections from members challenging the vote totals reported by particular states. But that was it, we thought; and yet it wasn't.

The strategy the campaign pursued in 2020 was the right one: right in two senses, for the campaign and for the system. This is not a claim of superior moral virtue. It was a strategy dictated by extraordinary circumstances. In the confrontation with Donald Trump, the inescapable question was whether we would act as a campaign not only on our own behalf but with some sense of responsibility for an embattled democracy whose defense was a central issue in the campaign. As Joe Biden has stated more than a few times, he is an institutionalist who decided to run against a president who consistently exhibited contempt for constitutional norms and legal requirements that got in his way. A campaign invariably reflects what the candidate in the most basic terms chooses to make of it. This was Joe Biden's choice.

The 2020 campaign did not settle the core conflict over democratic values. My own work on these issues has moved increasingly into the nonprofit, nonpartisan world, as I have joined with others, principled Republicans included, to defend election officials and mobilize civil society institutions to defend the electoral system and the voters of all parties. I am still a Democrat, and I will play any part I can in voting rights and election protection in the 2024 election. But the process itself will need close attention and care. The candidates giving their all to win, and lawyers and advisers who give their best advice on what it will take, have to remain, as the Biden campaign strove to be, advocates for the "soul" of the democratic process. Win or lose.

Choices will have to be made. The story of the 2020 election was a story of those choices made by a host of individuals. Election officials who braved threats and a public health emergency to run an election. Judges who would have no part of the charade that Trump and his lawyers put on in the courts. The U.S. military establishment who made clear they would not be conscripted for political service to their commander-in-chief. The Senate Republican Leader who recognized the Biden victory right after the Electoral College met and cast their votes. The vice president of the United States refusing to abuse his presidency of the Senate in a conspiracy to subvert the decisive congressional process for tallying the electoral votes. Members of Congress who insisted after the attack on the Capitol on reconvening without delay and completing the vote count, which dealt the final blow to any last hope Trump had of subverting the election.

Frequently, when I lay out my roster of those to whom we owe our respect and appreciation in 2020, I am met with either skepticism or vehemently expressed objections about the role of Mike Pence. The complaint goes something like this. Why would you praise Pence for behavior that should have been expected of him? Why should there ever have been a question that he would go along with Donald Trump in a constitutional *coup d'etat*? Sometimes the objections are put more broadly. Should we not evaluate Pence on his entire conduct during the Trump presidency, holding him responsible for the number of times he did not speak out when he should have but instead stood side by side with the former president in apparent full support of or acquiescence to conduct never seen before in the history of the office?

Now and then I struggle with the question. The vice president of the United States is the hand-picked running mate of the president and yet, at the same time, an independent, elected constitutional officer. He's not the president's subordinate, not required to comply with his orders, not compelled to quietly abide presidential misconduct or abuse of power. A reliable and trusted partner, yes, in the normal course of governance, but not at the expense of conscience. I do not disagree that, whatever may have taken place behind closed doors, I would have hoped for more evidence that Pence as vice president did more in his four years in that office to defend the basic norms of the presidency. The fact remains, however, that at a crucial moment, Pence took the decisive step of breaking with Trump and meeting his constitutional obligations, and he did so when to have acted differently would have had grave and lasting consequences for the democracy.

It would be a mistake to simply rely on this experience of 2020 in assuming that the next assault on the system will be countered with the same success. The system requires strengthening at all points of vulnerability, from the resources we provide to our election officials to the reforms that will support those who choose wisely and complicate the schemes of those who don't. When in 2022, Congress enacted the Electoral Count Reform Act, amending the law that governed the January 6 vote count and exhibited weaknesses that Trump and his allies conspired to exploit, there was reason to hope that difficult, bipartisan institutional reform is still possible. And it is, because there are individuals who choose to make it so.

CHAPTER 11

On the Nature of Political Ethics

Democracy is costly, exacting a price for its benefits: accepting the pain of loss and giving up certain—and potentially very effective—strategies for winning. I sometimes see this clearly, and other times I don't. I use "guerrilla" tactics on behalf of Barack Obama, in his primary contest with Hillary Clinton, to make the point that candidates should have good reasons to question election results. I have to be talked out of an ill-conceived plan to "send a message" from the White House to a nasty foe of the president. I am reminded that constitutional crises like Watergate are as much about basic political ethics as they are about criminality.

A dispute over the legitimacy of an election led to an unusual confrontation between two candidates over allegations of "irregularities" in the vote count. In this instance, it was not the 2020 election. It was the primary battle twelve years earlier between Hillary Clinton and Barack Obama.

After a split of the first four, or early, primaries, Barack Obama began running up the score in his surprisingly successful challenge to Hillary Clinton for the Democratic Party nomination. He did exceptionally well in caucus states, where the voters assembled to cast ballots in living rooms or special caucus locations in a collective enterprise very different from the familiar one in which a voter goes off to a polling place, casts a ballot in privacy, and leaves. In Iowa, which Obama won by a wide margin, voters gathered for hours in living rooms and other designated locations to deliberate on choices, argue with one another, and cast ballots through multiple rounds of voting until delegates are allocated to the candidates who exceed the threshold for winning delegates. The caucus process is complex enough that a candidate might win the most votes overall, but still split evenly the delegates awarded or wind up with a few less than the popular vote loser.

Nevada held a caucus next in line after Iowa, but while Clinton won the overall vote, Obama secured half the delegates. In one caucus state after another, Obama was well organized in the conception and execution of this strategy and began picking up delegates at a crisp clip.

Texas had both a primary and a caucus. Election night would conclude with a primary popular vote winner and, in a separate proceeding conducted the same evening, a caucus that apportioned the delegates to each candidate. By the time of this Texas "two-step," the Clinton campaign began grumbling about "irregularities" in the caucus process. It served the campaign's interests to raise questions about the legitimacy of the gains that Obama made with his more skillfully executed caucus strategy. Texas was a particular sore point. Clinton won the preference primary with 51 percent of the vote but came away with only four more delegates than Obama won. She did not do as well in the caucuses, losing it by six points while Obama netted nine more delegates. The combined impact of these contests was an Obama gain overall of five delegates.

The Clinton campaign arranged a press call to level charges of irregularities in the caucus procedure. On calls of this kind, reporters queue up to ask questions once the campaign has made its statement. I slipped into the queue: the operator managing the line was unaware I was not a reporter, but instead a lawyer for the opposing campaign. This was a breach of campaign etiquette. I was crashing another campaign's event. But we had concluded that what was in effect an allegation of a fraudulent or irregular vote count required a bit of norm-busting.

The Clinton campaign began taking press questions, and then, suddenly, there I was on the line, challenging, as groundless, opportunistic, and cynical, the doubt that her campaign was casting over the caucus. I declared that these claims in Texas was merely one of "a string of accusations [the Clinton campaign] launched against the caucus process on no principle" other than their failure to win the delegates they hoped for.[1] Nothing was wrong in Texas except for one campaign's unwillingness to accept the results.

The Clinton campaign spokesperson, Howard Wolfson, and I went back and forth in this exchange. He called on me to stand for the "fair and equal opportunity" for all who wished to participate in the caucus; I repeated that the campaign's attacks on the process were based solely on its electoral failings.

The *New York Times* reported my intervention, likening it to a guerrilla attack, which I quite liked, while a *Slate* reporter described it as "the best slap-down of the cycle, and the entire press corps has front-row seats."[2] I liked that, too. But behind this exercise in political theater was a more serious question of when a candidate should claim that a loss was the product of fraud.

Whatever lay behind the Clinton campaign's questioning of the caucus results, I thought very highly of Howard, whom I had represented when he was a senior Democratic party official. I certainly did not suspect him of putting out a claim he believed to be false. I may well have adopted the same line of attack had I been representing the Clinton campaign's interests. And yet whenever a losing (or about-to-lose) campaign, in this instance or any other, makes a charge of voting fraud or irregularity, it is a question of political ethics: not *whether* the campaign could make this kind of claim, but when and under what circumstances it *should*. Partisans are all ready to hear from their party and their candidate that they didn't lose, that they could not have lost but for the shenanigans. It falls to the campaign and the candidates to judge whether the allegations are so strong, amenable to proof, that they are worth the high cost to public confidence in the electoral process.

The law in every state, structured in different ways, provides for avenues of redress—recounts and contests—if a campaign is convinced that there was an error in the voter count. A campaign has not committed an ethical infraction in availing itself of these processes. It may have a basis for bringing such a claim, especially in a very close race where there is reasonable evidence-based possibility of error. Elections can misfire, tired officials can make mistakes, and machines can malfunction. Some form of cheating might not be ruled out, as exceedingly rare as it is, and any such illegal activity with the potential of affecting the outcome is even rarer.

Still each individual instance when a candidate, their supporters, or their party might raise doubts that an election produced the true winner is a test of political ethics. It pits the personal and political self-interest of the candidate against a wider obligation of care for the democratic process itself. Public confidence in that process binds voters to the results, which is an indispensable requirement for respect for democratic choice.

In a particular race, the election of the candidate whose victory is challenged as fraudulent strikes at the right to assume office and the authority they claim for their exercise of political power. When the system comes under systematic attack, such that its legitimacy is constantly called into question as a defining feature of a political party's platform, the consequences are severe, as the election denialism led and fostered by Donald Trump has made all too apparent. Trump could not abide a loss, and so he brought his wholesale indifference to ethical considerations, evident throughout his business career, into the heart of American politics and seriously weakened confidence in the electoral process across a broad swath of the American public.

The cost cannot be reckoned solely in the poll results showing that a large segment of Republican voters are now convinced that Trump was cheated out of victory by a corrupt electoral process. A rotted political ethics has a long tail. We may see how long in 2024 and beyond. For election denialism looks both backward and forward. It rewrites the history of the last election to make its case that fraud triumphed and those who took office were imposters. It has also spawned a movement to roll back voting rules enacted to make voting more accessible to voters—an accessibility that its detractors falsely insist serves no purpose other than to encourage fraud and elect Democrats.

The effect of this is to cut still more deeply into confidence in the political process, except now the doubters are also gathering on the other side of the political spectrum. Democrats perceive—with justification—that much, if not most, of these "antifraud" policies are another version of system-rigging. Republicans may and do allege that permissive rules undermine the credibility of elections, but Democrats allege the same about the purported tightening of the rules. So, in 2024, while Republicans supporting the Republican candidates have a ready-made argument for rejecting the results of a lost election, so do their adversaries, who may make the case that the rules clamping down on voter access achieved their partisan goal but made impossible acceptance of the results. This is the bitter fruit of Trump's politics and ethics, and it may extend well into the future, long after he is gone from the scene.

The constitutional crisis that was Watergate also arose out of a president's unwillingness to lose an election and the steps he was prepared to take to ensure that it could not happen. It, too, was an episode in fallen political ethics, as some observers recognized at the time. This may seem odd. This version of the Watergate episode focused on "ethics" might seem too slight, not up to the task of describing an assault on constitutional government made up of many discrete violations of law. Criminal laws were violated and those committing offenses such as burglary or money laundering were properly called to account. The standard Watergate narrative seems to rest on what is solid, indisputable, and enduring: ours is a government of laws, not of men and women.

But in 1974, in a report requested by the Senate Select Committee on Presidential Campaign Activities, known as the Watergate Committee, the National Academy of Public Administration put the collapse of ethics at the center of its explanation of what had gone very wrong. Written by a panel of scholars, prominent members of the business community, and other notables, the analysis did not overlook various contributing failures. It worried about the centralization of power in the White House and the power grab by White House staff who were routinely assuming the authority that belonged to cabinet officials confirmed by the Senate. It considered ways that the Department of Justice could be kept out of partisan politics. Its proposals for Congress included bringing clarity to the standards for impeachment. But it concluded that "ultimately, the ethical and moral quality of government depends on the individuals who administer it, especially those who provide its leadership."[3]

The panel did not dispute that the law was implicated, and violated, at a serious level in Watergate: "burglary . . . forgery . . . the laundering of money through Mexico." But the criminal laws "set outer limits" for what is permissible in politics, and only that. "What was most important," however, were "the attitudes of mind, the modes of conspiring, and the narrow goals of those behind them. Most of these kinds of matters lie behind the range of criminal law."[4] It approvingly cited this conclusion from a publication of the Center for the Study of Democratic Institutions: "It was the unethical, not the illegal, actions in 1972, that did this country down [in Watergate]."[5]

It was a question, the panel wrote in an epilogue to its report, of how those in power understood the character of democratic government:

> A democratic government is not a family business, dominated by its patriarch; nor is it a military battalion, or a political campaign headquarters. It is a producing organization which belongs to its members, and it is the only such organization whose members include *all* the citizens within its jurisdiction. Those who work for and are paid by government are ultimately servants of the whole citizenry, which owns and supports the government.[6]

Individuals in Watergate had committed crimes. But *how* these many individuals came to commit these crimes was a story about grievous ethical collapse. It was in having choices to make and making them poorly that, in the most extreme forms, propelled Nixon and senior aides onto a course toward prosecutions and jail terms. The ones who went to jail were most visibly at fault and held responsible with the direst of personal consequences: the ruin of reputation and loss of liberty that comes with criminal charges, conviction, and incarceration. Others escaped legal penalties but had played along and enabled the corrupt mindset of the Nixon White House.

These others also chose poorly—behaved unethically—even for actions that did not result in a day in the dock or in jail. John Dean, the White House counsel who served time for false statements and obstruction of justice, was not, however, prosecuted for writing a memo recommending the use of government agencies to "screw" Nixon's political "enemies." But the thinking behind the memo defined—as did his White House colleagues' apparent readiness to receive and entertain this level of advice—the ethical void out of which the more spectacular legal trials and tribulations emerged. As a lawyer, Dean had assumed that the White House could operate as a political campaign headquarters, and he decided that this campaign could consist in part of excluding "enemies" from effective participation in the political process. They were not to be argued with and defeated at the polls, but "screwed" through the use of government power.

We might think: the law does not allow what Dean proposed, and so the issue remains a legal one.

But there is a wide gap between the unethical and the illegal. A smart but unethical lawyer, less reckless than Dean in those days, could counsel on the use of agencies to prefer allies over enemies, showing solicitude for friends and far less for foes. Policies can be shaped to these political purposes, with sophistication but also with effect. Government does not—and does not have to—run altogether evenhandedly. Up to a point, this is OK "politics."

In our time, the right of politicians to respond warmly to friends, giving them the preferential treatment denied to enemies, has become enshrined in the constitutional law. The Supreme Court has ruled in campaign finance cases that the very notion of representative government means that those who hold office may reward those who helped get them there. "Ingratiation and access" go with the territory: they "embody a constitutional feature of democracy—that constituents support candidates who share their beliefs and interests, and candidates who are elected can be expected to be responsive to those concerns."[7] For this reason, while an official cannot sell a law, by pocketing cash or a campaign contribution in exchange for a vote, special access is available. If you bet correctly on the winner in an election, the win may entitle you to a quick return of your phone calls or scheduling of a meeting so you can argue for your policy or legislative or rule-making preferences. Those who sat out the race, or supported the opponent, may have the longer wait. To the winner goes some measure of spoils. A politician will advance the policies she committed to during the campaign, and will show supporters, as she will not adversaries, special consideration.

CHAPTER II

To this point, Jimmy Carter was a president known for his recti-
tude, which was also often criticized as a political weakness, and yet his
administration successfully defended a lawsuit charging that he had put
government resources illicitly to use in strengthening his hand in his
1980 contest with Ted Kennedy for the Democratic nomination.[8] Kennedy supporters alleged that the Carter administration employed government power and resources in various ways to aid the president's
campaign and undermine his opponent's. Hiring policies distinguished
between supporters and others; states and local governments whose officials favored Carter were more likely to receive grants and "the timing
of the announcement [of those grants were] coordinated to provide the
maximum benefit to the President." Smaller advantages came the way
of the president's political friends who enjoyed the frills of presidential
favor, while Kennedy supporters were "not invited to attend Presidential
functions or to travel on the President's 'Air Force One.'"

But the challenge failed because the courts could not figure out a way
to disentangle the motivations behind a range of discretionary decisions
a government makes each day. Carter and his team knew not to go too
far. The court noted that while Kennedy won the New York primary, the
Carter administration pledged that substantial federal financial assistance to New York City would continue. The politics overall—and the
advantages of incumbency—are complicated, and the courts are not well
situated to perform a policing role.

Dean, however, was not simply concerned with seasoning discretionary decision making with more kindness to friends than to opponents.
He wanted more: a systematic program to treat adversaries as "enemies"
and to "screw" them. His proposal was to turn government directly
against political opponents, to rule them out of the "public" it was meant
to serve. But not entirely. They would receive attention, except that it
would take the form of punishment. Democracy rests on a fundamental
requirement that you accept as fully enrolled members of the political
community those with whom you disagree. Win or lose, they retain this
membership and, along with it, the right to enjoy the benefits of their
victories and to contest their losses in the next round of elections. They
are not to be destroyed, excluded, muzzled, cast out.

Dean was revealing his ethics. His felonies were yet to come. The ethical failings foreshadowed the legal transgressions. It was not only a matter of poor word choice—the "screwing" of their political opponents. The proposed use of the government's vast power to accomplish the screwing was the logical next step and eventually confers on this line of thought its deeper ethical significance. For the government that "belongs" to all its members has been turned against them, expelling them from its protections.

This course taken by the Nixon administration resonates in our time with the war waged by the Florida State government led by Governor Ron DeSantis against the Disney Corporation after the company objected to the state's Parental Rights in Education Act, or "Don't Say Gay," law, which imposed restrictions on the classroom discussion of sex education and gender issues. Disney pledged to seek its repeal and support actions against it in the courts. The governor declared openly his intention to retaliate against the company for opposing his administration on this controversial issue of public policy. He took the action of dissolving the special district through which Disney administered its vast entertainment properties and threatened still more punitive measures as the dispute escalated. His stated purpose was to punish Disney and send a clear message to other businesses that they should stay out of divisive public debate—if their position did not align with the government's. "Go woke, go broke" became the motto of the DeSantis politics of retribution.

Both Jimmy Carter's and Ron DeSantis's governing choices were enmeshed with political considerations. Each of their administrations wound up in court, the issues having been cast into legal form.

Carter was found to have kept to a safe, the legal, side of the line; DeSantis was accused of going well over it. The law will always have its say about when things have gone too far, beyond what is allowed in ordinary politics, but it is not a fine measuring instrument. It is useful only for the more extreme or dramatic cases. Long before the lawyers and courts become involved, the question to be asked—can government authority be used for political ends—is an ethical one. A bad ethics can result in legal scandal and consequences, but even if it does not, it remains a serious threat to democratic institutions. It weakens them and the norms vital to their functioning. Bad ethics is a source of democratic decay.

This ethical failure carries over by its own relentless logic to the conduct of antidemocratic politics as a whole. The use of government power to punish is allied with other measures to deny adversaries full membership in the political community and equal access to the processes by which leadership is chosen and policies formulated. The same enemy who becomes a target of its own government is by the same reasoning subject to other forms of political discrimination and harassment. Those in power take actions to suppress their voice in the process. A legislature may decide to expel members for expressing their views a certain way, as in Tennessee in 2023, when members of the General Assembly protesting its failure to advance gun control legislation were stripped of their seats. Or in the same year, when the majority-white Alabama legislature enacted state-level police and judicial arrangements to govern the majority-Black city of Jackson, replacing their elected prosecutors and courts with appointed ones—essentially establishing a white citizens' protectorate. These measures can become integral to a party program and national in scope, as has been seen throughout the country in recent years, when state legislative majorities have concluded that it is in their political interest to put up obstacles to the right to vote.

The slide to democratic exclusion can build slowly from a simple memo or conversation to a program of corrupted democratic governance. I look back now on one such moment when I was tempted to move in this direction to send clear messages, but to send them in the entirely wrong way, to Republicans who I thought—I knew—were manifesting a lack of respect for President Obama. I suspected that in some cases race was the obvious explanation. I had learned of a Republican member who had been without justification utterly rude and disrespectful in an exchange with the president over health care reform. It was, for this member, a grandstand play: he was going to show his colleagues he did not have to stand for a lecture from this snooty, Harvard-educated Black man. Composed as ever, the president did not take the bait and the tense moment passed.

I was enraged, however, and raised the possibility that we communicate our displeasure by freezing out all interactions with this representative's office throughout the government for a two- or three-month period. All inquiries to agencies on behalf of constituents, all routine requests for White House tour passes, all access to the executive branch, would be put on hold, and no calls returned. And we would quietly let it be known why. Message sent.

And as I thought about it at the time, in a foul state of mind at my desk in the West Wing, this message would help establish that this president, smart and thoughtful as he was, could play hardball. There was talk in Washington at the time that Obama could not master Congress as Lyndon Johnson did. LBJ could bully and cajole and mix it up with Congress. By contrast, the opinion was that "Obama is a far different person than Johnson. He is cool, cerebral and detached. Johnson was the earthy, insecure political seducer."[9] So perhaps, I thought, this was the occasion to make it clear that the 44th president was no naïf, not so new to the political game that he had no idea how it was played. He had a command of the levers of power. If he could make his point about the behavior of this insolent member of Congress, who knew what else he might do to overcome unreasonable partisan opposition to the policies he was elected to develop and implement?

Bad, bad idea, as I was quickly persuaded by others in the building. It was not Barack Obama's way. It sank us, even if only briefly, to the sorry level of the miserable character whose conduct we rightly found objectionable. And it was not impossible to imagine that once this sort of response passes for acceptable, a repetition of the same maneuver, and it's more dangerous expansion, becomes all the more likely. Barack Obama could achieve a great deal in his presidency, as I believe he did, and none of what he did required hardball of this kind.

The standard notion of government ethics does not have this sharp focus on the effects of political behavior on democratic practices and institutions. It is more typically a manual of dos and don'ts intended to prevent elected or other public officials from taking advantage of power for their own self-enrichment or personal gain. This anticorruption ethics is certainly important to the legitimacy of democratic self-rule. It protects public assets from plunder, our citizens from being "ripped off," and it is a needed defense against private interests using officeholder greed to buy them off and infect the government with their own policy preferences. We have a slew of laws and ethics rules in place to attack these threats.

They are of limited help in dealing with the dangers of a Nixon or Trump presidency. Nixon's Watergate crimes were political in nature, through and through, committed to vanquish his enemies in the pursuit of a second term. Nixon did not care all that much about money; Trump did—he always has—and critics rightly questioned the efficacy and transparency of the trust he established to hold his business interests during his presidency. His practices in charging the government for expensive lodging on his resort properties for the Secret Service and his hope to cash in by holding a major international conference at his Doral golf course resort were all ethically troubling to the core. Yet it is hard to imagine that Trump's greed, and his taste and aptitude for grift, will define for future generations what was most disturbing about his vision of the presidency and his conduct of the office.

The horrified reaction to Trump's norm-busting was mostly triggered by his contempt for institutions of self-governance as they must function in a democratic society. He expressed the view that as president he could do as he liked: his powers were unlimited. He chafed openly at the norm that law enforcement should operate independently of political influence. He delighted in getting around the Senate's constitutional process for confirming senior officials: he preferred to find ways he could install officials to his liking on an indefinite "acting" basis. He was surprised and angered that the justices and judges he appointed did not show the requisite loyalty by ruling in his favor in the ludicrous cases he brought to challenge his loss to Joe Biden in 2020.

Critics like Ben Wittes and Susan Hennessy have argued that Trump was not to be taken lightly as some amateur who blundered into the White House and had no idea what he was doing. He was redefining the presidency, imagining it as an "expressive" institution that serves only to amplify his voice and impose his will.[10] That is, in fact, the problem. A democratic institution subjugated to the will of the incumbent is no longer democratic, and it may no longer qualify as an institution. The Trump administration was more like the Trump Organization as it served its master's business interests. It was all about him, only about him, and not a "producing organization which belongs to its members, and it is the only such organization whose members include *all* the citizens within its jurisdiction."[11]

Until Trump, there was only sporadic attention to a political ethics dictated by a concern for the defense of democratic institutions. This view did surface in the 1990s, when congressional ethics commanded much attention and Dennis Thompson of Harvard's Kennedy School of Government pushed for institutions to come to the fore of the debate. "Legislative ethics," he wrote, "are not just about how members of Congress should behave but also about how a democratic process should function."[12] Individual wrongdoing was important enough, but if the institution itself had become a "shadowy world of implicit understandings, ambiguous favors, and political advantage,"[13] then the ethical problem was systemic. A revived set of ethical standards should "guide the actions of individuals, but only in their institutional roles and only insofar as necessary for the good of the institution."[14]

This is the cause for looking hard at systemic ethical corruption in these times, and the reasons for it. Its source tracks across generations, from Nixon to Trump; and from Joseph McCarthy to the MAGA insurgents in today's House of Representatives: a lack of understanding, or active contempt, for democratic institutions. It may be surprising that Nixon—who came to the presidency from a lifetime in politics, having served in the House, the Senate, and then as vice president—would be considered in this way like Trump, whose experience consisted of a controversial business empire and reality TV entertainment. Yet Nixon believed himself to be an outsider, never welcomed into the established inner circles of power. He thought that institutions to which he paid lip service were conspiring against him, and he needed to undermine and circumvent them to achieve his purposes. Once he could not count on the FBI to do his bidding and conduct illegal surveillance of his political opponents or "black bag" jobs to bring them down, he created his own private investigative team. This is how the Watergate burglary—a black bag operation if there ever was one—became possible.

Those who worked most closely for Nixon were more in the mold of Trump: recruited from careers in the private sector, ignorant about the role and normal operation of institutions, indifferent to anything but what was needed to achieve what their president wanted done. They could not make ethical choices because an ethical choice grounded in democratic sensibilities requires an appreciation of how that choice relates to institutional values and principles.

The ethical question—"what should I do?"—can only be answered with reference to those values and principles. If, however, that answer looks only to other goals and considerations—we have to win the election, we have to discredit the election we lost, we have to hound our enemies and undercut their capacity to be heard—it lacks the ethical vision that those in public life must share, honor, and strive to bring to life in concrete situations, if democratic institutions are to be maintained and nurtured.

Rebuttals to this line of argument usually begin with an appeal to realism in politics. It calls for an eyes-wide-open recognition that politics is always dirty, and that any moral limits reside at the very margins of political activity and are enforceable only—if at all—by criminal laws. In the extreme form, it allows for a vision of everyday politics that knows no bounds, making room for disregarding the law when the stakes are high enough.

Richard Nixon gave voice to that view when he was demanding that his aides arrange for a burglary and firebombing of the Brookings Institution where he believed that documents politically damaging to him were stored. He railed against those who "don't understand politics," who imagined that it was conducted in fidelity to "legal niceties." His rant bears full quotation, drawn from the tapes he was running in the office to record his every word:

> I want the break-in. Hell, they do that. You're to break into the place, rifle the files, and bring them in. . . . Just go in and take it. . . . Clean it up. These kids don't understand. They have no understanding of politics. They have no understanding of public relations. . . . Do you think, for

Christ sakes, that the *New York Times* is worried about all the legal niceties? The sons of bitches are killing me.[15]

"Politics," as he understood it, required doing what it took, whatever it took. His enemies did not respect those legal niceties, he declared, and so it was foolish to expect that he should. And he did not.

It now seems to me that the test of this ethics is not resisting a president's order to launch burglaries or arson. It is hardly a serious test of ethical fiber to balk at a flagrantly illegal order to commit an illegal attack on political adversaries. Better that someone speaks up rather than they don't, that they resist rather than give in; but better still that this moment does not arise because of all the decisions—or failure to make the right decisions—that brought it to pass. Nixon did not direct this criminal scheme out of the blue: he ran a White House in which this "understanding" of politics, namely, that one did what it took, was standard.

Nixon's aides did not execute that particular order, but when it was issued, no one in the room dissented, protested, walked out, or resigned. Other orders at other times to break the law would be followed, and in the ethical culture of the Nixon White House, this is hardly surprising.

A more tempered version of "that's politics" is often described as that of "dirty hands." A politician has grave responsibilities and has to dirty her hands to serve the people who elected her, or if appointed, in whose name she serves. She knows what she is doing is ethically fraught or condemnable, but she could not be responsible and fail to act as she does. It's a hard job and someone has to do it. In a famous article on the subject, the political theorist Michael Walzer asserts that "no one succeeds in politics without getting his hands dirty."[16] All that we can ask is that the politician take this action with appreciation that in one sense, she is doing wrong. Unlike Nixon, she respects the very limits that she, in a particular case and for good reasons, has to violate. She acknowledges and regrets what it is that she has to do. Not Nixon though, who was a dirty hands politician acting without regret, determined not to let his enemies get the better of him.

However, even if we credit the dirty hands politician with a moral conscience, we have to know what in the action or speech proposed or contemplated should trigger conscience. The "dirtied hands" are presumably at work on matters the politician reasonably believes to be in the public interest—not just, say, to win an election, or suppress the voice of opposition in the public debate. And even where there are grave policy issues at stake and the politician believes he has to play dirty to serve his constituency or the nation, what are the ethical issues and how are they to be weighed in proceeding?

This is where a rule-driven, anticorruption ethics go only so far in illuminating the path. Ethical sensibilities are partially a matter of character. Little can be expected of politicians who just lack it. For those possessing this character, what counts in the end is the quality of their judgment. The choice these politicians make may be controversial but at least they can be expected to be aware that there was a choice—and that they are responsible for it.

This applies not only to the seeming marquee ethical decisions, such as creating a government enemies list or refusing to concede a recount. A concern with the truth also matters: in words and not only action. "To speak is to govern."[17] Ethical speech is also ethical democratic politics and ethical government.

So when does "spin" become a serious and dangerous lie of consequence? Spin is fine: in politics, there is license for the best, most persuasive argument to be made for your side. A government that cannot distinguish the lie from the spin strains the foundation of trust between the rulers and the ruled. Each day in politics, numerous people work over press releases and statements and speeches, and the judgments they make about what constitutes an embellishment or exaggeration or sharp spin varies with the nature of the communications. Embellish a tribute to the deceased? Sure. Misrepresent the facts to win a policy fight or the case for war? No. And so much in between, all calling for speech that is ethically appropriate to the context and the medium. All the little things, which can later become big things.

In my experience, the little things that make up the writing of a speech or a comment to the press are not always, under the pressures of the moment, on the mind, or in focus, for the people who hold the pen or have their hands on the keyboard. There are now books and articles pouring out with despair about a posttruth politics, and to be sure, it is a major problem for the democracy, complex in its development. It is powered as never before by the possibilities presented by social media; its dangers have increased with the capacity enabled by microtargeting to sneak false messages to target audiences. What can be done about it is occupying creative minds, and so far, the solution seems out of reach, caught between anxieties about free speech and a likely hopeless chase to catch up with and curb the evolving technologies.

It does not minimize these alarming new dangers to remain concerned with the less spectacular assaults on truth in daily political life. The responsibility for this rests with the many people responsible day by day for political speech. The absence of a robust accountability for speech is, in part, the worry that any more muscular protection against political lies will be costly to First Amendment freedoms. We are asked to accept that the answer to bad speech is more speech, and to expect that bad speech will eventually crumble under the weight of exposure. There isn't all that much reason to hold onto that hope—nothing in our political history, particularly recent history, would give us that reason—but it is also an excuse for failing to argue for an ethics of political speech.

The case of George Santos stands out as an example of how our political ethics struggles with the outright lie. Santos was found to have lied his way through his campaign for the House, which was successful: it was hard to find one aspect of his life, professional or personal, he did not lie about to the voters. One might think that the House of Representatives ethics code would speak to an ethical calamity on this scale. It allows for members to be disciplined for behavior, including behavior prior to assuming office, that brings discredit on the institution. Santos was brought before the Ethics Committee, but it would only judge Santos on those falsehoods that would involve potential violations of law, such as the failure to meet his personal financial or campaign finance disclosure requirements. The pure lies about everything else was not the sort of offense against the institution the House had the will to address. These persuasive falsehoods somehow did not bring discredit on the institution.

Lying is not a topic covered in the Executive Branch Code of Ethics for Government Service. This code does touch on certain questions of ethics in speech, and the way it does so is revealing about what utterances of those in power it takes to be ethically consequential. It bars "private promises of any kind binding upon the duties of the office" and commands that, "wherever discovered," corruption be "expose[d]."[18] That is all. The knowing falsification of a communication made in the course of official duties is absent from the code's proscriptions.

Another ethical issue in political speech, much in the news, is that of "civility"—a certain decorum and restraint in the expression of one's views or response to those of others. Donald Trump was the first president to specialize in insult and personal abuse. Partisans clashing over issues they care about in a charged, polarized politics are resorting ever more visibly, and with less shame or evident consequence, to the same incivility. Members of Congress scream at the president of the United States during a State of the Union address. Vitriol is the rhetorical order of the day.

The ethical stakes in the loss of civility implicate the very viability of democratic conversation. Incivility breaks off conversation, leaves any reasoned exchange with nowhere to go. As one thoughtful political philosopher has noted, it is not necessary in valuing civility—"mere civility"—that one must concede the validity of the adversary's views or show those views, however odious, respect. However, the adversary must be heard, and the conversation must continue, which leaves open the chance that, if only as a distant possibility, it will take a productive turn. Civility in this sense is "an essential virtue of . . . deliberative democracy."[19] Democratic politics requires taking a bet on that.

In this way, the lie and incivility as unethical speech are closely linked to speech that is more generally associated with attacks on the democratic order, like those of a politician withholding a concession in a lost election on a claim that he, in fact, won it. This is just speech, but even if it is not followed by legal action to vindicate the claim, or more speech to rally supporters to violent protest, this speech is a problem of political ethics. It reflects, as does incivility and many kinds of lies, an unwillingness to bet on democratic institutions and norms.

In its most virulent form, speech on the order of pure demagoguery is a program of speech striking at the heart of the democratic order. The demagogue, it has been said, is the "enemy of democracy."[20] This politician weaves falsehoods into a divisive appeal for support that would elevate them to being the sole true expression of "the people." Free and fair elections and the willingness to abide by them, along with respect for facts and acknowledgment of the legitimate opposition, are all swept away in the person of the demagogue who blends in their appeal lies, incivility, and an attack on democratic institutions.

The consequence is not just to the quality of speech in democratic debate. Demagogic speech, as the expression of unbounded devotion to self-interest, goes hand in hand with the demagogue's resistance to institutional and legal limits on his power. The demagogue may, as he sees fit, "threaten an outright . . . break with established rules of conduct, institutions, and even the law."[21] When an adversary demanded that he heed the state constitution, the Louisiana governor and first-class demagogue Huey Long infamously responded: "I'm the constitution around here now."[22] To violate or circumvent the law, the demagogue believes that he requires only the proclaimed validation of the "people" who stand behind him.

The demagogue's ultimate aims lead relentlessly toward the maintenance of high-pitched rhetoric and its ready escalation. If constitutional laws and legal limits must give way, so too must the objections and opposition of adversaries. The demagogue specializes in lashing out. Former senator Joseph McCarthy specialized in personal attacks guided by a belief that, as his leading biographer has written, he was required "when attacked [to] return a blow twice as hard."[23] Like Trump.

When the partisans perceive their interests and values are under extreme threat, they are susceptible to the call of the demagogue. The appeal to ethics in speech and action leaves them cold.

So where is there found any possibility of ethical renewal in our politics? It starts with the recognition that it can contribute to the defense of our democracy, with the emphasis on "contribution" and no attempt to suggest that salvation lies in that direction. But without it, any prospect of arresting the deteriorating conditions of democratic debate and engagement seems fanciful. Political reforms have their place, but it is evident from every measure of public trust in institutions that those reforms cannot bear the weight of reversing its steep decline over many decades. The political theorist and commentator Bill Galston understates the case when he writes of liberal democracy that "the operation of liberal institutions and the functioning of liberal society are affected in important ways by the character and beliefs of individuals (and leaders) within the liberal polity."[24] Though I would remove the parentheses he placed around the reference to "leaders."

The next step is to take ethical issues seriously and bring them into the contemporary debate about democracy reform.

CHAPTER 12

Ethical Action in Politics

After the 2020 election, I commit myself to bipartisan political reform, even as I remain a committed Democrat, and get ready for 2024. Cochairing President Biden's Presidential Commission on the Supreme Court, I study and observe with dismay how poor ethical choices in our politics damage the standing of one branch of government that had maintained high levels of public trust for years. I join with Republicans as well as Democrats to support reform of Congress's role in the last stage of our presidential elections and protect against a repetition of the January 6, 2021, assault on the Capitol. Also working across the partisan divide, I participate in programs to defend election officials under attack in this era of election denialism.

My father came to the United States in the 1940s, and by early 1953, he was an American citizen and an official at the Voice of America (VOA), an international broadcast operation within the Department of State that provided news and other programming to overseas audiences in the service of United States foreign policy interests. He had first entered government service during the war; as a native Austrian, he was chosen to broadcast news of the D-Day invasion in 1944 to German-speaking audiences overseas. He embraced his new country passionately.

By 1953, he also found himself caught up in the anti-Communist McCarthy crusades of the 1950s, testifying before Joe McCarthy's Senate Permanent Subcommittee on Investigations to establish his loyalty to this country. Another VOA official had complained to the committee that my father's Latin American programming—in particular a radio program titled "Eye of the Eagle"—was ineffective in communicating an anti-Communist perspective and a waste of money. He had suggested that my father's performance reflected "stupidity," but he also implied that something "worse" could explain these failures. McCarthy asked whether the witness thought "individuals"—such as my father—"responsible for the type of material put out were loyal to America, and want to give the truth about this country to the rest of the world, or what type of individuals do you feel they are?" The witness replied that while he could not say that my father was a "subversive," "because I have no proof of that," he also did not think "[my father] saw the truth of the country as we did in the Latin American Division."[1]

My father was an immigrant who spoke with a heavy accent that stayed with him for the rest of his life, and now a question had been raised about whether he was truly American, whether he "saw the truth" of his adopted country the way real Americans did. At one point, my mother picked up the phone in my parents' New York City apartment to hear an anonymous caller ask whether her husband was a Communist. My father demanded to be heard before the committee.

On March 6, 1953, he testified. But before he entered the hearing room, he was summoned to a private conversation with the committee's chief counsel, the notorious Roy Cohen. This does not have to go badly for you, Cohen told him, but it would help if you helped identify others in the VOA whose loyalty might be an issue and should be investigated. My father rejected this insidious offer to save himself by casting suspicion on others, and he proceeded to testify.

The hearing went well. My father defended himself in detail and ably on the merits, as the transcript shows, and McCarthy retreated. Toward the close of the questioning, he disingenuously stated for the record, in a comment directed to my father: "You do understand that no one here has accused you of being pro-Communist or un-American or anything of that kind. You do understand that, do you?"[2]

What seems to have made all the difference in McCarthy's decision not to persist in smearing my father was the choice made by Senator Karl Mundt of North Dakota. Mundt was a hard-core Republican conservative with few beliefs in common with my Democratic parents who adored, as the senator certainly did not, FDR. But it was Mundt who pressed the committee to afford my father the opportunity to answer the charge against him, and it was Mundt who came to my father's defense during his testimony. The senator credited his testimony as effective and stressed that "we are not in a position to doubt" his loyalty. "I would like to lay this one on ice and see if we cannot find something a little bit more important."[3] McCarthy was stung and it was then that he began to pull back, hurried the hearing to a conclusion, and affirmed that my father should not consider his patriotism to have been doubted. Whatever my father would think of Mundt's politics, he would never forget that in that episode, Mundt chose the ethically responsible choice: to make sure that an accused person had the chance to respond and, at least in this instance, to separate himself from the groundless smear that McCarthy and his counsel Cohen were pursuing.

It was during this toxic period in American politics that a group of Americans came together in 1954 in what might seem a quixotic venture to challenge unethical McCarthyite politics and uphold standards for democratic debate. Viciousness in the political dialogue was a recurring subject of anxious discussion in editorial pages and even in congressional hearings. One of the hearings, chaired by Iowa Senator Guy Gillette, resulted in the recommendation that "a continuing committee of eminent members of both parties, working jointly for higher and cleaner standards of campaigning, can do as much as the enactment of laws to rid this nation of abuses which are reaching alarming proportions."[4] The committee that came into existence was the Fair Campaign Practices Committee.

The committee's board members included businessmen, newspaper publishers, lawyers, former members of Congress and party leaders, clergy, and the honorary cochairs were two former presidents, Harry Truman and Dwight D. Eisenhower. Their focus was campaigns, and one of their publications, a booklet titled *Fair Play in Politics*, carried an epigraph from the nineteenth-century British politician and writer John Morley: "Those who would treat politics and morality apart will never understand the one or the other."[5]

The committee could do nothing more than attempt to elevate the significance of ethics in politics, and particularly in political campaigning. Its role was "wholly educational—to enable voters (and future voters) to spot smear tactics when they are used, and to encourage study and thought about campaign tactics."[6] It went about its business in three ways: establishing, promoting, and challenging candidates and parties to commit to a Code of Fair Campaign Practices; setting up a procedure for receiving complaints for violations of the code and providing those accused of violations the opportunity to answer those charges; and in an especially ambitious move, offering in conjunction with the American Arbitration Association a process for candidates to seek arbitration of disputes over code violations.

The code reflected a specific concern with McCarthyite demagoguery, calling on candidates to desist from "malicious or unfounded accusations . . . which aim at creating or exploiting doubts, without justification, as to [an opponent's] loyalty and patriotism." Also encompassed within the code were prohibitions on racial or religious prejudice.[7]

These and other ethical requirements under the code applied to how candidates would argue the case against opponents. The code also called for attention to the "right of every qualified American voter to full and equal participation in the electoral process," and to any "unethical practice which tends to corrupt or undermine our American system of free elections or which hampers or prevents the full and free expression of the will of the voters."[8] In this way the code sought to limit how candidates might conduct a winning campaign against another—how they present the reasons why they, and not their opponents, were the best choice—but also how campaign ethics had to be understood within the broader context of the rights of voters and the "system of free elections" as a whole.

And so what? The committee did not have a long run. By 1974, its doors had to close, the money having dried up. Perhaps it could not outlast the fall of Joe McCarthy. Its time and influence were limited.

That is not the whole story. During the period that it was active, it could claim some success in keeping the question of campaign ethics alive. The major party chairs signed on, professing agreement with the code, and candidates availed themselves of the chance to complain—and to publicize their complaints—about their opponents' and opposing party's conduct in alleged ethical violations. The committee encouraged news organizations to cover those complaints. The press responded with some useful coverage. It treated the committee as meaningful, notwithstanding that it was constrained in what it could do to enforce its code. In reporting on one such complaint in 1971, the *St. Louis Post Dispatch* noted that, while lacking enforcement power, the committee's code has been accepted [in national campaigns] as the campaign standard by the Democrats and Republicans."[9]

Fifty years later, this whole episode may seem quaint, if not slightly ridiculous. Not to me, as I consider that I started my career when American politics was undergoing the most comprehensive reform in the nation's history and, some four decades later, here we are: our institutions at ever lower levels of public trust, and declining. Polls suggest that a sizable number of Americans, not a majority but fast closing in on one, doubt that democracy, as they observe and experience it, has much to offer.

To some commentators, retaining a sturdy confidence in legal reform, the answer lies in better, more innovative reform, updated to meet the demands of the era. Much is under discussion, in books and papers, and in conferences held around the country: gerrymandering, the institution of new forms of voting like ranked choice, the revision of communications laws to impose more accountability on social media platforms for the mis- and disinformation they carry, refreshed regulation of money in politics, and more. And, certainly, this is valuable work. Some good may well come of it.

It is not enough. We need political ethics—we need to care about political ethics—to go with our fascination with the rules of politics. In a splendid little book, *Ethics: The Art of Character*, Gregory Beabout writes:

> Problems arise when ethics is conceived only in terms of rules. Life is complex, so no set of rules can be specific enough to cover every circumstance. A rule-based approach tends to encourage searching for loopholes and "gaming the system." Rules can conflict, and often require interpretation. If ethics is nothing but rules, then further rules

will be needed to decide what to do when rules and interpretations conflict. Such problems show why it can be seen as better to understand ethics having to do, first and foremost, with character.[10]

In the years after I left full-time law practice, reflecting on the steady erosion of democratic norms and practices and my own experiences as a political lawyer, it seemed that ethics in politics had to be taken seriously, not dismissed as a fantasy. It made no sense to speak of norms and not appreciate that the maintenance and defense of democratic norms is, in very real and practical terms, a matter of ethics—a matter of what political actors *should* do, rather than just what the law, which can only reach so far, *requires* them to do. And the ethics of paramount concern in our time is an ethics attentive to the protection of democratic institutions and norms.

By definition it cannot be the work of only one party or system of political beliefs. Democrats have to find Republicans who might fight them on every major public policy issue but are open to a discussion of political ethics in this period of trial for our democracy. If the members of the two parties can find enough common ground for this conversation, then those Americans who identify as independents might join in.

This is how I have come to spend a lot of time in recent years on nonpartisan democratic reform, after a very long spell as a committed partisan warrior. I am still a Democrat, very much so, and I will continue to do what I can to help elect Democrats to the White House, Congress, and other offices around the country. But at this time, democracy reform cannot succeed as a one-party endeavor. I have joined with others, Republicans and independents, in the defense of democratic institutions and norms. The work includes legal reform, but it often has an explicit component to shore up ethical standards for the conduct of politics. This brand of reform reinforces failing norms, directs attention to them, and brings more clearly to light the ethical considerations on which the defense of those norms inevitably rests.

One such reform initiative, the Electoral Count Reform Act (ECRA), has brought me together with Jack Goldsmith, who was one of my most prominent critics during the war powers controversy around

Libya in 2011. We have also worked together and with others on reform of the presidency to make it less likely that an aspiring autocrat can take advantage of the office's awesome power to undermine the democracy.

I have found in Jack, formerly assistant attorney general in the George W. Bush administration, a superb advocate for the reasoned, ethical defense of democratic norms and practices in the Trump years. He has written a much-admired article in the *Atlantic*, succinctly capturing the assault on norms Trump has made famous as almost the signature feature of his government:

> Donald Trump is a norm-busting president, . . . without parallel in American history [who] told scores of easily disprovable public lies; he has shifted back and forth and back again on his policies, often contradicting Cabinet officials along the way; he has attacked the courts, the press, his predecessor, his former electoral opponent, members of his party, the intelligence community, and even his own attorney general; he has failed to release his tax returns or to fill senior political positions in many agencies; he has shown indifference to ethics concerns; he has regularly interjected a self-regarding political element into apolitical events; he has monetized the presidency by linking it to his personal business interests; and he has engaged in cruel public behavior.[11]

Jack did not stop there, but also warned that the response to Trump from the bureaucracy, the courts, and the press could fall into the danger of fighting fire with fire—norm-busting to counter norm-busting. He understood that "these institutions have risen up to check a president they fear. But in some instances, they have defied their own norms, and harmed themselves and the nation in the process. Unfortunately, many of these norm violations will be hard to reverse."[12] Officials in the executive branch, horrified that Trump leaked intelligence intercepts and other confidential information, committed to taking steps within the government, including hiding and altering documents, to thwart him. Goldsmith expressed concern that judges rushed opinions to constrain Trump, as on immigration issues, slighting the care and self-restraint indispensable to their judicial craft and institutional norms. Members of the press decided that norms of objective coverage could not be afforded or honored to the same degree when confronted with the threat that was Trump.

Jack had well-publicized occasion to absorb in the course of government service the issues involved in preserving norms, and by doing so, institutional integrity and accountability. He had joined the Bush administration in 2003 as the Senate-confirmed assistant attorney general heading the Office of Legal Counsel, the office within the Department of Justice that opines on major executive branch legal issues presented for analysis by the White House or government agencies. He was immediately confronted with White House pressure to find legal authority for controversial "war on terror" counterterrorism measures, such as the application of international law to the treatment of Iraqi terrorists held in their country and the international and domestic legal constraints on techniques used to interrogate terrorist suspects. He famously stood his ground against this pressure, an experience he recounted in his book *The Terror Presidency*.

One such stand, which unsettled White House senior staff and enraged the counsel to Vice President Cheney, was his withdrawal of the "torture memos," referred to within the bureaucracy as "enhanced interrogation techniques," on the basis that they were seriously lacking in legal grounding. Jack firmly believed that he had to play his part, as a senior government official, in

> try[ing] to build, sensible and durable institutions that allow the terror presidency to meet this threat within a scheme of democratic accountability. Ultimately, however, our constitutional democracy will not be preserved by better laws and institutional structures, but rather . . . by leaders, with a commitment to the consent of the governed who have checks and balances stitched into their breasts.[13]

Jack was the ideal partner to pursue reforms that would highlight and, where possible, restore failing norms in the aftermath of the wreckage of the Trump years. Together we wrote a book, published in 2020, titled *After Trump*, and laid out a reform program in detail across a broad range of problems that Trump and many of his predecessors had exposed in the norms and law constraining the presidency. And once we had finished the book, we set up an organization, the Presidential Reform Project, to identify realistic priorities among these reforms and, along with others, pursue them.

The law can be reformed to address presidential abuses of power. It can, for example, restrict in important ways the partisan misuse of the Department of Justice and the power to pardon. There are constitutional limits to be reckoned with in designing reforms, but it is possible to revise the criminal laws to subject the president to liability for obstruction of justice. While these reforms are of the utmost importance, they can affect some conduct and not others: they cannot fully answer the threat of a president who decides to pervert the mission of a Justice Department committed to the rule of law. In the end, those who populate our executive branch in positions of authority have to make the sort of decisions that many of Richard Nixon's cabinet members and aides did not. They have to step in when things are going wrong, but before the worst has happened. They have to uphold norms through sound ethical decisions when a choice has to be made.

There are ways that these ethical responsibilities can be defined. Jack and I have proposed that the Department of Justice strengthen by regulation the ethical standards that its officials must follow. In September of 2021, we wrote to the attorney general to urge revisions of the department's ethical guidelines so that it is clear that their lawyers "answer not to partisan politics but to principles of fairness and justice." We also recommended that department regulations be amended so that the current prohibition on the misuse of official authority target any "improper partisan political purpose of influencing an election to public office."[14] As of 2023, this has not yet happened: we will keep trying.

One might fairly ask: what possible difference can the lofty formulations make to the day-to-day performance of government officials? There is meaning in every articulation of ethical standards. Often, they begin at the highest level of generalization, but they are there to be cited, to be relied on, when there is a question about whether to accept, reject, or modify a proposed course of action. And they are there to be used by others, in the watchdog community or Congress, in arguing the case that the administration is not adhering to its own ethical commitments.

In our work together on the ECRA, Jack and I co-chaired a bipartisan working group hosted by the American Law Institute (ALI). The group consisted of an even number of Democrats and Republicans who recognized that the 1877 law governing the congressional electoral count, which was a mess of a statute, was a standing invitation to more calamities on the order of January 6.[15] In a matter of months, we reached agreement on principles to guide reform, and it was well received by members of Congress such as (among others) Senators Susan Collins, Amy Klobuchar, and Joe Manchin, who were exploring what would be possible in a bipartisan initiative. On behalf of the ALI group, Jack and I worked with senators and staff, with allied organizations and individuals, and on testimony before the Senate.

The ECRA settles for good certain questions we should not have had to ask, such as whether the vice president of the United States, as urged by Donald Trump, can simply reject the electoral count from the states and demand that state legislatures reconsider who won the election. It does more than that. It expresses an expectation of how democratic institutions must operate in the all-critical democratic moment of presidential selection, communicating this message to Congress, state legislatures, and the courts. In clarifying their various roles—a constitutional map of sorts—it necessarily directs the attention of political actors to their own choices.

To this end, the reformed law sharply increases the number of members from each chamber whose objections to a state's certification of the winner require Congress to formally consider their complaint—from just one each in the House and Senate to no less than 20 percent. Objections failing to meet the threshold fall by the wayside. This is meant, of course, to rule out objections that are either frivolous or lacking substantial support. Along with specifying the kind of objections deemed acceptable, this reform sends a norm-fortifying message: Congress does not decide elections, the voters do, and members pondering objections intended to cancel out voter choice as certified by the states are on notice that they should advance serious arguments to support them. Every objection a member considers will have to be evaluated not only against the specific legal requirements, but against this overall goal of the reform: the people, not the politicians, decide.

In 2024, Jack and I joined again with others in an ALI working group to address reform of another statute long recognized to be antiquated and potentially dangerous: the Insurrection Act. Federal law provides that armed forces are not to be used "to execute the laws," except in cases "expressly authorized by the Constitution or act of Congress."[16] The Act is one such express authorization. It dates back to the 18th century and confers on the president apparently unlimited authority to deploy troops within the United States to quell insurrections and rebellions, but also more vaguely worded threats, such as unlawful "assemblages," "combinations," and "obstructions." This language lacking any settled or accepted meaning, together with the absence of other measures to ensure executive accountability, invites executive overreach and abuse. The working group assembled to consider the issue included retired senior members of the military and others who held high-level positions in both Democratic and Republican administrations, including both the Obama and Trump administrations. Our purpose was to call attention to the basic flaws in the statute—its dangers irrespective of who controlled the White House at any time—without centering the debate on Donald Trump and his advisers who have displayed an alarming interest in potential misuses of the law. And we did reach an agreement, released in April 2024, of broad principles to govern Insurrection Act reform, which included the elimination of vague terms; more clarity on the conditions for a president's invocation of the statute; requirements for consultation with the Congress and the states within which deployments would be made; and time limits on deployments without congressional authorization.[17] This reform initiative was a further demonstration that these conversations can take place productively among people with very different political backgrounds and views.

The work I have done with Jack Goldsmith on the ECRA, the Insurrection Act, and other reforms has been Washington-directed, centered on executive branch norms, ethics, and legal reform. But this is not a mission that can take place only in Washington. On key issues, it has to penetrate into communities across the country. An example is the work of state and local election officials who bear the responsibility of ensuring access to the polls, and an accurate vote count, for all eligible voters. It is in these communities that I have joined with a lifelong and committed Republican, Benjamin Ginsberg, to support election officials around the country who have come under attack by partisans for just doing their job impartially and in fidelity to professional standards.

I met Ben in 1982 when he and I were on opposite sides of a contest over election results in an Idaho congressional race. Congress can hear such cases under the Federal Contest Elections Act, and in the course of this Idaho proceeding, I defended the victory of Democratic congressman Richard Stallings against a Republican challenge. Ben was a young lawyer on the challenger's legal team. As I was arguing my case, I spotted him in the audience giving me what I would call, and construed at the time to be, unfavorable "audience reaction" to my presentation. I would not quite charge him with making faces at me—but whatever it was, it was distracting, and afterward I complained to the partner in charge of the Republican crew of lawyers. Ben then called me to clear the air. It was thoroughly cleared—perhaps I overreacted, who knows?—and we became friendly adversaries.

In 2012, we faced each other as general counsels to opposing presidential campaigns, Barack Obama's and Mitt Romney's. When the election ended, President Obama decided that he would set up by executive order a commission to study administrative problems with the conduct of elections. His primary concern was the long lines and hours of waiting some voters experienced at some polling places in the 2012 general election. Because long lines are a symptom of a host of other administrative problems election officials face, the commission was to study them all and report back in a year after field hearings around the country.

The president asked me to cochair the commission, reserving the other cochairmanship for a Republican. I recall the doubt expressed at the Obama White House and elsewhere that Ben would agree to do this so soon after a hard loss in the presidential election. I know from experience that the pain of this disappointment takes time to ease. There was also the possibility that Republicans would have little use for

Ben's agreement to serve on a commission on a political topic—election administration—established by a Democratic president.

Ben accepted the president's request that he serve on the commission. He did so because he believed that the parties had to support a basic proposition, one without which the "right to vote" is bled of its fullest meaning: voters are owed nonpartisan, professional administration of the elections, which gives full effect to voting rights, from registration through voting days to the vote count. He exhibited the courage of his conviction then, and again in 2020, when on the eve of the presidential election, he published a now-famous opinion piece in the *Washington Post* calling out the nominee of his party for an "all-out, multimillion-dollar effort to disenfranchise the voters—first by seeking to block state laws to ease voting during the pandemic, and now, in the final stages of the campaign, by challenging the ballots of individual voters unlikely to support him." This attack on the right to vote, Ben wrote, "is as un-American as it gets."[18]

The ten-member commission Ben and I cochaired in 2013 and 2014 was bipartisan in composition and those appointed had experience in election administration—or, in the case of the vice president of Disney theme parks, a special expertise in the administrative challenge of managing long lines! We held public hearings in four states, meeting with election officials and listening to voters, and we heard from other experts across the country. We produced for President Obama a bipartisan report with concrete recommendations, such as management techniques for shortening lines, which if followed would improve election administration for the benefit of all voters. Philanthropies offered to fund, and then did finance, an implementation program involving close cooperation with election officials of both parties.

In this time, Ben and I became fast friends. We could hold very different political opinions—to understate the point—and yet we shared a respect for political differences and for the democratic process that led us to new joint undertakings beginning in 2021.

One such project was the establishment and cochairmanship of the Election Official Legal Defense Network (EOLDN). EOLDN makes available pro bono lawyers to assist election officials in defending themselves against personal threats and extraordinary partisan political pressure to run elections the way preferred by politicians. Hundreds of lawyers and major national firms have signed up around the country to provide this service. This is not legal reform, but an expression of a commitment to democracy on the part of Democrats and Republicans alike. In defending these election officials without regard to party affiliation, these lawyers are upholding an ethics of public service. Election officials who resist political pressure in the performance of their duties are acting ethically—where the relevant ethical considerations are those concerned with the integrity of the democratic process.

Our work in support of election officials has led to our forming and again cochairing another nonprofit, nonpartisan program—Pillars of the Community. The Pillars project is intended to help build coalitions at the state and local level, among ordinary citizens, who despite their political differences share a commitment to free elections and to professional, nonpartisan election administration. The public hears often enough from partisans, and they need to hear the defense of democratic norms and practices from those who run local businesses, preach or minister at local religious institutions, head up the local community college, and otherwise command the respect of their fellow citizens. In partnership with other organizations sharing the same goal, we are recruiting these leaders—the "Open Pillars"—for ongoing dialogues with election officials. By fully understanding and helping to explain to the public what these officials are doing to serve the voters of these communities, these leaders can do much to break through the partisan shouting and bullying and build critically important support for the democratic process.

This work Ben and I have done together and with others has no end date. It will go on as long as we have conflict over the integrity and quality of our election systems, and it appears that this conflict, even if it does not worsen, will continue to fester in the polarized politics of the times. It is encouraging that so many organizations, a few of them newly formed and others well established, have sprung up to do the work of strengthening and defending our voting systems.

And while the problem to be solved has to be attacked from various directions, the role of individual ethical choice is always central. In 2023,

Ben and I headed up an American Law Institute working group, modeled after the one Jack Goldsmith and I co-chaired on electoral count reform, to collaborate with election officials on a model ethics code for their profession. Officials from both parties participated in both the development of the code and the drafting of its provisions, and the venture relied crucially on the leadership of senior research director Charles Stewart III, an MIT political scientist and expert on election administration. The code this group developed was adopted and then published through ALI in January 2024. Our hope is that, together with other work of this kind, including an important project by a national association of election officials, the Election Center, the code will reinforce public understanding that election administration is professional, not political work—that those who do it aspire to the highest standards of impartiality, integrity, and professional excellence. This professionalism, expressed in clear ethical commitments, is indispensable in the defense against poisonous polarization and its threat to public confidence in our voting systems.

There is perhaps no more serious development than the effects of polarization on the Supreme Court of the United States, which have included claims by its severest critics that the court is suffering a crisis of legitimacy.

Of course, the root of it all is the Court's power, and its intervention to resolve through the decisions of nine individuals major social, political, and cultural issues on which Americans are deeply split. President Biden's Commission on the Supreme Court, which I cochaired along with Yale Law professor Cristina Rodriguez, stressed that "[t]he role the Court plays in major political and social conflicts has long made its composition and jurisprudence subjects of debate in the nation's civic life."[19] And this is true, too, of the angry battles over nominations to the Court in the last year of the Obama administration through the Trump years: "Throughout American history, including in recent decades, conflict over the Court has played out with varying degrees of intensity in the processes by which the President nominates and the Senate confirms new Justices."[20] The ethics of those charged with upholding the norms buckle under intense struggles over power, and so go the norms themselves.

As usual, partisans will accuse each other of firing the first shot in the escalating wars over the Court. Not all such accounts are entitled to equal weight. On the account I believe to be the correct one, the Republican Senate majority committed an egregious offense against norms by entirely ignoring President Obama's nomination of Merrick Garland to succeed Antonin Scalia: no hearing, no debate, no vote. The reason given was that in the case of an election year vacancy, the voters should be heard. The constitutional process of nomination followed by Senate consideration was abandoned.

Trump won, and the Gorsuch nomination replaced Garland's; but when another election year vacancy developed, upon the death of Ruth Bader Ginsburg, the Senate Republicans decided to rush the nomination of Amy Coney Barrett ahead of voter choice only months off. The argument Republicans had advanced in 2016 somehow lost its force for them in 2020, when the nomination was theirs to make, the seat theirs to fill.

Had arguments like these been heard before in the history of the Court, when a congressional majority wished to prevent a president from having a nominated justice confirmed? The history indicates that, yes, there were maneuvers like this—not quite the same, but close. No one could make the case that it was the norm, defensible on constitutional principle, and the problems with it are obvious, which is that this constitutional defiance of the president's authority to make nominations for Senate consideration may itself become the norm. If the "voters should be heard" is an exception to the constitutional process by which presidents nominate and the Senate considers Supreme Court nominations, then it may follow that an appeal to the opinions of the voting public is not confined to presidential election years. Why not also after midterms when a president fares poorly, or if she suffers consistently poor public opinion polling on her job performance? Or the pendency (see chapter 8) of an impeachment process? And the argument on principle collapses completely when the same majority embracing it chucks it altogether when their party comes into control of the presidency.

The controversies outside the Court began to erupt inside it. For the first time ever, someone with access to the most confidential Court records leaked a draft opinion of a pending decision—the Court majority to overrule *Roe v. Wade*. Was the leaker hoping to rally public pressure on the Court to retreat from this position? Or to apply pressure to stand firm on wavering justices in the majority? Either way, the Court's commitment to confidentiality was breached presumably by someone convinced, on whichever side of the issue, that ethics had to take a back seat in emergency circumstances. More support for Jack Goldsmith's argument in the *Atlantic*, that norm-busting can become a two-player game.

Other ethical issues have confronted the Court as questions have been raised about its commitment to basic ethical responsibility, such as avoiding conflicts of interest or the appearance of partiality. Much of the public reporting and commentary has focused on Justice Thomas and his acceptance of undisclosed gifts and hospitality by a longtime friend whose conservative politics included affiliation with organizations active before the Court. In part the concern was the absence of disclosure, and in part the purported failure by the justice to see that these financial ties might present questions of impartiality. These same concerns drove criticisms of the justice's continued participation in consideration of 2020 election challenges brought before the Court while his wife was active in election denialism. Republicans countered by arguing that other justices, among them Democratic appointees, had also committed ethical infractions or shown comparably poor judgment in failing to safeguard the Court's integrity.

The bipartisan Biden Commission was directed to study and report on these and other issues in the role and operation of the Court. It was not called on to make recommendations, only to provide a critical analysis of reform proposals, of which "court packing" was only one. It did, however, seek to be truly critical, indicating where it could on a unanimous basis the strengths or evident weaknesses of particular arguments. On the issue of Court ethics, it pointed clearly in a specific direction: the Court's adoption of a code of ethics, which "could promote important institutional values."[21] Even if the Court were left to self-regulate, determining on its own how to encourage compliance and address apparent violations, "experience in other contexts suggests that the adoption of an advisory code would be a positive step on its own."

The commission was far from the first of the voices calling on the Court to adopt a code. The Court balked, seemingly unwilling to give in to public pressure. Then, in November of 2023, it relented and published a Code of Conduct. It was a step in the right direction, but the Court could not resist introducing the code with a "Statement" attributing to its critics a "misunderstanding" of its posture on ethics. The rules and principles in the code were not "for the most part . . . new: the Court has long had the equivalent of common law ethics rules."[22] It also largely built its code around general principles and maintained for each individual justice the discretion to apply them. For example, the Biden Commission had noted the consensus among scholars and judicial reformers that, in anticipating and addressing financial conflicts of interests, the justices should not own individual, publicly traded securities. No such restriction made it into the code that the Court adopted.

Still, the code was something, in an era when that is decidedly better than nothing.

The Court has now joined other governing institutions in the crisis of democratic distrust in which the country finds itself in the third decade of the twenty-first century. The source of these difficulties has been the flouting of norms, achieved by a series of specific choices by institutional actors. A Senate majority's refusal to even consider a president's nomination on a basis which it then disregarded when it suited its own purposes. The Court's lapse into internal conflicts, reflected in the leaked opinion draft, mirrors the divisions and ethical free-for-all in the other governing institutions. The justices' resistance to adopting, then producing a tepid version of, an ethics code.

Each choice or decision provoked yet another, and the Court, no longer high above the political muck, has seen public confidence in its operations plunge. By 2023, the Court that has long looked to stay out of sordid political battles had begun sinking deeply into them.

In worrying about the ethical failures that have produced this sad state of affairs, I run up against an objection that haunts my own conversations and actions on this subject. I am confronted with the complaint that the times call for a toughness of mind and a hard practicality, that the other side is not playing by ethical rules and will run over opponents lost in fairy tales about an ethical politics. What is needed, it is argued, is a version of what some political scientists refer to as "militant democracy." In this view, a democracy under siege must protect itself. It may mean taking steps that, in more ordinary times, would be unthinkable: ruling out of bounds political speech that promotes hate or engenders fear of physical harm, or banning forms of nonviolent political activity that pose a threat under contemporary conditions to the democratic order. It may involve steps of a lesser but still fundamentally militant nature, such as accepting that, in emergency circumstances, the observance of norms may have to be suspended in order to protect democratic institutions in the long run.

This has caused some Democrats and progressives to ask—why not just "pack" the Court with more justices to remedy the norm-breaking power play by which a Republican Senate majority added Justices Gorsuch and Barrett? As court packing supporters see it, two can play the norm-busting game: it is intolerable that one side would allow the other to play it and not answer in kind. Two members of the Supreme Court commission I cochaired made the public case for it. They contended that this harsh medicine is the only answer to illegitimate appointments, the conservative policies infecting the Court's decisions, and what they viewed as the antidemocratic character of those decisions. And if, they and others have argued, the first round of packing does not work as intended, there is always another round or more to go, as needed.

This is the case for court packing. Those in positions of power, who might act on those arguments, have basic choices to consider. What would it mean for the Court, and the democratic system as a whole, if the party in control of Congress engages in systematic court packing to rectify past norm-breaking and to reshape its ideological composition? Of course, once this begins—in the name of exigent conditions—it is far from clear where it ends. The attacks on the Court might cease being temporary as it becomes a routine target of political intervention. Each party in control of the presidency and the Senate would have the accepted option of adding justices, as deemed necessary. The norm of "forbearance"—resisting certain uses of political power that pose a danger to the democratic process—rests on the very specific decision whether to adopt this course of action.

Of course, Congress bears a large share of responsibility for the woes besetting the Court. The confirmation process is in shambles, a partisan sideshow that has brought discredit to the Congress and shadowed, fairly or unfairly, the justices who emerged from it. The commission heard testimony from a former senior Senate aide, Jeffrey Peck, who consulted with others, Republicans and Democrats, and who reported agreement across parties that the nominating process was a "circus," a "farce," a "charade." The only answer was for senators from all parties to agree that they had a responsibility to act in the interests of both institutions, the Court and the Senate. They could agree that all nominees would receive a hearing, a committee vote, and an up-or-down vote on confirmation. They could establish schedules for the various phases of deliberation and voting. They could agree on fair procedures for background investigations. They could also lay down new norms for the consideration of election year nominations, taking up nominations until August 1 of an election year and agreeing that no such consideration need be afforded after the election to a "lame duck" president who had lost the election. These new rules, if adopted, would remain in place unless changed by unanimous consent "in order to eliminate the ability of the majority party to jettison the new policies for political expediency by simple majority vote."[23]

The commission decided to make an appendix to the report of this testimony. Members might have different views of the various recommendations. It seemed to me that, as in the call for the Court itself to adopt a code of ethics, it was important for the commission to elevate for public discussion why those in positions of power should be willing to sacrifice some measure of their freedom of action—the Court's freedom to reject the pressure for an ethics code, the Senate's freedom to pursue "hardball" confirmation politics. The reason, of course, would be to protect the integrity of these governing institutions and the public confidence in them. Especially now. It would be the right thing to do—a political sacrifice in the service of a political ethics.

When, as a young political lawyer, I was reviewing the best literature on the role of money in politics, I came across a major study written in the 1950s by notable political scientist Alexander Heard, *The Costs of Democracy*. The cost to which he was referring was a financial cost: the money needed to organize and run campaigns, build parties, underwrite the expense of a robust democratic politics. The cost exacted by a democracy is higher still. It is the cost that responsible political actors must bear in accepting and acting on ethical limits: on what they say and how they say it, how they pursue and use power, and how they treat political opponents.

This is the duty of all responsible political actors—including, but not only, the lawyers.

Last Words

In October of 1939, in flight from his native Austria that would end a year later in New York City, my father joined and became a writer and radio broadcaster for a "freedom" station on the coast of Normandy, in the town of Fécamp. It was a clandestine operation, set up so that the German regime would have difficulty determining whether it was located within or outside occupied territories. My father broadcast under the name "Rudolph." For two hours a night, he combined political analysis with ridicule and mordant humor to enrage the Nazi occupiers and support the station's mission of giving hope to oppressed populations.

He found an audience where he hoped he would, and even others in Allied nations took note. One columnist for an English paper wrote about this "Rudolph, lone speaker of the mystery Austrian freedom station," who was "[putting] up an act which must cause Dr. Goebbels to choke." He concluded: "Go to it, Rudolph—wherever you are, whoever you are. We are listening—and wishing you luck."[1]

In a broadcast on December 26, 1939, which I have in translated form in a binder assembled by my mother, my father spoke of the elements of what he termed "the tragedy of our time . . . confusion of the minds, moral decay, lies, fraud committed against the people, slander, Machiavellianism, hypocrisy...." Sorting through the translated transcripts, I see more of his references to the ethical underpinning of a decent political order.

This was how he understood the democracy's undoing: a profound moral failure, a collapse of an ethical politics. This is how I have come to understand it. The responsibility to defend against this failure—to avert a tragedy in our own time—is a very individual one for those who have the privilege to play a direct part in our civic life and bear the first line of responsibility for the safekeeping of our democratic institutions and norms.

And it is a responsibility, too, of the citizenry, who are obligated to hold politicians, political consultants and lawyers, elected and government officials, members of the press, judges and justices, accountable for the choices they make.

So go to it—wherever you are, whoever you are.

Notes

Preface

1. Benjamin Ginsberg, *The American Lie: Government by the People and Other Political Fables* (New York: Oxford University Press, 2007), 3.

2. Ginsberg, *The American Lie*, vii, 3.

3. Frank Sorauf, *Party Politics in America* (Glenview, IL: Scott Foresman/Addison Wesley, 1988) 245, 408.

4. Kristen Holmes, "Trump Calls for the Termination of the Constitution in Truth Social Post," *CNNPolitics*, December 4, 2022, https://www.cnn.com/2022/12/03/politics/trump-constitution-truth-social/index.html.

5. Bernard Crick, *In Defense of Politics*, 4th ed. (Chicago: University of Chicago Press, 1992), 154, 146.

6. "Gravely Ill, Atwater Offers Apology," Associated Press, January 13, 1991, https://www.nytimes.com/1991/01/13/us/gravely-ill-atwater-offers-apology.html.

7. Donald A. Ritchie, preface to "F. Nordy Hoffmann, Senate Sergeant at Arms, 1975–1981," Oral History Interviews, June 28–August 30, 1988, Senate Historical Office, Washington, DC, https://www.senate.gov/about/resources/pdf/hoffman-f-nordy-full-transcript-with-index.pdf.

8. "F. Nordy Hoffman, Senate Sergeant at Arms, 1975–1981," Oral History Interviews, June 28–August 30, 1988, Senate Historical Office, Washington, DC, https://www.senate.gov/about/oral-history/hoffman-f-nordy-oral-history.htm.

Chapter 1

1. James Comey, *A Higher Loyalty: Truth, Lies, and Leadership* (New York: Flatiron Books, 2018), xii, 137.

2. Tim Miller, *Why We Did It: A Travelogue from the Republican Road to Hell* (New York: Harper, 2022), 213.

3. Steven Levinsky and Daniel Ziblatt, "This is how democracies die," *The Guardian*, January 21, 2018, https://www.theguardian.com/US-news/commentisfree/2018/jan21/this-is-how-democracies-die.

4. Steven Levitsky and Daniel Ziblatt, *How Democracies Die* (New York: Crown, 2018), 8.

5. "Rule 2.1: Advisor," American Bar Association, Model Rules of Professional Conduct, https://www.americanbar.org/groups/professional_responsibility/publications/model_rules_of_professional_conduct/rule_2_1_advisor/.

CHAPTER 2

1. *United States v. Myers*, 635 F.2d 932 (2d Cir. 1980).

CHAPTER 3

1. Bruce L. Felknor, *Political Mischief: Smear, Sabotage, and Reform in U.S. Elections* (New York: Praeger,1992), 220.

2. John Dean, "Memorandum: Dealing with Our Political Enemies," August 16, 1971, https://upload.wikimedia.org/wikipedia/commons/9/94/Dean-enemies-1.jpg.

3. U.S. Congress, Hearings Before the Select Committee on Presidential Campaign Activities, 93d Cong. 1st sess., 1973, 1526.

4. Kimberley Strassel, *The Intimidation Game: How the Left Is Silencing Free Speech* (New York: Twelve, 2016), 35.

5. Mariecar Frias, Katie Escherich, and Kate McCarthy, "Tom DeLay on 'Dancing with the Stars,'" *Good Morning America*, August 18, 2009, https://www.goodmorningamerica.com/news/story/tom-delay-surprise-contestant-dancing-stars-8350260.

6. Jim Vandehei and Greg Hitt, "Democrats Sue GOP's DeLay, Claim He 'Extorted' Donations," *Wall Street Journal*, May 4, 2000, https://www.wsj.com/articles/SB957385409975903169.

7. Michael Kelly, "Hammering DeLay," *Washington Post*, May 10, 2000, https://www.washingtonpost.com/archive/opinions/2000/05/10/hammering-delay/cc4a36b0-7d7d-4bec-8386-9cc3e940bce9/.

8. Juliet Eilprin, "Democrats, DeLay Settle Racketeering Suit," *Washington Post*, April 6, 2001, https://www.washingtonpost.com/archive/politics/2001/04/06/democrats-delay-settle-racketeering-suit/40bf23e7-833a-41f8-80cb-97e809d90be2/.

9. Eilprin, "Democrats."

10. Caitlin Oprysco, "Joaquin Castro Doubles Down Amid Backlash over Tweeting Names of Trump Donors," *Politico*, August 6, 2019, https://www.politico.com/story/2019/08/06/joaquin-castro-trump-donors-1450672.

11. *Americans for Prosperity Foundation v. Bonta*, 141 S. Ct. 2373, 2388 (2021).

CHAPTER 4

1. U.S. Congress, Senate, Committee on Finance, Hearing before the Subcommittee on Taxation and Debt Management, 97th Congress, 1st sess., 1981, 74.

2. Committee on Finance, Hearing, 68.

3. Robert L. Jackson, "The Resignation of Jim Wright: Speaker's Downfall," *Los Angeles Times*, June 1, 1989, https://www.latimes.com/archives/la-xpm-1989-06-01-mn-1334-story.html.

4. Sheryl Gay Stolberg, "Gingrich Stuck to Caustic Path in Ethics Battles," *New York Times*, January 26, 2012, https://www.nytimes.com/2012/01/27/us/politics/the-long-run-gingrich-stuck-to-caustic-path-in-ethics-battles.html.

5. Julian E. Zelizer, "A 1985 Recount Is Suddenly Relevant Again," *The Atlantic*, November 12, 2018, https://www.theatlantic.com/ideas/archive/2018/11/florida-recounts-message-matters/575614/.

CHAPTER 5

1. Claire McCaskill, "How I Helped Todd Akin Win—So I Could Beat Him Later," *Politico*, August 11, 2015, https://www.politico.com/magazine/story/2015/08/todd-akin-missouri-claire-mccaskill-2012-121262/.

2. Jennifer Epstein, "Obama Team: Romney Committed a Felony or Lied to Voters," *Politico*, July 12, 2012, https://www.politico.com/blogs/politico44/2012/07/obama-team-romney-committed-a-felony-or-lied-to-voters-128757.

3. "Transcript, Democratic Presidential Candidates Debate in Des Moines, Iowa," American Presidency Project, UC Santa Barbara, January 8, 2000, https://www.presidency.ucsb.edu/documents/democratic-presidential-candidates-debate-des-moines-iowa.

4. "The Bradley Campaign: A Pre-Mortem," *Slate*, January 31, 2000, https://slate.com/news-and-politics/2000/01/the-bradley-campaign-a-pre-mortem.html.

5. Katharine Q. Seelye with John M. Broder, "The 2000 Campaign: The Vice President; Questions of Veracity Have Long Dogged Gore," *New York Times*, February 17, 2000, https://www.nytimes.com/2000/02/17/us/the-2000-campaign-the-vice-president-questions-of-veracity-have-long-dogged-gore.html.

6. Philip Gailey, "The Difference between a Negative Campaign and a Dishonest One," Tampabay.com, last updated September 3, 2005, https://www.tampabay.com/archive/2002/09/01/the-difference-between-a-negative-campaign-and-a-dishonest-one/.

7. Seelye, "The 2000 Campaign," *New York Times*.

8. The Annenberg Working Group on Presidential Campaign Debate Reform, "Democratizing the Debates," University of Pennsylvania, June 27, 2015, https://www.annenbergpublicpolicycenter.org/feature/democratizing-the-debates/.

9. A different Benjamin Ginsberg from the one who wrote the book *American Lie*, discussed in the preface.

10. Valerie Biden Owens, *Growing Up Biden* (New York: Celadon Books, 2022), 258.

CHAPTER 6

1. Teddy Davis, "Bauer Helped Reshape Democrats' Views on Campaign Finance," *Roll Call*, July 29, 2005, https://rollcall.com/2005/07/29/bauer-helped-reshape-democrats-views-on-campaign-finance/.

2. "Federal Election Oversight," C-SPAN video, July 14, 2004, https://www.c-span.org/video/?182694-1/federal-election-commission-oversight.

CHAPTER 7

1. Thomas Jefferson to Edward Carrington, January 16, 1787, The Founders' Constitution, Volume 5, Amendment I (Speech and Press), Document 8, University of Chicago Press, https://press-pubs.uchicago.edu/founders/documents/amendI_speechs29.html.

2. Thomas Jefferson to John Norvell, June 14, 1807, The Founders' Constitution, Volume 5, Amendment I (Speech and Press), Document 29, University of Chicago Press, https://press-pubs.uchicago.edu/founders/documents/amendI_speechs29.html.

3. "Statement from Bob Bauer, Personal Attorney for the President," *Politico*, January 12, 2023, https://www.politico.com/f/?id=00000185-b616-de44-a7bf-fe177dea0000.

4. Alex Raskin, review, "*Honest Graft*: Big Money and the American Political Process," *Los Angeles Times*, October 16, 1988, https://www.latimes.com/archives/la-xpm-1988-10-16-bk-6318-story.html.

5. Jack Beatty, "The Road to a Third Party," *The Atlantic*, August 1995, https://www.theatlantic.com/magazine/archive/1995/08/the-road-to-a-third-party/667707/.

6. Josh Getlin, "Media Stirred Ethics Furor, Coelho Says," *Los Angeles Times*, June 28, 1989, https://www.latimes.com/archives/la-xpm-1989-06-28-mn-4185-story.html.

7. Charles Rothfeld, "On Legal Pundits and How They Got That Way," *New York Times*, May 4, 1990, https://www.nytimes.com/1990/05/04/us/on-legal-pundits-and-how-they-got-that-way.html.

8. Steven V. Roberts, "Parties Finding Ways to Evade Spending Laws," *New York Times* October 29, 1986, https://www.nytimes.com/1986/10/29/us/parties-finding-ways-to-evade-spending-laws.html.

CHAPTER 8

1. Ken Gormley, ed., *The Presidents and the Constitution, Part Two: From World War I to the Trump Era* (New York: NYU Press, 2022), 572.

2. Ken Starr, *Contempt: A Memoir of the Clinton Investigation* (New York: Sentinel, 2018), 259.

3. Robert W. Gordon, "Imprudence and Partisanship, Starr's OIC and the Clinton-Lewinsky Affair," *Fordham Law Review* 68, no. 3 (1999).

4. Gordon, "Imprudence," 649.

5. Peter Baker, *The Breach: Inside the Impeachment and Trial of William Jefferson Clinton* (New York: Simon & Schuster, 2000), 112.

6. Baker, *The Breach*, 114.

7. Transcript: "Lead House manager Hyde gives final summation of case against president," *CNN*, January 19, 1999, https://www.cnn.com/ALLPOLITICS/stories/1999/01/16/transcripts/hyde.html?cid=ios_app.

8. "Byrd: 'Begin . . . the Process of Healing,'" *Washington Post*, January 12, 1999, https://www.washingtonpost.com/wp-srv/politics/special/clinton/stories/byrdtext012299.htm.

CHAPTER 9

1. Gene Healy, *The Cult of the Presidency: America's Dangerous Devotion to Executive Power* (Washington, DC: Cato Institute, 2008), 7.

2. George E. Reedy, *The Twilight of the Presidency* (New York: World Publishing Company, 1970), 17.

3. Ben Terris, "Senators Oppose White House Disclosure Plan for Contractors," Government Executive, May 12, 2011, https://www.govexec.com/oversight/2011/05/senators-oppose-white-house-disclosure-plan-for-contractors/33958/.

4. Robert Houghwout Jackson, *That Man: An Insider's Portrait of Franklin Roosevelt* (New York: Oxford University Press, 2003), 59, 74.

5. Office of the White House Press Secretary, "Memorandum from White House Counsel Regarding the Review of Discussions Relating to Congressman Sestak," May 28, 2010, https://obamawhitehouse.archives.gov/the-press-office/memorandum-white-house-counsel-regarding-review-discussions-relating-congressman-se.

6. Rich Lowry, "Psst, Buddy, Want a (Legally Murky, Not at All a Bribe, Oh So Innocent Job," *New York Post*, May 30, 2010, https://nypost.com/2010/05/30/psst-buddy-want-a-legally-murky-not-at-all-a-bribe-oh-so-innocent-job/.

7. William A. Burck and David A. Rivkin, Jr., "Primaries and Patronage, the Chicago Way," *Pioneer Press*, June 6, 2010, https://www.twincities.com/2010/06/06/burck-rivkin-primaries-and-patronage-the-chicago-way/amp/.

8. Jack Goldsmith, "President Obama Rejected DOJ and DOD Advice, and Sided with Harold Koh, on War Powers Resolution," *Lawfare*, June 17, 2011, https://www.lawfaremedia.org/article/president-obama-rejected-doj-and-dod-advice-and-sided-harold-koh-war-powers-resolution.

9. Libya and War Powers: Testimony before the Committee on Foreign Relations, 112th Cong. 11 (2011) (statement of Harold Koh, State Department Legal Adviser).

10. Bruce Ackerman, "Legal Acrobatics, Illegal War," *New York Times*, June 20, 2011, https://www.nytimes.com/2011/06/21/opinion/21Ackerman.html.

Chapter 10

1. *Bluman v. Federal Election Commission*, 800 F. Supp. 2d 281 (D.D.C. 2011), aff'd, 565 U.S. 1104 (2012)

2. Sarah K. Burris, "Trump Can 'Rage from the Balcony' But He 'Will Not Succeed': Dem Super Lawyer Promises to Protect the Vote," *RawStory*, October 20, 2020, https://www.rawstory.com/2020/10/trump-can-rage-from-the-balcony-but-he-will-not-succeed-dem-super-lawyer-promises-to-protect-the-vote/.

3. Melissa Quinn, "Trump Targets Drop Boxes in Effort to Discredit Vote-by-Mail," *CBS News*, August 26, 2020, https://www.cbsnews.com/news/trump-mail-in-voting-ballot-drop-boxes/.

4. Donnie O'Sullivan and Daniel Dale, "Fact Check: Trump, Jr. Touts Baseless Rigged-Election Claims to Recruit 'Army" for His Dad," *CNN*, September 23, 2020, https://www.cnn.com/2020/09/23/politics/donald-trump-jr-baseless-rigged-election-fact-check/index.html.

CHAPTER 11

1. Chadwick Matlin, "Bauer and Wolfson Exchange," *Slate*, March 4, 2008, https://slate.com/news-and-politics/2008/03/bauer-and-wolfson-exchange.html.

2. Tobin Harshaw, "Crash the Party Line," *New York Times*, March 4, 2008, https://archive.nytimes.com/opinionator.blogs.nytimes.com/2008/03/04/crash-the-party-line/.

3. National Academy of Public Administration, "Watergate: Its Implications for Responsible Government," March 1974, vii.

4. National Academy, "Watergate," 135.

5. Milton Mayer, "From Deliquescence to Survival," Center for the Study of Democratic Institutions, February 1974.

6. National Academy, "Watergate," 136.

7. *McCutcheon v. Federal Election Commission*, 134 S. Ct. 1434 (2014).

8. *Winpisinger v. Watson*, 628 F.2d 133 (D.C. Cir. 1980).

9. Dan Balz, "Obama and LBJ: Measuring the Current President against the Past One's Legacy," *Washington Post*, August 12, 2014, https://www.washingtonpost.com/politics/obama-and-lbj-measuring-the-current-president-against-the-past-ones-legacy/2014/04/12/672718fe-c258-11e3-bcec-b71ee10e9bc3_story.html.

10. Susan Hennessy and Benjamin Wittes, *Unmaking the Presidency: Donald Trump's War on the World's Most Powerful Office* (New York: Farrar, Straus and Giroux, 2020).

11. National Academy, "Watergate," 136.

12. Dennis Thompson, *Ethics in Congress: From Individual to Institutional Corruption* (Washington, DC: Brookings Institute Press, 1995), 9.

13. Thompson, *Ethics in Congress*, 7.

14. Thompson, *Ethics in* Congress, 11.

15. Garrett M. Graff, *Watergate: A New History* (New York: Avid Reader Press / Simon & Schuster, 2022), 64.

16. Michael Walzer, "Political Action: The Problem of 'Dirty Hands,'" *Philosophy and Public Affairs* 2, no. 2 (Winter 1973): 160–80.

17. Pierre Ronsanvallon, *Good Government: Democracy beyond Elections*, trans. Malcolm DeBevoise (Cambridge, MA: Harvard University Press, 2018), 225.

18. "Code of Ethics for Government Service," Legal Information Institute, Cornell Law School, https://www.law.cornell.edu/cfr/text/21/19.6#:~:text=1.,a%20party%20to%20their%20evasion.

19. Teresa M. Bejan, *Mere Civility: Disagreement and the Limits of Toleration* (Cambridge, MA: Harvard University Press, 2017), 145.

20. Harvey C. Mansfield, Jr., *Taming the Prince* (Baltimore, MD: Johns Hopkins University Press, 1993), 234.

21. Michael Signer, *The Fight to Save Democracy from Its Enemies* (New York: St. Martin's Press, 2006), 35.

22. Arthur M. Schlesinger, "Messiah of the Rednecks," in *Huey P. Long: Southern Demagogue or American Democrat*, ed. Henry C. Dethloff (Boston: D. C. Heath and Company, 1967), 79.

23. Thomas C. Reeves, *The Life and Times of Joe McCarthy* (Lanham, MD: Madison Books, 1997), 196.

24. William Galston, "Civic Education in the Liberal State" in *Liberalism and the Moral Life*, ed. Nancy L. Rosenblum (Cambridge, MA: Harvard University Press, 1989), 92.

CHAPTER 12

1. U.S. Congress, Senate, Committee on Government Operations, Hearings Before the Subcommittee on Investigations, 83d Cong. 1st sess., Part 2, February 18, 1953, 91.
2. Hearings Before the Subcommittee on Investigations, Part 7, March 6, 1953, 540.
3. Hearings Before the Subcommittee on Investigations, Part 7, 539.
4. Fair Campaign Practices Committee, *Fair Play in Politics*, rev. ed. (Washington, DC, 1962), 6.
5. Fair Campaign Practices Committee, *Fair Play in Politics*, 3.
6. Fair Campaign Practices Committee, *Fair Play in Politics*, 7.
7. Fair Campaign Practices Committee, *Fair Play in Politics*, 11.
8. Fair Campaign Practices Committee, *Fair Play in Politics*, 11.
9. Thomas W. Ottenad, "McCloskey May File Complaint against Agnew," *St. Louis Post Dispatch*, December 2, 1971.
10. Gregory R. Beabout, *Ethics: The Art of Character* (New York: Bloomsbury, 2018), 5.
11. Jack Goldsmith, "Will Donald Trump Destroy the Presidency?," *The Atlantic*, October 2017, https://www.theatlantic.com/magazine/archive/2017/10/will-donald-trump-destroy-the-presidency/537921/.
12. *Id.*
13. Jack Goldsmith, *The Terror Presidency: Law and Judgment Inside the Bush Administration* (New York: W.W. Norton, 2009), 216.
14. Bob Bauer and Jack Goldsmith, letter to Attorney General Merrick Garland, September 8, 2021, https://www.potusreform.org/wp-content/uploads/2021/09/PRP-Letter-to-AG-Garland-PDF-edited-9.8.21.pdf.
15. "ALI-Convened Group Issues Principles for Electoral Count Act Reform," *American Law Institute*, April 4, 2022, https://www.ali.org/news/articles/ali-convened-group-issues-proposals-electoral-count-act-reform/.
16. *Posse Comitatus Act, U.S. Code* 18 (1878) §1385; *Homeland Security Act, U.S. Code* 6 (2002) § 466.
17. "Guidance for Insurrection Act Reform Issued by Bipartisan Group," *American Law Institute*, April 8, 2024, https://www.ali.org/news/articles/guidance-insurrection-act-reform-issued-bipartisan-group/.
18. Benjamin L. Ginsberg, "My Party Is Destroying Itself on the Altar of Trump," *Washington Post*, November 1, 2020, https://www.washingtonpost.com/opinions/2020/11/01/ben-ginsberg-voter-suppression-republicans/.
19. Presidential Commission on the Supreme Court of the United States, *Final Report*, (Washington, DC, 2021), 7.
20. Presidential Commission, *Final Report*, 13.
21. Presidential Commission, *Final Report*, 216.
22. Supreme Court of the United States, Code of Conduct for Justices (Washington, DC, November 13, 2023), https://www.supremecourt.gov/about/code-of-conduct-for-justices.aspx.

23. Presidential Commission on the Supreme Court of the United States, Final Report, (Washington, DC, 2021), 258.

LAST WORDS
1. Jonah Barrington, "Heil Hitler? NO! Good Luck Rudolph," *Daily Express*, October 31, 1939.

Index

confirmation process, 203;
ethical responsibility of, 200–1;
Justices' nominations in, 199–
200, 201, 203; Pennsylvania,
158; Presidential Commission,
185; standard of review, 137

Tampa Bay Times, 63
Tennessee General Assembly, 174
The Terror President
(Goldsmith), 192
Texas, 166–67
Thomas, Clarence, 201
Thompson, Dennis, 177
Thomson, Bob, 14, 16
Thorsness, Leo, 23
Truman, Harry, 138, 187
Trump, Donald: abuse of power
by, 38; attack on voting system,
158–64; civility and, 182; on
constitution, xv–xvii; debate
with Biden and, 67–68; electoral account and, 194; ethics
of, 169; Georgia case, 32;
impeachment of, xiv, 105, 106,
108, 109, 121–22, 124; lawyers
of, 138, 139, 153–54, 156, 162;
negative campaign against, 54;
Obama birth certificate and,
128; as president, 8, 176–77,
191–92, 199; presidential
campaign of, 29, 33–34; press
and, 191–92; 2016 elections, 99,
152–55; 2020 election, xiii–xiv,
xv–xvi, 31–32, 34, 57, 58, 137,

152, 157, 168; as unethical
political actor, 3
Trump, Don Jr., 160
Trump Organization, 154, 177
Twitter, 83, 101, 103

Ukraine, 105, 121
United States (U.S.). *See specific
topics*
University of Pennsylvania,
Annenberg School of
Communication, 65
U.S. *See* United States

Verrilli, Don, 157
vice president: Biden as, xix, xxi;
Pence as, 161, 163
violations, of campaign finance
laws, 152, 154
violence: of campaigns, 23, 32;
political, 46
Voice of America (VOA), 185–86
voters, xvii, 194–95, 197; African
American, 50; attack on, 46–48;
favor of, 19; intimidation of,
158; manipulation of, 53–54,
57–60, 79
voting: accessibility, 168–69;
deadline for, 158; illegal, 48; lies
about, 160–61; mail-in, 159;
military, 156; rights, 152, 196
voting system, 198; attack on,
158–64; defense of, 158–60,
162; fragility of, 151, 155–56

About the Author

Bob Bauer has been involved in many of the biggest political struggles in the five decades since the post-Watergate 1970s. He has been a leading legal adviser to the national Democratic Party and to its candidates on strategies for winning elections and protecting voting rights, and he has represented the party in national political conflicts and controversies. He was the chief counsel to both of President Obama's presidential campaigns and was the President's White House counsel. He was counsel to the Democratic Senate leader during Bill Clinton's impeachment trial. He was a senior adviser to the Biden presidential campaign on voting rights and election protection, and on vice presidential selection, and his responsibilities included playing the role of Donald Trump in preparation for the general election debates. Bauer is also now on the faculty of the New York University School of Law, teaching political reform and the ethical challenges facing lawyers in public life. He coauthored with Jack Goldsmith *After Trump: Reconstructing the Presidency*.